T0312004

"I'm delighted to finally see a compendium of rich examples where academics and practitioners share their experiences of applying human-centred design methods and techniques to higher-education."

Sarah Drummond, Director of School of Good Services

"This book is one of those rare and valuable anthologies that enables creativity and innovation, and serves as a playbook for designing thoughtful, iterative change in our universities."

Professor Jeff Grabill, Deputy Vice-Chancellor: Student Education, University of Leeds

"This book gives many examples where the cycle of service design of exploring, creating, reflecting and implementing has led to great results."

Professor Zoe Radnor, Pro Vice-Chancellor and Executive Dean, College of Business and Social Sciences, Aston University

"This book will be of enormous interest to educators everywhere - whether employed in academic or professional roles."

Debbie McVitty, Editor of WONKHE

Transforming Higher Education With Human-Centred Design

Encouraging a collaborative and thoughtful approach to the wicked problems facing Higher Education (HE), this book is a showcase of pioneering educators who believe that well-designed education is good for everyone – learners, teachers, education administrators, the learning organisation and the world.

Through case studies, thought pieces and practical advice, this book takes a fresh look at the application of Design Thinking and Service Design in a variety of university contexts. Human-centred design perspectives show up the fact that decades of rhetoric about student-centred learning have often left the student still effectively marginalised from change processes. The reader will encounter ample tools and techniques of design and co-creation that can enhance the student experience, from applicant to alumnus. More importantly, the book sets out, in actionable ways, how we can make our universities more effective at supporting students for success and to become places where people are more empowered to make those changes.

University academics, learning support staff, managers and professional staff, as well as HE policy makers and professional bodies, will appreciate this clear and practical guide to exploring service design in the new context of education.

Radka Newton. Radka's personal experience of being an international student contributed to her professional calling to ensure that as educators we create challenging yet attainable education environments. As a continuous improvement and service excellence scholar, she has grown a significant expertise in combining executive coaching, organisation change practice and service design. Radka is a Personal Chair in Management Education and Innovation and a co-founder of the Service Design in Education network.

Jean Mutton. Following a degree in Educational Research, Jean began a career in Higher Education academic administration where she managed many Registry and Faculty-based administration teams, covering the student journey from Admissions to Graduation. Since 2015, Jean has been working as a consultant across the sector, using human-centred design for process improvement to enhance the student and staff experience. Jean is a co-founder of the Service Design in Education network.

Michael Doherty. Michael is Professor of Law and Associate Head of the Law School, at Lancaster University. He is co-author of *Public Law* (3rd ed., Routledge, 2023). He is active in legal education scholarship, co-created the Connecting Legal Education online community and is a former Chair of the Association of Law Teachers. Michael's work in legal and service design encompasses education, cultural studies and disciplinarity. He is the founding editor-in-chief of *Legal Design Journal*.

Transforming Higher Education With Human-Centred Design

Edited by
Radka Newton, Jean Mutton and Michael Doherty

 Routledge
Taylor & Francis Group

NEW YORK AND LONDON

Designed cover image: Molly Northcote

First published 2025
by Routledge
605 Third Avenue, New York, NY 10158

and by Routledge
4 Park Square, Milton Park, Abingdon, Oxon OX14 4RN

Routledge is an imprint of the Taylor & Francis Group, an informa business

Library of Congress Cataloging-in-Publication Data
A catalog record for this title has been requested

ISBN: 978-1-032-46769-6 (hbk)
ISBN: 978-1-032-46763-4 (pbk)
ISBN: 978-1-003-38316-1 (ebk)

DOI: 10.4324/9781003383161

Typeset in Galliard
by Taylor & Francis Books

We wish to acknowledge a special person, designer, artist and educator, who showed us the importance of creativity, kindness, generosity and caring – the late Andy de Vale. Andy's support and encouragement kept us going and this book is a tribute to Andy's mentorship and also to his most beautiful smile. The illustrations for this book were originally supposed to have been created by Andy de Vale, founder of WorkVisible. You can see his visualisation art work of the online EDUJAM 2020 on the inside cover of the book. Andy was a brilliant human and an absolute pioneer in the field of working visually, being an inspiration to many. Andy's family business continues under WorkVisible Studios, run by talented brother and sister duo, Marcus and Emily de Vale.

Contents

List of figures   xii
List of tables   xiv
List of contributors   xv
Foreword   xx

Introduction   1
RADKA NEWTON, JEAN MUTTON AND MICHAEL DOHERTY

Drawing inspiration from the Human-Centred Design process:
How the illustrations in this book were created   6
MOLLY NORTHCOTE

Human Understanding and Behaviour Go Hand-in-Glove:
Making a Difference through Human-Centred Design   11
MICHAEL DOHERTY

SECTION I
Design As We See It   21

Foreword   23
SARAH DRUMMOND AND DEBBIE MCVITTY

1 "It all just clicked": Experiences of finding and using service
   design in higher education   24
   MICHAEL DOHERTY, RADKA NEWTON AND JEAN MUTTON

2 Service Design solves the right problem   35
   ADAM LAWRENCE

SECTION 2
Building Capacity, Developing Mindsets   46

Foreword   47
PAUL MORAN AND ANNETTE ROBINSON

3   Change HEROs: Scaling Service Design as a Core Competence
    for Professional Services Staff   48
    PAMELA SPOKES AND JEAN MUTTON

4   Inspiring change at all levels: The personal and professional impact
    of service design training   59
    SONIA VIRDI AND KATIE MURRIE

5   Untangling networks: Using design methods to grow
    collaborative innovation beyond the classroom   75
    LARA SALINAS

6   Mindsets Eat Methods: Human-Centred Design for organisational
    change in Higher Education   86
    PHILLIPPA ROSE AND SHARON JONES

7   Prototyping educational change: Learning from a ten-week service
    design programme   102
    SARAH DYER AND KSENIJA KUZMINA

SECTION 3
Institutional Change   117

Foreword   119
SHEILA MACNEILL AND ANDY YOUELL

8   An exploration of the relationship between Lean and Service
    Design for Service Improvement   120
    MILA BOMBARDIERI AND NICHOLE DUNNE-WATTS

9   Moving from silos to integrated services – a case study of three live
    experiments   132
    SVEIN ARE TJELDNES AND KARIN EILERTSEN

10 Futurelib: Prototyping library services at the University of
    Cambridge   145
    JENNY EGAN AND DAVID MARSHALL

11 Designing for a Gender-Inclusive Campus 158
BERNADETTE GEUY, DAPHNE OGLE AND RACHEL HOLLOWGRASS

12 Intelligent Automation: Integrating human-centred design
thinking into an Automation Service 175
JENNIFER ROBERTSON

SECTION 4
Student Experience 186

Foreword 187
SUE MORRISON AND JACQUI JACKSON

13 Warwick Secret Challenge: Design thinking for re-imagining
student engagement 189
BO KELESTYN

14 Service Design in Education: A mindset towards Inclusive and
Accessible Learning Experiences 203
KIM ANDERSON AND CHRISTOPHER SZE CHONG LIM

15 Reflection by Design: Embedding Reflective Practice into the
Student Learning Journey 218
KSENIJA KUZMINA AND JAMES MORAN

16 Discovering the untold story: Emotional journey mapping of
learners' educational experience 230
RADKA NEWTON

17 'Know thy student, for she is not thee': User personas as a way to
give agency to student voice 243
RADKA NEWTON AND MICHAEL DOHERTY

18 Seamless Student Journey: Fact or Fiction? 258
JEAN MUTTON AND CHRISTINE STEWART

Index 266

Figures

0.1	Human-Centred Design guiding the illustration process	8
1.1	Crowd-sourced insights	25
2.1	Service design activities	39
2.2	Service design learning loop	43
3.1	Legacy Systems	55
4.1	Sonia and Katie's takeaways	72
5.1	The three missions of universities converge	76
5.2	Look at what we do	81
6.1	Assumptions Mapping	90
6.2	WREN model	98
7.1	Elements of the Innovation Lab	109
8.1	Emerging from the tunnel of conventional thinking: expanding problem-solving horizons	126
9.1	Cross-organisational service-map	137
9.2	After the experiment, the participants in the service pilots were asked how important it is for UiT to work with service design. The answers are given in percent and N=48. Mean value for service co-ordinators = 4.4 and service team members = 4.0	139
9.3	The service leadership model with the five key elements with two underlying conditions	141
11.1	Designing for a Gender-Inclusive Campus	162
11.2	Ecosystem map, designing for gender-inclusive learning	165
11.3	Entering Gender Data, Risks and Rewards	166
12.1	Humans at the centre of automation choice and selection	177
13.1	Student Challenge roadmap	194
14.1	The approach of inclusive design	205
14.2	Framework of motivated behaviour for learning	209
14.3	An example of a persona created from mapping disability support information to UDL	211
15.1	Opportunities for Reflective Touch Points in the Student Journey	227
16.1	My EDUJAM journey	234

16.2	My learning journey	236
16.3	Student journey map	238
17.1	Student persona	245
17.2	Persona profiling guide	252
18.1	Student standing on islands representing silos	260

Tables

5.1	Guiding principles to define the problem and solution space	79
7.1	*Innovation Lab projects. See Exeter Education Incubator (2021)*	103
7.2	The Lab Programme	103
7.3	Coaches' schedule	109
10.1	Number of chairs, mean and maximum observed occupancy, in prototype iterations of a space	149
11.1	Gender Data Elements	169
11.2	Pronouns Questions and Options	169
11.3	Gender Identity Questions (3) and Options	170

Contributors

Adam Lawrence is a co-author of *This is Service Design Doing*, a top-selling handbook and textbook for service design. He is a co-initiator of the Global Service Jam, the world's largest service design event. A professional actor, he applies his expertise in psychology, customer experience and showbusiness to co-create value with clients and users. He co-founded Work-PlayExperience, a global consultancy helping organisations integrate service design in their culture and processes.

Pamela Spokes has worked in Higher Education (HE) for more than 15 years and is a fierce promoter of service design in professional services. She has studied, lived and worked in Canada, the UK, Sweden, Finland, Russia and Japan and utilises this international perspective. Since completing her MBA in Service Innovation and Design, she has trained innovators through in-person and online service design training. She is a service designer at Metropolia UAS in Finland as well as an entrepreneur.

Katie Murrie graduated in Law from the University of Dundee then completed a Masters in Leadership and Innovation where she discovered her love for service design. Katie joined at the launch of the Service Design Academy, contributing to the co-creation of the learning content for the Professional Development Award in Service Design. Katie was the first to achieve the Service Design Network Accredited Master Trainer in Scotland and is a co-founder of the Service Design in Education network.

Sonia Virdi is a graphic designer, service designer and product owner with over 20 years' experience in Higher Education. Currently at the University of Edinburgh, she specialises in technical and creative projects, utilising her passion for design to drive impact and positive change. She facilitates the learning of design practices and approaches in teams across the university and is continuously inspired by the diverse range of users with whom she works, shares and collaborates.

Lara Salinas is a design researcher, practitioner, educator and co-director of Service Futures Lab at London College of Communication, University of the Arts London. She leads research on design for place-based climate action across sectors, with a focus on public sector innovation. With over a decade of experience in academia, she has played a pioneering role in shaping knowledge exchange in creative disciplines.

Phillippa Rose is a leading practitioner and educator in human-centred design and innovation with 20 years' experience working across government, the private sector, healthcare and education. She is a design coach with Design Thinkers Academy and an appointed design expert for the UK Design Council. Phillippa regularly speaks and writes about design and enjoys teaching service design at Hyper Island and the University of the Arts London.

Sharon Jones specialises in transformational change and strategic service design using a human-centred approach to reimagine existing services and creating new services for users that are worthy of their investment in time and money. Her professional background is in Higher Education leadership and management. She is currently working as a Higher Education Consultant, helping universities to transform education and services using design thinking methods.

Sarah Dyer is based at the Manchester Institute of Education. She is an Associate Dean for Teaching and Learning in Manchester's Faculty of Humanities. She undertook the work explored in this book in her role as Inaugural Director of the Exeter Education Incubator. Sarah has been recognised for her commitment and innovative pedagogy as an Advance HE National Teaching Fellow. Her inclusive innovation leadership helps accelerate mindset change and collaboration across silos.

Ksenija Kuzmina is a Senior Lecturer and a Programme Director of MA/MSc Design Innovation programme at Loughborough University, London. Her research looks at the role of design in ecological and just transitions, contributing to the contexts of education, community development and everyday living. Ksenija is a co-lead of the Centre for Doctoral Training on homelessness and a guest editor of the Special Issue, Sustainability, entitled *Sustainable Design Education and Implementation.*

Jennifer Robertson has over 20 years' experience in Higher Education (HE), while prioritising the enhancement of student and staff experiences, leading the design and implementation of responsive services and specialised teams. As Head of Automation at the University of Glasgow, Jennifer leads a service integrating technology and service design principles, streamlining tasks for organisational efficiency. Her persistent commitment to innovation and service excellence defines her professional journey, driving meaningful contributions to HE services.

Mila Bombardieri has worked in both the private and public sectors in project management and process improvement roles. Passionate about innovation, creativity and the user experience, she moved to HE in 2017 to drive business improvement at a London university. She is focussed on contributing to the development of creative problem solving skills across the institution and on harnessing technology to improve the student and staff experience.

Nichole Dunne-Watts has worked in HE since 2014. She began her career in administration, moving to a student facing role and then onto process improvement. She is now applying her knowledge of continuous improvement, problem-solving and service design in her current position where she supports students in a London University. Nichole is passionate about human-centred design and providing services to students that they need and want, ultimately to improve their experience within HE and their wellbeing simultaneously.

Svein Are Tjeldnes is a Lean manager, design thinker and experienced facilitator at UiT the Arctic University of Norway. Svein Are has a passion for sharing knowledge and experiences within continuous improvement and human-centred approaches. He is co-creator of the video blog #bærekraftigfacilitation, an extensive online resource for facilitation. Since 2020 Svein Are has led a large-scale design thinking project, designing interconnected services at UiT.

Karin Eilertsen is a Lean and improvement specialist at UiT the Arctic University of Norway. As part of the continuous improvement team, she facilitates improvement processes using various tools and techniques, as well as supports and mentors staff with their own projects. Since 2020 Karin has facilitated a large service design project by designing services for academic staff and students.

Jenny Egan is a Service Design Lead at the University of Cambridge. She works on strategic service design projects centred around improving the University's web estate and digital experiences. She enjoys crafting user-centred services within complex environments and is passionate about uncovering behavioural insights and latent needs through appropriate research methods. She has experience in a range of industries, including IT, healthcare, financial services, publishing and environmental conservation.

David Marshall leads a team of user researchers and data scientists working on the design and improvement of services at the University of Cambridge. He has experience setting strategy and direction for user research, building and maintaining teams, advocating for the value of user research and embedding it in organisation-level ways of working. David has a particular interest in research ethics in the context of user-centred service design.

Bernadette Geuy is a service design strategist and change-maker who consults with Higher Education clients on improving service experiences and student success. She has a BA and MBA from the University of California, Berkeley. Her projects include understanding the student portal experience, reimagining academic planning and enrolment, designing for accessible learning, improving the billing and payments experience and designing for gender inclusivity. Bernadette enjoys weaving and knitting.

Daphne Ogle is a designer, strategist and user advocate. Her passion is to help organisations design experiences that improve people's lives. Together with users and stakeholders, she specialises in co-designing holistic, customer-focused experiences that enable organisations to thrive. Daphne has recently been helping Higher Education institutions create more gender-inclusive campuses through enhancements to technology, culture and policy. She holds a BBA and an MSI from the University of Michigan.

Rachel Hollowgrass is a user experience researcher and designer. She has contributed to consumer applications at Apple, interactive math curricula at Stanford, student information systems at University of California Berkeley and climate research at the Lawrence Berkeley National Laboratory. She leads an internship program at UC Berkeley that amplifies the student voice. The interns' academic and professional growth spurs teams and technology to be more student-friendly.

Bo Kelestyn is a design thinking academic and practitioner, Associate Professor and the Undergraduate Student Engagement Lead at the Warwick Business School, University of Warwick, UK. Bo is the creator of the Warwick Secret Challenge, a problem-solving workshop with elements of design thinking, which has become a key methodology to tackle innovation challenges at Warwick through authentic student-staff co-creation. Bo also hosts the Student Experience by Design podcast.

Kim Anderson is a service designer and educator based in Scotland. A graduate of Abertay University in Computer Arts, she discovered design thinking through sprints and holds a Master's degree in Design for Business. Kim utilises her passion for inclusive and accessible design in her role at Dundee and Angus College, where she is continually seeking to develop and improve the experience for learners via professional development courses in service design.

Christopher Lim is a design educator, researcher and designer and also a Fellow of the Higher Education Academy. Chris teaches product design, interaction design and human factors subjects at Duncan of Jordanstone College of Art and Design, University of Dundee. He advocates a Human-Centred Approach in Design, involving people in the process of design thereby encouraging the Inclusive Design of products and services.

James Moran has worked in various HE institutions since 2009, encompass-ing roles in education, curriculum development and student support. Cur-rently, as a Senior Lecturer in Curriculum Design at the University of Westminster, he teaches the Postgraduate Certificate in Higher Education, oversees the intensive course design process and advocates for innovative approaches in curriculum development throughout the university.

Christine Stewart is a Lean, continuous improvement specialist with over 30 years of experience in various sectors. Since 2007 she has been using Lean methodology to provide advice, facilitation and training to institutions, helping them harness the skills and capabilities of their people, engaging them in developing and delivering a strategy for improvement and build-ing ownership of their daily activities to make continuous improvement the norm.

Molly Northcote is a Bristol-based service design consultant, illustrator and artist. Molly loves working with people and applying design, creativity and critical thinking to problem-solving and communication, whether that be for a service design project, creating a mural or live illustrating an event. Her love for human-centred design blossomed from previously working in Human Factors Engineering, specialising in medical devices, and stemmed from an education in Product Design.

Foreword

Student expectations are increasing, and many are more likely to ask about 'value for money' before committing to one of the biggest financial decisions they are likely to make. At the same time, institutions face the challenges of inflation and interest rates while the marketplace for students becomes increasingly competitive.

Many universities are asking themselves, "are we an educational establishment or part of the service industry?" Adopting a human-centred design approach helps tackle these challenges head on, yielding many benefits including:

An enhanced student experience. By designing services that meet student needs, organisations create more inclusive, accessible and effective learning environments.

Promotes collaboration. It breaks through operational silos, by involving stakeholders, such as educators, administrators and students to facilitate a more cohesive joined-up approach.

Fosters innovation. An emphasis on agility and continuous improvement ensures organisations are able to respond quickly to evolving technological and educational needs.

Improves operational efficiency. By identifying and addressing pain points in administrative processes and prioritising work that delivers the most value.

Through practical examples, this comprehensive book 'demystifies' the mindsets and methods of human-centred design, equipping tutors, teachers, managers and administrators with practical insights, helping them transform their organisations for the future.

Paul Bailey, Head of Design, SPARCK

Introduction

Radka Newton, Jean Mutton and Michael Doherty

Do you remember when you last attended a seminar, workshop or any other learning event? Did you have enough information about what was expected, did you know what to prepare, who your peers were going to be, how many assignments you would have to complete? Did you feel comfortable in your environment and know how to get around, where to eat and what to take with you? Hopefully you did and that made your learning journey a seamless experience. Or perhaps you stumbled at the first hurdle of a registration form or a failed login to an online platform. Education is not only about the excellence of the content, it is also about understanding how to deliver and reach diverse audiences with different needs and learning backgrounds. Students have told us that they are prepared to struggle and work hard but they really need to know what is expected of them so that they can immerse themselves in an education that is challenging yet attainable. In this book, we explore how academic and professional services staff from across the global Higher Education (HE) sector are seeing the value in applying new work practices with human-centred design (HCD) that can be defined as a mindset towards problem-solving that puts people at the centre. As people working in HE, we should know what learners need, not only in their teaching and learning, but from a pastoral and wellbeing perspective. HCD enables us to explore more deeply how students navigate their way around their learning experience focusing not only on the explicit student needs but also on these latent needs that are often left unexplored.

Herbert Simon (1969) summarised the notion of design for us in this excellent quote: "*Everybody designs who devises courses of action aimed at changing existing situations into preferred ones ...*", and we would add "*... and does it with empathy, a listening ear and consideration*". We see design as not just a discipline for the artists and creatives, but as an integrative field that also invites us as educators to approach our actions consciously and from the learners' points of view. Importantly, we see design as a capability that helps educators navigate complex challenges and equips them with a mindset of collaboration, empathy and co-creation. In the book you will read not only about how design has been applied to HE but how educators adopted design principles as a

DOI: 10.4324/9781003383161-1

guidance towards new skills, knowledge and enhanced abilities in designing good education experiences.

Universities have been described as thirty or more different companies that share a car park, and having spent many years working in HE, we can see why. Staff working in the non-academic side or 'back office' functions run myriad systems and processes, and they may have direct or indirect contact with students right across the student journey from prospect to alumnus. However, there is little engagement with students themselves in the design of these services. Too often the different aspects of education are delivered by staff who have the highest intentions but who can only 'see' their part of the journey, which is one piece in the jigsaw puzzle of the total student experience. Considering the perspectives of others through the empathy of putting ourselves in their shoes, and looking beyond silos, is what we understand as a core activity of human-centricity.

Education exists in a system of schools, colleges, universities and other learning providers who operate complex administrative networks to try to ensure quality and good learner experience. In addition, the system is impacted by regulatory bodies and external accreditation organisations, and also by regional and national policies, economic growth and political contingency. A change of one part of the system affects another and sometimes even an improvement carried out in a silo may actually result in quality or experience deterioration in other parts of the system or further down the line. The ripple effect is not always good waves. That's where the application of service design can deliver the holistic view and consideration of the whole system, its culture, values, structures and norms. Service Design encourages cooperation and integration of different disciplines – in education it may be collaboration between the organisation managers and leaders, the teachers, the facilities providers, the caterers, all those striving for a common goal of enhancing the student experience.

Book anchoring

The book provides a wide range of references to excellent work of others who have written about Design Thinking and Service Design so that you can go deeper into the concepts that you will encounter in the chapters. There are two anchor publications that we, as editors, find essential for anybody keen to explore the underpinnings of our book further.

One of our main inspirations was a publicly co-created set of principles of good services curated by Lou Downe in 2020 – *Good Services: How to Design Services That Work*. Lou's definition of a service as 'helping someone do something' helped us re-invigorate our calling to help learners, our students, to achieve what they have set themselves to do; to get that degree, complete the next apprenticeship level and progress to their dream job. Lou, who made her career in public services, speaks to us in education with clear and uncomplicated language making design accessible and usable. Many of our chapters will also refer to a book that sits proudly on our desks without a spot of dust. Edited in 2018 by a quartet of service design practitioners, *This is service design doing: applying service design thinking in the real world*, provides a detailed guide to design methods, tools and case studies encouraging anybody to 'have a go'. We are grateful that one of the editors of that book, Adam St John Lawrence, has given us many mentoring hours, guided us through our first design applications and given us the courage to continue, fail and get up again to 'fail better' next time.

We use HCD as an umbrella term for designerly approaches to education transformation applying Design Thinking and Service Design practices to HE. We draw on design thinking principles championed by the UK Design Council and promoted through a variety of design frameworks, such as the Stanford d. school Design Thinking Process, that are all underpinned by a set of design-led commonalities that we have applied to education.

In addition, our practice has been informed by staff at two design agencies, Snook and SPARCK, that have generously offered time and expertise to help us experiment with design in the context of HE, learn from other industries and grow our experience with their guidance. This mutual knowledge co-creation and learning development has been highlighted by Anne Dhir (2024), a Creative Strategist at SPARCK, who has followed our progress and constantly reminded us of design being a capability that educators ought to nurture.

The service aspect of designing comes from our appreciation of education as a system. By putting applicants, students and alumni at the heart of our systems and processes, we can ensure that they are fit for purpose and tailored towards the end user. That does not mean that we should ignore any internal or external imperatives or directives, but we have found that by taking a holistic approach, looking beyond the silos, asking open questions, working with the end users to understand when and how students struggle helps to get to the right problem and takes us beyond the quick fix.

Designing the book

The book itself was a two-year design project collaboratively co-created with a global community of educators, prototyped with potential readers and expertly guided by our very supportive publisher. But before the book, there were years focused on design doing, trying the concepts out in education settings, adapting, discussing and pondering. A significant milestone was a Lean HE conference in 2018 that facilitated a debate about Service Design as an approach to continuous improvement, complementary to the Lean practices now widely adopted in HE. Following the positive response from the Lean community and encouragement to pursue the topic of design further, the Service Design in Education (SDinED) network was formed in 2019 with the support and endorsement of the Service Design Academy in Dundee. In collaboration with the Academy we set out on a journey of building partnerships and networks, learning from each other and sharing our expertise, connecting with design professionals and trying to absorb as much knowledge and practice as we possibly could. Over the past five years we connected with hundreds of educators searching for doing things differently to address increasing challenges in the HE sector where the old ways of working did not seem to work any more.

In the book, you will come across the *jam* concept, inspired by Global Jams, weekend gatherings open to all those keen to learn about design process through a practical design challenge delivered in a true 'jazz jam'-like improvising manner. With the generous support of the Victoria and Albert Museum in Dundee, who shared our passion to open design to educators, the SDinED network ran two global EDUJAMs with over a hundred attendees committed to designing better futures for education. The subsequent increased demand for mentoring in the design approach to education transformation and frequent requests for sharing of our experience gave us the confidence to dream up this book project. We knew we had to finally put pen to paper and share the great stories of the network members who embraced design as their new superpower. The EDUJAM also gifted us our wonderful illustrator, Molly Northcote, who herself completed service design training and simply clicked with the community to bring the book alive through fun and thoughtful drawings.

The most perfect prototype

The transition from doing to writing about it has been tough. We spent a lot of time thinking about you, the reader. We also reflected on ourselves, the practitioners connected through a common purpose of championing design principles in education and yet struggling to reflect on our practice. To gain some inspiration from the widest possible audience, we put an open call out for insights that have been collated into the Crowdsourced chapter. That really got us going, and with all our contributors, we agreed to prototype our chapters first as short public presentations and seek feedback from the audiences to further refine our message. The book got its own website through which we have been able to collect feedback on our topics, format and approach ensuring relevance. From those sessions, we learned that jargon may be a barrier to implementation. In our practice we rarely tell people that we apply Design Thinking or Service Design, and instead we often have to work our magic by stealth. It is the mindset, the empathy for others, the collaboration and co-creation that matters most. But in writing about it we believe that it is important to acknowledge the discipline and consequently we have had to stick with some of the language from that discipline.

During the book design process, we have seen many new stories of design in education all over the world. We have witnessed the rise of new HE roles in

Service Design connected to digitalisation as well as degree programme design and the design of systems and processes, as well as services.

This book is a showcase of pioneering educators who believe that well-designed education is good for everyone - learners, teachers, education administrators, the learning organisation and the world. We aim to showcase the application of Design Thinking and Service Design in a variety of HE contexts ranging from central university teams adopting designer mindsets, breaking silos and designing a more holistic experience for all, to smaller scale yet impactful applications of design tools and methods acknowledging emotions and personal socio-cultural contexts of staff and students. We hope that this book will inspire you on your own journey to an educational experience that, with good design, becomes rehumanised and focused on transformation above transaction.

The diversity of contributions speaks to the potential of adopting design principles, practices and mindsets to university administration, curriculum design and learning experience design as well as insights into how we as educators refined and developed our own design capabilities. To enrich the perspective of applying design to education, we invited global experts from the world of design and education to share their opinions of why they believe Design Thinking and Service Design practices are good for the HE sector. These are interwoven in the book as candid testimonials providing compass pointers to the work of those we respect, those we have ourselves learnt from, and hopefully you will, too.

Our book may be a prototype but we hope that there will be many more new success stories to come. Education deserves good design; now, over to you.

References

Dhir, A. (2024) Human-centred design in higher education is a culture change challenge. Available at: https://sparck.io/journal/human-centred-design-in-higher-education-is-a-culture-change-challenge (Accessed: 5 February 2024).

Downe, L. (2020) *Good Services: How to design services that work.* Amsterdam: BIS.

EDUJAM. (2020) Edujam 2020 and 2022. Available at: https://edujam.co.uk (Accessed: 9 January 2024).

Global Jams. Available at: http://globaljams.org (Accessed: 9 January 2024).

Simon, H. A. (1969) The Science of the Artificial. The MIT Press.

Stickdorn, M., Hormess, M. E., Lawrence, A. & Schneider, J. (2018) *This is service design doing: applying service design thinking in the real world.* Sebastopol, CA: O'Reilly.

Drawing inspiration from the Human-Centred Design process

How the illustrations in this book were created

Molly Northcote

Phase 1: Discover

Initial research: One of the first steps in creating illustrations for the book was to figure out what type of illustrations it would include. Constrained only by the need to be black and white illustrations, I set off on a discovery journey to understand what is 'typical' for books of this nature, gaining inspiration from other book genres and illustration styles too.

In practice, this involved lots of in-person book shop visits and desk-based research. Findings were collated on a Miro board to make sense of the 'data' I had collected.

Understanding the users: Who are the stakeholders and what do they want and need? The stakeholders for the illustrations were split into four 'user groups'; the editorial team, the chapter authors, the publishers and most importantly the readers – that's you! I conducted research on the wants, needs and requirements of each user group.

In practice this involved asking simple questions to each user group to understand their perspective, such as "What do you want or need from these illustrations, and why?".

Phase 2: Define

Ensuring the team was aligned: After I had gathered lots of juicy insights from the discovery phase, it was time to define a style which was both desirable and feasible.

In practice this involved creating three design style concepts based on the discovery phase. I then presented these to the editorial team via a Miro board, where feedback was gathered. As a team, we then collaborated together and aligned on a final style to move forwards into the develop phase.

Defining what is important: At this stage, I also outlined the defining principles to guide all work created in the 'develop phase', much like a set of design guidelines or general objectives.

DOI: 10.4324/9781003383161-2

In practice, the key considerations which emerged from the discovery phase were ensuring that each and every illustration was easy to understand, intentional and fun. These considerations were fundamental in defining the overall style and finalising designs later on in the process.

Phase 3: Develop

Experimentation: After the design style and guiding principles were defined, now it was time to create! I spent hours and hours over many months creating illustrations for the many different chapter authors, using various tools which offered me flexibility and inspiration.

In practice this involved lots of rough paper sketches, paper collaging and even the use of Artificial Intelligence (using a tool called Vizcom) to help brainstorm ideas through new perspectives and different lenses.

Collaboration and iteration: I worked closely with authors to ensure the illustrations I developed were in line with what they had in mind. I created multiple iterations in order to 'fail fast' and get to the final illustration more efficiently.

In practice, this involved closely working collaboratively and flexibly with all authors and the editorial team. This involved feedback on early, rough pencil sketches, all the way through to near-finished digital drawings later in the process.

Phase 4: Deliver

The bigger picture

The bulk of this project's activities involved working with multiple different authors on their different chapters. To bring the book together in the final stages, I needed to take a step back from the detail of individual activities and see everything as 'one'.

In the middle of 2023, I was blown away by an exhibition by Takeshi Murikami in San Francisco. Murikami inspired me when he presented his 'behind the scenes' process alongside the relevant final artwork in the gallery. His process involved printing smaller versions of his paintings and then manually overlaying his improvements using tracing paper, different coloured pens and Tipp-ex. I took inspiration from this process as a way to help me easily and visually analyse whether all drawings worked not only on an individual basis, but as a whole family of illustrations which spoke the same language.

In practice, this meant printing physical copies of all the digital drawings and laying them all out closely together on my kitchen table. From this perspective, I then identified new weaknesses and strengths across all illustrations after reviewing them as a 'whole'. To capture this, I used a different coloured pen to scribble notes on each physical copy, which were then referenced when making final updates ready for print.

My three key learnings

1. There is immense value in following a human-centred design process, whatever your background

To be perfectly honest, this was the first time I had illustrated a book. I've done a lot of the things it takes to illustrate a book on separate occasions, such as drawing for others, responding to a brief and liaising with clients. However, this was the first time all of these activities were wrapped up together for the purposes of publishing a book, and I had the official title of 'Book illustrator'.

It's funny what impact a job title can have on people.

For me, this initially felt like I was closing a door to what I had done in the past and putting on a new hat and fancy dress; doing things a 'book illustrator' should and would do. This way of thinking seeped into my initial steps into the project, where I would take myself off to cafes, open my sketchbook and start waiting. Waiting for the 'aha!' moment. I'd order a flat white coffee … then a peppermint tea, then a little cake thing, to show the cafe staff I wasn't just there for the wifi. So much waiting, scribbling random ideas on paper that were driven by the notion of '… *but what would look cool*?'. It's fair to say this process didn't last long until I hit peak frustration. My mind was blank, and I started to question my own capabilities to even start, never mind finish this project. I stepped back to analyse the situation and ask myself why I was feeling like this. The answer was simply **'I don't know where to start or which direction to go in'**. This was the moment I realised what had happened.

Despite practicing and encouraging others to follow a Human-Centred Design Process in my day job, I would hang this hat up on Friday evenings, and then put on my 'Book Illustrator' hat ready for the weekend's work. But the principles and ways of thinking of Human-centred design are not owned

Figure 0.1 Human-Centred Design guiding the illustration process

only by those with 'designer' in their job title. It's for everyone, whatever the job title may be, and can be applied to most challenges that need to be solved. And that's why it's really special. After this realisation, I quickly set into motion a plan to incorporate a Human-Centred Design process, which is detailed in the 'How to' section above. This process guided me throughout the whole illustration project, allowing me to regain confidence in knowing where to start and which direction to go in.

2. When making things easier for others, ensure you're also making things easy for yourself

Fortunately, and also unfortunately, I am a default people pleaser. This trait, which I share with many other people, has meant that I don't often prioritise the things I could do in my daily life and work which could make my life easier. After finishing this project, there are three things I learnt through the process which would have made my life easier, which readers may find helpful.

Ensure important discussions are captured effectively for future reference

Despite being very used to recording and taking notes while conducting research in my day job, for some reason this logic didn't carry over to this project. There were some amazing meetings which I didn't record or take the time to write cohesive notes for. When following up on illustration updates at a later date, I wasted lots of time having to re-jog my memory as to what was discussed during the meeting and decode the squiggles on the page that was my handwriting.

Use the tools that make the most sense to what you need to achieve, not just what you think you should be using

At first, I was logging the progress on each and every illustration on Miro, an online, visual whiteboard tool. I thought '*hey, this is a very visual based project, so my admin and organisation should be visual too*'. After lots of time repeatedly uploading images to Miro and organising everything into fun, visual groups to keep track of progress, I realised I was spending too much time 'organising the organisation'. I quickly transferred only the key information needed to track progress into an Excel spreadsheet and was then able to filter and organise myself efficiently moving forwards. (Don't worry, I still got my visual fix by a nice bit of coloured conditioning formatting in Excel.)

Create fast and dirty concepts, early

This is a classic example of the 'fail fast' approach, whereby there are many known benefits to iterating quick and 'rough' concepts early, to get more quickly to the desired result. This is opposed to running with the first concept you come up with and perfecting it, only for you need to start all over again if it proves not to be the right thing you should have made. When in the development phase of creating an illustration, the focus should be on capturing the essence of the idea for communication purposes through quick sketches; rather than exhausting energy on creating a polished piece (think of neat lines, correct proportions and shadows), which is susceptible to needing changes after feedback.

3. Service design is a very approachable and strong community

I first met the editors and some of the authors of this book at the 2022 EduJam at the V&A in Dundee, Scotland, organised by the Service Design in Higher Education organisation. My involvement in EduJam was to support the late Andy de Vale in live-scribing the entirety of the event. You can see some examples of his work at this event, in the beautiful drawings that are in the inside covers of this book.

Attending this event was my first insight into the service design community. What struck me was how genuinely approachable, friendly and passionate all the service design practitioners were, and how engaged the various participants were in the two-day workshop. Working on this book has further strengthened my appreciation for this whole community. It's no surprise that when service design puts empathy at the heart of their processes and tools, this transcends beyond the 'job to be done' into the people and the community values as a whole.

Human Understanding and Behaviour Go Hand-in-Glove

Making a Difference through Human-Centred Design

Michael Doherty

The great theorist of design, Don Norman, wrote about the complex psychology of the interactions between people and 'everyday things', such as kettles and doors. To paraphrase Norman, 'Design is concerned with how things work ... and the nature of the interaction between people and [things]. When done well, the results are brilliant and pleasurable. When done badly, the [things] are unusable, leading to great frustration and irritation' (Norman, 2013, pp. 5–6).

For us in Higher Education (HE), our 'things' are generally more complex. They are the teaching, learning and assessment opportunities within our programmes and modules. They are the systems of student support and all the administrative processes needed to make institutions function so that they can provide this learning and support (plus all the other research and engagement activities in universities). All those working in HE, though, will be familiar with both sets of results and emotions that Norman describes. They come from our own experiences and in feedback from students and colleagues. We do not always connect these reactions to design decisions that we and others in our institutions have made.

Norman goes on to explain that when people fail to follow the detailed complex operating rules for things like washing machines and microwave ovens, then it is the operators who are blamed for not understanding the 'thing'. He argues that 'it is time to reverse the situation' and that it is the duty of those who design 'things' to understand people. Likewise, the chapters in this book are a provocation to all of us in HE to understand our people (our students, our colleagues) better and to design our systems of education and support to create more brilliant and pleasurable experiences and fewer that are marked by frustration and irritation.

Discussions of understanding and meeting human needs often circle back to Maslow's foundational theory of human motivation (Maslow, 1943). He presented a hierarchy of needs with physiological needs at the base and moving upwards through safety needs, social needs, esteem needs and, at the peak, growth needs of self-actualisation. It is interesting to note how many of the chapters explain how to identify and meet these needs in multiple ways. Design

DOI: 10.4324/9781003383161-3

approaches, though, go beyond this. They are not tethered to a pre-ordained list of objectives. As Gasson explains, even ostensibly user-centred projects will often 'fail to promote human interests because of a goal-directed focus on the closure of pre-determined technical problems' (Gasson, 2003, p. 41). Effective design projects need to privilege the actuality above the theory and direct us to really see the people before us in all their complexity and diversity. They challenge us to understand and empathise with them in particular timeframes and in situated circumstances. Giacom (2014, p. 6) emphasises 'the situatedness of human-centred design, which must of necessity ask questions which are specific to the individuals involved and the target environment'.

Authoritative statements of what human-centred design actually means and what it involves are hard to come by but one official statement, as highlighted by Giacom (2014), is found in ISO9241–210 'Human-centred design for interactive systems'. This indicates core characteristics of:

- Multi-disciplinarity
- An explicit understanding of users, tasks and environments
- User-centred evaluation
- Consideration of the whole user experience
- Involvement of users throughout design and development
- Iterative processes.

It is interesting to compare the (seemingly) cold functionality of engineering standards versus the warm and aspirational rhetoric of student-centredness in HE. One example of this is in the Bologna Process for a European Higher Education Area; 'Student-centred learning requires empowering individual learners, new approaches to teaching and learning, effective support and guidance structures and a curriculum focussed clearly on the learner' (European Higher Education Area, 2009). Yet, what is revealed by even a cursory thought experiment on how these things are being done in practice, is how far existing conceptions of student-centredness in HE have failed to use the human-centred approaches listed above, and how radical the changes could be if those mindsets, approaches and practical tools were applied to HE.

There is a great deal of angst in HE about the ability (or inability) of institutions and staff to influence student behaviour on issues like attendance, engagement (with learning, with feedback, with student support processes), and attainment. Yet, as Krippendorf (2004, p. 48) says 'Human centredness takes seriously the premise that human understanding and behaviour go hand in glove'. The approaches outlined in this collection are very practical and pragmatic, but they also engage with the affective domain, the emotional responses to being in HE (as student, academic, professional services), more explicitly than most models of change in HE.

It is in this exploring and open-minded spirit that the authors have approached the task of advocating for human-centred and service design approaches. They explain why they used these approaches to address challenges in their institutions and in their practice. They outline the impact of human-centred design and how this differs from more traditional processes of review, development and change management in HE institutions.

Design has a deep well of conceptual thinking to draw on but is ultimately a 'doing' field of practice. The authors therefore conclude their chapters with a short list of takeaways. They are practical tips, suggestions for scalable first steps, and provocations. The 'situatedness' of human-centred design, discussed above, is important here. It means, paradoxically, that the methods outlined in these case studies are very portable and flexible. The authors are not detailing projects that are limited to their own discipline or domain of HE, just how they have leveraged general design mindsets and toolkits to address situated challenges.

This is what you have to look forward to. The book is principally structured around three broad themes: a) building the capacity and mindsets to undertake service design projects in HE institutions; b) using human-centred design approaches to effect change in services and processes that operate at a cross-institutional level; and c) how thinking in human-centred ways can positively impact what happens in programmes and in the classroom. Each section is fronted by insightful forewords from designers and educators who wanted to share their relationship with design with the readers. We have also included an endorsement section with supporting statements from our mentors, peers and colleagues who have given us much needed support and encouragement on our journey.

Section 1: Design as we see it

The first section starts with you, the community that has grown around this book. In our crowdsourced chapter, "*It all Just Clicked!*", edited by **Michael Doherty** you will read your own words, your own recollection of the first encounter with design, your first connection, first experience. We asked you whether you managed to make it stick in your organisation, and in your practice. This is a chapter we thank you for, and one to cherish.

We continue with an overview chapter from someone who inspired many of us to explore the potential of service design, and whose work equipped us to undertake design projects. In '*Service Design solves the right problem*', **Adam Lawrence** draws on his wide experience to argue that service design is an important, powerful, effective, and accessible approach to change and improvement which reflects the realities of today's organisations. Despite a long history, it is also widely unknown. In this introductory chapter, he maps out what service design is, why it is useful, what happens in service design projects, and why HE should be adopting it more.

Section 2: Building capacity, developing mindsets

There are a range of, thankfully surmountable, challenges to those wanting to apply human-centred design within HE. Our first substantive section addresses these challenges and outlines how we can build the capacity to undertake human-centred design projects and developing the sort of empathetic and innovative mindsets, in ourselves and in others, to see opportunities for change and to make them happen.

In 'Change HEROs: Scaling Service Design as a Core Competence for Professional Services Staff', **Pamela Spokes and Jean Mutton**, look back at the learning journeys they have had as professional services staff working in HE who adopted service design to enhance the student experience and improve the efficiency and effectiveness of business processes. They explain how they drew upon their extensive experience in administrative and operational roles to create a course specifically for people like them; those wanting to make sustainable service enhancement in systems and procedures, created or re-designed using human-centred research. They explore how the tools and techniques of service design have helped them to appreciate the importance of getting the right mindset to flourish in an environment often hostile to co-creation in change management.

Katie Murrie and **Sonia Virdi** similarly explore the transformative effects of service design, but in this case from the perspective of the impact of service design education on Sonia, as a student/practitioner, and on Katie, as a lecturer. In '*Inspiring change at all levels: the personal and professional impact of service design training*', they look at Sonia's journey, as a graphic designer, undergoing further training at the Service Design Academy and showcase how she applied core techniques and principles to real-world scenarios. Additionally, they draw upon valuable insights from Katie to distil essential lessons from the training, emphasising the capabilities required of service designers. Their narrative outlines the importance of practising service design in HE and sheds light on how it can reveal established operational inefficiencies that hinder seamless end-to-end user experiences. As education institutions become increasingly service-oriented organisations, it becomes paramount that individuals can drive change at all levels. They argue that by cultivating a service design mindset we can, as institutions and staff, place the needs of those we serve at the core of our endeavours.

Collaborative innovation is the focus of **Lara Salinas's** chapter. In *Untangling networks: Using design methods to grow collaborative innovation beyond the classroom*, she delves into the design and implementation of a canvas tailored to foster a culture of collaborative innovation within an HE institution. This chapter presents a case study centred on the development and deployment of a canvas: an online visual tool that supports academic teams to have a structured conversation. This offers a platform for reframing teaching and learning activities as conducive to collaborative innovation. The canvas operates at both macro and micro scales. At a macro level it drives organisational change by revealing the dynamic interplay between teaching, research, and knowledge exchange. At a micro level the canvas supports academic teams in unpacking the intricate network of collaborations that underpin project-based learning and align them with institutional strategic objectives. The chapter outlines the design journey of the canvas and prompts reflection on the distinctive advantages of employing these design approaches compared to traditional practices in HE.

There is a real focus on methods and tools in design thinking, but **Phillippa Rose** and **Sharon Jones** argue otherwise in their chapter *Mindsets Eat Methods: Human-Centred Design for organisational change in HE*. In this chapter they recount their shared experience of introducing Human-Centred Design (HCD) interventions into two different HE live organisational projects. In each institution the practice of Human-Centred Design was applied in response to real-world design challenges, to build HCD capability and drive wider change and transformation. They contend that HCD offers more than a method for bringing about improved services for users. HCD disrupts thinking and builds capability to surface innovation in group settings through shared problem/solution finding that is relevant and meaningful to participant-learners, users, and wider stakeholders.

Finally in this section **Sarah Dyer** and **Ksenija Kuzmina** outline *Prototyping educational change: Learning from a ten-week service design programme*. They share their experiences of designing and running a ten-week service design programme – The Innovation Lab. The programme was designed for educators and students at the University of Exeter who had been awarded institutional grants to undertake education change projects. This chapter outlines the programme's five defining characteristics as a structured service design programme, addressing real world problems, with a cohort of educators and students, coached by designers and that the programme was a pilot itself. They consider three tensions that emerged during the programme: service design and business as usual; people and projects; design and implementation. The discussion is framed by the intention to provide readers with a set of prompts for planning their own programme of service design activities.

Section 3: Institutional change

The contributions to this section all address changes that have been implemented across significant parts of the operations of HE institutions. Some draw on existing change concepts (Lean, automation) or focus on different operational domains (library services, information systems), and they all highlight the distinctiveness and potential of human-centred approaches.

In *An Exploration of the Relationship between Lean and Service Design for Service Improvement*, **Mila Bombardieri** and **Nichole Dunne-Watts** examine the challenges, insights and successes experienced by a team of process improvement specialists at Middlesex University while pursuing the integration of Service Design and Lean methodologies. Starting with an overview of the context and motives around the team's inception, the chapter discusses how a culture of Continuous Improvement was embedded, how integration came about, how challenges were overcome and the lessons learnt along the way. Drawing on evidence from various case studies, this chapter shows how two conceptually different approaches – one broadly paradigmatic, rooted in analytical and rational thinking, the other focussed on empathetically understanding human needs and generating new ideas through creative co-design – can helpfully and successfully complement each other so organisations can create new possibilities.

Svein Are Tjeldnes and **Karin Eilertsen** explain *Using Service Design to increase the student and staff experience – a case study of three live experiments* in an overview of a service design project carried out at UiT the Arctic University of Norway. The project was undertaken to increase the customer experience for students and staff by improving administrative services. Instead of a classical structural re-organisational approach, the project focused on reorganising the way of working. The main body of the chapter discusses why the service design methodology was chosen to approach the problem and how the project was initiated. The chapter then presents three live experiments that were conducted as part of the project: developing a cross-organisational service-map, designing and running five service pilots and creating a model for service leadership.

Work conducted by Cambridge University Libraries' Futurelib programme, is the focus of **Jenny Egan** and **David Marshall** in *Futurelib: prototyping library services at the University of Cambridge*. The chapter reflects on the project, which employed service design methods to design, test and refine concepts for library services. Two of these services are discussed in detail: Spacefinder (a service to help Cambridge students find appropriate places to work); and Protolib (design of user-centred workspaces to optimise productivity and wellbeing in libraries). These case studies are used to discuss key tenets of service design and their application in an HE context, as well as wider themes around organisational culture, relationship management and advocacy. The chapter covers the barriers to introducing service design at a UK university and steps that were taken to overcome those challenges. It presents a critical view of what worked well and less well, with the intention of enabling those currently adopting or advocating for service design in their own institutions.

In *Designing for a Gender-Inclusive Campus*, **Bernadette Geuy, Daphne Ogle** and **Rachel Hollowgrass** explore the application of human-centred design to structural information systems in HE institutions. On every campus there are vulnerable people who are trying to make sense of the world around them, navigating structural systems with only male/female gender options and feeling like they do not belong. All campus community members deserve to be recognised in respectful and inclusive ways by acknowledging their gender through *pronouns* and *lived names*. This chapter serves as a best practice guide describing how the authors worked with universities in the United States to design and enable new gender data options in campus systems to further a culture of inclusivity. The work of enabling gender data is complex and transformational. During these projects, many nuanced needs emerge along with the potential of harming vulnerable, gender-nonconforming people. A Service Design approach provides the framework and methods for centring research on human needs, desires and experiences. These must be evaluated against the institution's business and technical constraints, and in a context of socio-political externalities. Adding the infrastructure for collecting and using gender data on campus has far-reaching impacts. It demonstrates that the institution values inclusion and begins to normalise expansive gender categories for campus community members and beyond. The authors further explain how working with and advocating for the needs of genderqueer, non-binary and transgender people touched them deeply, as they designed for and led change efforts at universities.

Finally in this section, **Jennifer Robertson** argues for *Integrating service design thinking into our Automation Service*. The chapter considers Automation, specifically Robotic Process Automation (RPA), as a tactical solution for HE to improve the efficiency and effectiveness of services. It introduces the idea of what 'automation' is and why universities may want to consider RPA as a service delivery option. It describes why institutions need to start viewing RPA (virtual workers) as another part of their service blueprints, providing enablement across user touchpoints and service interactions, and how service design approaches can and should be used across the RPA lifecycle. The chapter also provides an overview of the Automation Service at the University of Glasgow, including the automation strategy and automation journey using service design approaches.

Section 4: Student Experience

This fourth section brings us into the classroom. We mean this broadly as anything from curriculum design to new ways of generating and responding to feedback that directly impact what happens in lecture theatres and seminar rooms.

In *Warwick Secret Challenge: Design thinking for re-imagining student engagement*, **Bo Kelestyn** argues that student engagement is transforming, with students seeking more active and constructive roles in the co-creation of innovation, beyond simply sharing their opinions. New tools for decision making, problem-solving and ideation have been created in the business and digital realms to reflect the complexity and uncertainty brought about by the accelerated levels of innovation and change, which old management tools could no longer speak to. These tools are also relevant for the HE context. Design thinking is one example, and the academic community is growing in familiarity in its uses of curriculum and learning design. Applying design thinking to student engagement, however, proposes new and exciting areas of innovation and research. Used for student engagement it allows for the creation of a new space outside of the formal structures of the University and the Students' Union, and of the tensions associated with these structures. Instead, it reimagines student engagement and creates several distinct affordances, such as in the case of the Warwick Secret Challenge (WSC). This chapter positions the WSC as a novel conceptual model for engaging students as partners in shaping their academic experience through design thinking.

Diversity and inclusion are fundamental values in HE and this theme is addressed in *Service Design in Education: A mindset towards Inclusive and Accessible Learning Experiences* by **Kim Anderson** and **Christopher Sze Chong Lim.** Their chapter explores the intersection between service design, inclusive design and education emphasising the importance of creating inclusive learning experiences. It begins by defining the relationship between Universal Design, Inclusive Design and Accessibility and its common goal of creating products, environments and services that cater to a diverse range of users. This is important because in the UK, the Equality Act 2010 legally obliges Further and HE institutions to provide reasonable adjustments in their approach to service provision to ensure they are accessible to people with disabilities. Lack of awareness and understanding, assumptions and stigma from others can create barriers to learning for people with disabilities. The Universal Design for Learning (UDL) framework is introduced as a means to make learning and teaching more inclusive. The framework focuses on three principles: multiple means of representation, multiple means of expression and multiple means of engagement. Drawing from the authors' praxis as educators in Further and HE, two case studies are presented exemplifying the integration of UDL principles and the application of service design mindsets and methods.

Ksenija Kuzmina and **James Moran** in *Reflection By Design: Embedding Reflective Practice into the Student Learning Journey* outline the multiple forms of reflective practice, such as models developed by Kolb and by Gibbs, which are routinely drawn upon within Higher Education teaching, learning and assessment. However, in the authors' experience, these are used in an *ad hoc* manner across different modules and activities with little attempt to embed a coherent longitudinal approach to support development of reflective practice across an academic programme or within the wider student journey. This chapter reflects on a project which used service design thinking to inform and develop student engagement with reflective practice across one-year postgraduate courses within a British HE institution. It reports on the authors' experience of: introducing reflective concepts; co-creating interventions with the students; embedding these within the student journey and evaluating the effectiveness of a pedagogical approach derived from service design thinking to engage students in the reflective process.

Radka Newton provides an insight into the value of visualising the learner's educational experience using an emotional journey mapping approach. In *Life beyond the classroom: Emotional journey mapping of learners' educational experience*, she explains how visualisation of the intangible can be presented as a powerful demonstration of how we experience learning throughout our lives, as well as in university settings during degree programmes, short courses or educational conferences and events. Every learning experience can be mapped as a journey from the point of our first interest to the time we complete the learning, reflect and take our learning to the future. The chapter discusses a variety of applications and purposes of journey maps and provides inspiration to incorporate this method as a reflection tool, design communication tool and a tangible articulation of learners' experience leading to the co-creation of education. It demonstrates a human-centred approach enhancing an understanding of the feelings, frustrations and emotions associated with learning activities.

In *Know thy student, for she is not thee': User personas as a way to give agency to student voice*, **Radka Newton** and **Michael Doherty** explore the application of human-centred research and user personas to the design of university curriculum and degree programme experiences. They link the user-centred principle of service design to student-centred education and explore how personas can help educators achieve more inclusive and human-centred learning. They argue that if we understand our students better and keep that understanding visible through our decision-making processes, then institutions and staff can make better educational decisions. The chapter emphasises that personas are an outcome of evidence-based user research, rather than assumptions, and that they synthesise and personify both quantitative and qualitative data. You will be transported to the actual life and experiences of students, their dreams and fears, hopes and frustrations. Empathy is a central theme of this chapter, and it considers how personas can enable better communication between lecturers and students.

And finally, *It's a Wrap.* **Jean Mutton** and **Christine Stewart** summarise our book themes in an intriguing piece titled *Seamless student journey – fact or fiction?*. As at the start, this section also ends with inspiration from crowd-sourced discussions collected by the authors to ensure that our own assumptions about the enablers and blockers to effective and sustainable change were either confirmed or challenged. The chapter ends our collection with the conclusion that while the sector has moved significantly towards designing better staff and student experiences it still has some way to go.

All of us involved in this collection, editors and authors, would feel that we have failed if having read the book, and found it interesting (as you surely will), for it then to have no impact on your practice as an educator, provider of professional services, administrator or other type of change-maker in HE. We want you to take away and use our key takeaways. When you do apply these methods in your own practice, you will necessarily do so in different ways, finding different challenges and opportunities and reaching different results. This will, though, be in a common framework that will bring greater understanding, empathy and insights that will allow you to make practical changes that actually work for your students and colleagues. Good luck!

References

European Higher Education Area. (2009) Ministerial Declaration 2009. Available at: https://ehea.info/cid101040/ministerial-conference-leuven-louvain-neuve-2009. html (Accessed: 24 January 2024).

Gasson, S. (2003) Human-centered vs. user-centered approaches to information systems design. *Journal of Information Technology Theory and Application*, 5(2), 29–46.

Giacom, J. (2014) What is Human-Centred Design. *Design Journal*, 17(4), 606–623.

International Organization for Standardization. (2019) ISO9241–210:2019 'Human-centred design for interactive systems'. Available at: www.iso.org/standard/77520.html (Accessed: 24 January 2024).

Krippendorf, K. (2004) Intrinsic motivation and human-centred design. *Theoretic Issues in Ergonomics Science*, 5(1), 43–72.

Maslow, A. (1943) A Theory of Human Motivation. *Psychological Review*, 50, 370–396.

Norman, N. (2013) *The Design of Everyday Things* (2nd ed.). New York: Basic Books.

Design As We See It

Foreword

Sarah Drummond and Debbie McVitty

These days, learning is more complex than just walking into a building. Our experience of learning doesn't happen in a vacuum – it's part of our messy lives. We sometimes learn remotely, across geographies, by ourselves, on the go, in groups. What learners need and the effectiveness of delivering our intended educational outcomes can and should be designed.

Our first thought of design is often physical objects, fashion, buildings, maybe websites. From shaping how we enrol on courses, to what kind of student support we provide, making Virtual Learning environments accessible, to wayfinding around complex campuses the whole end-to-end learning experience should be shaped. We must ensure that we meet both the needs of learners and the intended outcomes for our Higher Education institutions.

I'm delighted to finally see a compendium of rich examples where academics and practitioners share their experiences of applying human-centred design methods and techniques to Higher Education. This will no doubt be a much-needed resource for institutions and educators embarking on consciously thinking how they design learning experiences for all.

Sarah Drummond, Director of School of Good Services

Across the globe, Higher Education systems are in need of practical wisdom on tackling the challenge of reimagining how large, complex and bureaucratic institutions achieve their educational mission to realise students' potential and improve their lives. Human-centred education and service design practice offers the practical tools to achieve this, underpinned by insight on how embracing connection, empathy and community can help to realise the continued value and importance of Higher Education to the contemporary world. This book will be of enormous interest to educators everywhere – whether employed in academic or professional roles – who care about the personal wellbeing and collective impact of the people who make up the Higher Education community.

Debbie McVitty, Editor of WONKHE

DOI: 10.4324/9781003383161-5

"It all just clicked"

Experiences of finding and using service design in higher education

Michael Doherty, Radka Newton and Jean Mutton

This is a crowd-sourced chapter. It draws on the accounts of 19 contributors who told us how they first made contact with service design ideas, how they incorporated service design methods into their perspectives and practices and how they have used service design tools to bring about positive change in their institutions and for their students and colleagues. As service designers this felt like a natural thing for us to do in putting this book together. Service design is a collaborative venture. It encourages us recognise the limitations of our own disciplinary and personal skills and perspectives and to work in teams. It values processes of co-creation. We also conceive of service design in Higher Education (HE) as a movement as well as a burgeoning field of practice. Our understanding of what it means to 'do' service design in HE should draw on a wide and diverse range of voices.

We make no claims that the survey is strictly representative, but it was circulated as widely as possible via social media, our book website and through our networks and contacts. The responses were really gratifying because a) these stories are powerful; and b) we really want this book to have impact, to empower you to start or continue your journey into human-centred design in HE. A challenge is often that people cannot see an 'in', an opportunity to take their first steps into a new field of practice. This chapter is full of diverse examples of how people have made that first step, built up their capabilities in service design and applied it to make positive changes to their institutions. Our thanks to the contributors who are listed at the end of this chapter.

Do you remember the first time?

We asked; 'What was your first encounter with service design, your first connection, first experience – do you remember?' There were some common themes that emerged from the responses, though with much overlap and interaction between them.

DOI: 10.4324/9781003383161-6

Figure 1.1 Crowd-sourced insights

Serendipity or post-hoc realisation

For some respondents, their first contact with service design happened by chance – perhaps we can call it serendipity. This could be as simple as hearing about mapping user journeys from podcasts. Some people had trained as designers but only later found – or fully appreciated – the value in HE of, service design: "Starting my career as a furniture and product designer, I've always designed with and for people and environments. The emotional connection, functionality and experience of an object were always important to me. I was exploring how I could use design for social impact when I came across a Design Thinking workshop at Wecon – a Women's Entrepreneur conference in Pakistan". One Content/UX Designer did user research into their university's virtual learning environment, where she considered students as 'the users' at the centre of her user-centred design process and found out about the things that students wanted to use the VLE for; "When I looked into achieving some of these 'wish-list' items, I really grasped what service design was about".

Others were in roles supporting student experience and their values drove them to take human-centred approaches often without realising that the mindsets and methods they had developed were well established concepts of service design: "I spent many years creating, designing and improving services with HE. I started to create 'student stories' and 'staff experiences' to demonstrate changes, not knowing at the time that these were called personas" and were a core part of the service design methodology.

Someone who is now Head of Person-Centred Design at a university said, "I was probably doing service design without knowing it in previous business transformation roles as I've always been interested in how we make things better for our students". Another explains that after ten years in HE, "I was working as a planner and I often joke that I was doing learning analytics before I knew what it was. My first interaction with service design is therefore much the same". This moment of discovery of service design was often described as exciting and revelatory; "The work I'd been doing suddenly had names, strategies and tools".

The itch you cannot scratch – purposefully searching for methods to address a problem

'The problem' is an important concept in service design. We are encouraged to spend a lot of time in 'the problem space' and to see it as the trigger for creativity and innovation. A theme that emerged from our survey was the realisation that existing approaches were insufficient or unsuited to resolving problems and the subsequent purposeful search for alternatives. A head of digital services at a university, for example, found that, "My team and I were constantly running into problems with the products and services we had been asked to work on", while an academic who became chair of an important university committee, "discovered that plagiarism was so widespread but that students were unaware of the university's plagiarism policy".

Others framed this searching out of human-centred approaches as triggered not so much by a specific problem, but the wider and ongoing challenge of making changes: "I was leading an institutional change project ... focussed on improvement and capability building, when I started reading more and more from IDEO about Design Thinking and then onto Service Design". Similar challenges were mentioned in relation to staff recruitment and selection processes and to seeking different approaches to teaching marketing students about services. People then were able to access either service design experts within their own institutions or external training providers such as Adaptive Path.

One take on this idea of 'the problem' as the trigger was placed in the context of previous failed attempts at change and the consequent cynicism about innovation buzzwords. It involved a move into academia to support a research institute in its formation phase, and "because of the empty (and therefore kind of burnt) buzzwords – people were reluctant to come along the proposed journey. And in those workshops I realised: what they'd actually need was a service design approach for what they were planning (building an inhouse innovation unit, identifying current trends in research in digital transformation, co-creating the research topics from the ground up with citizens, etc.) ...".

Through the pleasures of education and training

Finally, several people had their first contact with service design as part of some sort of education or training event. Among the things mentioned were a Master's programme in entrepreneurship and innovation; "One of my modules was in innovation and design thinking. I was introduced to service design processes, tools, and how it can help with problem-solving and to drive innovation".

One respondent took up a research fellowship in a management school, and another took part in an internal training day on service design for HR services. One was working as a project manager in an education incubator that had already adopted service design methods. Conferences were also important sources of first exposure to service design including the Adaptive Path Service Experience Conference in 2014 and the Service Design Network's global conference in San Francisco in 2012.

Lightbulb moments

We asked, 'When did you first feel that 'lightbulb', that 'aha' moment?' Again, there was a lot of overlap, but three distinct themes emerged.

Epiphany

"It was clear early on that the process involved made absolute sense. Too often we looked at the solution from 'our' perspective and needs, and not that of the service user. So, by creating personas and getting into that character you are better able to understand the challenges they face".

This feeling of 'fit' or the immediate sense of the potential of service design came through in other responses:

"Attending the conference was like an epiphany – here was an approach and set of practices to examine and problem-solve the issues I saw in my work", and "it all just clicked. For so long we had done student experience at students, rather than with them in mind. I spend every day now challenging the idea of who we are aiming student experience at".

Some respondents described this effect in quite emotional terms; "It was so inspirational, and I connected with many people who have become important members of my professional network" and, "I never felt that I fitted into what peers were doing, 'keeping the lights on' … I felt like I found my tribe!". The impacts of this epiphany went wider than work "This experience changed my perspective on life, and I started to look at so many things in a different way".

Digging deeper

For some it was only by digging deeper into the literature and practice of service design that its potential became clearer. "I spent a considerable amount of my own time, reading, learning and practicing, to develop my approach and confidence as I created a service from nothing to where it is today". The activities mentioned by respondents in exploring service design further included attending events like EduJam2022 in Dundee, reading books like Andy Polaine's *Service Design: From Insight to Implementation*, articles such as 'Designing Services that Deliver' by G. Lynn Shostack in the *Harvard Business Review* and materials from the Livework consultancy.

Application

The most common response to how people found their way to a 'lightbulb moment' though was through application. As examples: "The real lightbulb moment came when process mapping the initial recruitment stages using our persona of a newly appointed academic employee who had experience of HE but none in a management role" and "I saw a method that could be useful so that my students could approach the management of services in a more creative, innovative and comprehensive way".

For some there was a point of revelation early in the application process; "The penny dropped that [the virtual learning environment] was more than a platform or an interface, it was a service, where operators' actions enabled users to achieve their tasks", and "the service was not designed in a way which would allow [the] technology to flourish and work. That was my lightbulb moment". For others the realisation came through the enactment of a whole process or "at the end of a service design challenge", even if this process was relatively swift; "the journey from a more Lean and metrics-based approach to one that was more open and embracing of Human-Centred Design was fairly rapid. My journey with it continues, embracing how it can be applied to anything from designing strategies to designing classrooms".

Making it stick with you

Many of us are neophytes at heart. We come across lots of new ideas and many of them seem terribly attractive, yet few of them stay with us as strongly as service design ideas. We asked what it is that makes service design so 'sticky'?

Internalised mindset

Some answers pointed to how these ideas are quickly internalised into everyday thinking and working, often in simple and direct ways: "I just talk about it everywhere now" and people described how they have "imbibed the thinking procedure taught into my everyday life and this has changed my perspective on how to approach a crisis and develop fundamental research".

It was often integrated into practices; "I immediately changed the way I approached my courses. I started adding Service Design to various strategic and tactical marketing processes". This internalised mindset can have an enduring impact; "I have left the organisation. However, I have kept with me the principles of service design, ensuring services are user-centred, co-created and evidence-based".

Some consciously reinforce this new way of looking at the world and defining problems by drawing on principles and guidelines such as "Turn on curiosity antennae to find problems" and one person describes how they create and follow key guidelines that "have helped me to keep the right mindset and be confident when I'm solving a problem or improving the design of a service or process". The guidelines include e.g., to try to stay curious, be okay with holding your nerve, not jumping to conclusions and to be user/human-centred obsessed.

Meets your needs and chimes with your values

We heard that service design ideas stayed with people because it met their needs. This was described in terms of sheer utility: "Using the design thinking methodology while designing a service or trying to solve a problem has been helpful in making it stick" and "I think it's stuck (for me at least) in the process of evaluating and evidencing improvements (however microscopic!) and getting student buy in". It also seemed to chime with peoples' values. This could be on a personal level, "Understanding the methodology has also helped me to focus on people and be inclusive in everything I do [values]", and also at a professional and institutional one, "Working in service design in Higher Education, I devote time to keep up with new developments in the academic literature. Anchoring my service design work in aspects of academia gives it more weight and gravitas in the eyes of academic colleagues".

Other people

The role of community and other people also emerged as an important factor in embedding service design ideas: "I think you need to surround yourself with good people". This included participating in "a series of experiences like online courses, hackathons, Service Design Fringe festivals, jams, for example EduJam, and being part of different communities". It extended to activities intended to build a sense of community; "My passion for service design led me to create a Service Design Book Club, mentoring people in Service Design and transitioning to Service Design", and this goes beyond the walls of the university: "As we are building our service design capability from scratch, I've done this mainly with colleagues from outside the university. I've partnered with a service design agency (Sparck) to create Service Designers Connect, a service design community centred in Nottingham".

Keeping the flame alive

Finally, we asked people what made service design endure in their practices, how they used it to create effective change and to build capacity and impact.

Our respondents had a realistic view of this process, based on experience; "Making service design stick relies on energy, time and patience", and "it was a long process, that took a lot of work that was kind of uncommon for some of my academic colleagues". Some spoke of the inertia and cultural resistance both to change and to new ways of creating change "Universities are no different from any other organisation. They tend to push back against new ideas or ways of working". However, they were not daunted by these challenges and shared a wide range of ways in which they made service design work effectively for them, their institutions and their students.

Sharing is caring

It was important to create and share resources and to make these as accessible as possible. In the words of one university head of service it was crucial to avoid "creating a 'wall of expertise' that blocked others from accessing and developing their understanding of service design". In a similar vein, one person said, "Allies are important, especially if they are in positions of influence".

Some of the activities to build momentum by sharing resources were impressive in their scale and ambition: "I share learning resources on Service Design 101 with key members of the Design Leadership team in the business organisation of IBM. I also created a case study on the SDN website about my work on a new mainframe product editor and how I worked collaboratively with the product stakeholders. And I spoke at the internal Design Conference at IBM in 2022 about my transition to Service Design from Design Research".

Nice and easy does it

There were some really interesting approaches to navigating university structures and reducing the more knotty problems to get people on board; "I reduced the use of jargon and referencing tools – focusing on the jobs to be done and what would take pain away". It was also important to understand institutional and disciplinary cultures; "I, as the facilitator, realised how important it is to take out all ego when guiding them through the jam, really meeting them where they are to encourage their creativity to unfold" and avoid trying "to appear extra-professional, cool, knowledgeable, better-by-default or by means of my title, etc".

This even extended to not mentioning service design at all: "we structured it along the double diamond, but because of my earlier experience with the burnt buzzwords I never mentioned we are using a service design approach". This was summed up in some very practical and actionable advice: "don't use buzzwords, speak the language, you don't have to call it service design to do service design (doing not talking), you need buy-in (trust) from upper management, create trust and psychological safety when involving so many stakeholders from different levels, backgrounds of society, really emphasising how you value their expertise".

The power of stories

In service design we know the power of stories. This worked for people at the meta level, using stories about service design to build support and engagement with service design; "To keep service design on the agenda I am always looking for new ways of communicating the same wisdom, fresh success stories, updated examples of lives improved by service design", and "I make it stick by sticking it to everything I do, showing it works and then sticking it on new things".

A Senior Director of Service Design explains how they manifested new institutional capabilities to do service design "through advocacy, seeking funding, sponsorship, many dozens (even hundreds now?) of projects to show and prove the work, referral word of mouth, community building, networking and evangelism across my institution". A User Experience Manager stresses the importance both of measuring and celebrating the impact of design-led changes, but also of the sustainability of the method; "Energy, time and patience to complete the cycle of researching the service, visualising the service through artefacts, identifying changes, making changes, researching the impact of the changes. And repeat ad infinitum".

The ripple effect

"Us humans like to know someone else has done it before, and then we often want a piece of it too". People talked about the power of making colleagues part of the solution, mentoring and empowering them to widen the impact of service design approaches within institutions; "I've also found that getting other people to talk about service design is helpful so that you are not a lone voice. I invited an academic colleague from our Product Design course talk to our University Leadership Team".

One former Head of Digital at a university usefully describes the process this way; "This is all about getting people more comfortable with the idea of service design and helping them develop empathy for their users. Once you've finished the research, get them to share what they have learned with their teammates in a 'show and tell' and identify the next steps". Others encouraged their academic colleagues "to take those learnings back into their training as educators to enable their future students".

This process of co-creating, in one case called 'the Ikea effect', appeared in several accounts of how to amplify the impact of service design; "let them be part of building the solution", and in another case "I designed a workshop to look at students' onboarding experiences and invited participants from across the departments ... Each participant was responsible for interviewing at least one student about their experiences and to bring that to the workshop. Together we mapped out the students' journeys".

Conclusion

A couple of our responses provided wider reflections on the nature of doing service design in universities and thoughtful advice on building this movement and making it inspire real and positive change. We cannot improve on them and are very happy to conclude the chapter with these words:

> "Service design can be a lonely existence in Higher Education. You are often on your own, pioneering your craft and advocating for it, all at the same time. For this reason, being part of groups like the Service Design Network, and attending conferences like Service Design in Government help dispel inevitable notions of imposter syndrome, instil a sense of camaraderie and help keep you inspired and motivated to keep flying the service design flag".

> "In summary, I don't think there is a 'secret sauce' to embedding service design in Higher Education, just a strong belief in the process and its universality and a will to keep going in the application of it to university services. If we keep practising and publishing our outputs and communicating the outcomes service design has achieved, we have the power to shift the narrative, to make Higher Education the service design sector and to grow and develop service design as a discipline to inspire the service designers of the future".

Contributors

Huge thanks to our contributors for sharing their stories, their insights and ideas. They are a stellar group of people bringing about human-centred change across the HE sector. They are:

Owen Beer – Head of Person-Centred Design, Nottingham Trent University, UK
Mauricio Bejarano – EAFIT University, Colombia
Dr Fiona Chambers – University College Cork, Ireland
Bernadette Geuy – Power of Design Services, USA
Emma Horrell – User Experience Manager, University of Edinburgh, UK

Arun Joseph – Service Designer, IBM, USA
Lekhana Manjunatha – Lancaster University Management School, UK
Megan Erin Miller – Senior Director of Service Design, UK
Tobi Ogunpehin – Lancaster University Management School, UK
Dave Rimmer – Centre for Ecology & Hydrology (previously Lancaster University, UK)
Tom Ritchie – University of Warwick, UK
Jennifer Robertson – Head of Automation, University of Glasgow, UK
Annette Robinson – Learning & Development Coach, Co-op, UK
Professor Dave Sammon – University College Cork, Ireland
Samuel Simon – Center for Advanced Internet Studies (CAIS), Bochum, Germany
Alice Trethewey – HEdway Group Ltd, UK
Sadaf Uddin – Service Designer and Educator, Pakistan/UK

References

Crowd-sourced resource list

These are the resources – articles, books, digital objects – that our respondents said helped them find and build capacity in service design.

IDEO. Designing for Public Services Toolkit. Available at: www.ideo.com/journal/designing-for-public-services (Accessed: 6 December 2023).

Livework. Service Design for Business. Available at: liveworkstudio.com/insight/service-design-for-business-behind-the-scenes (Accessed: 6 December 2023).

Lynn Shostack, G. (1984) Designing Services that Deliver. *Harvard Business Review* (January). Available at: https://hbr.org/1984/01/designing-services-that-deliver (Accessed: 6 December 2023).

Polaine, A. (2013) *Service Design: From Insight to Implementation.* Los Angeles, CA: Rosenfield Media.

Risdon, C. (2013) Mapping the User Experience. Available at: https://walkerux.wordpress.com/2013/12/15/mapping-the-user-experience-w-chris-risdon (Accessed: 6 December 2023).

Spool, J.Resource Library on UX. Available at: https://aycl.uie.com/experts/jared_m._spool (Accessed: 6 December 2023).

Stickdorn, M., Lawrence, A., Hormess, M. & Schneider, J. (2018) *This is Service Design Doing.* Sebastopol, CA: O'Reilly.

Vargo, S. & Lusch, R. (2004) Evolving to a New Dominant Logic for Marketing. *Journal of Marketing*, 68, 1.

Events

We know these have been and gone, but they should give you a sense of what is out there and what has been really useful.

Adaptive Path, Service Experience Conference. (2014) www.sausalito.com/event/ The-Service-Experience-Conference-2014-Hosted-by-Adaptive-Path/183858.

Design Council, Leading Business by Design Summit. www.designcouncil.org.uk/ our-resources/archive/reports-resources/leading-business-design.

EduJam. (2022) Dundee. www.vam.ac.uk/dundee/whatson/events/edujam.

Lean HE Annual Conference. (2018) Everyday Lean – from your story to my story. Tromsø www.leanhe.org/conference/our-conference-archive.

Service Design Network conference, San Francisco. (2012) www.service-design-net work.org/chapters/san-francisco.

Service Design in Government conference 2021 and 2022. https://govservicedesign.net.

Wecon – Women Entrepreneurs Conference, Pakistan. www.wecon.pk.

Chapter 2

Service Design solves the right problem

Adam Lawrence

Introduction

Service design is an important, powerful, effective and accessible approach to change and improvement which reflects the realities of today's organisations. Despite a long history, it is also widely unknown. In this introductory chapter, I will map out what service design is, why it is useful, what happens in service design projects and why Higher Education (HE) should be adopting it more.

The educators and the airport toilet

I often stand on a conference stage and look out at a room full of lawyers, or engineers, or government workers or educators. There might be 80 or 800 of them, looking at me sceptically across folded arms. My session is entitled "Service Design", and they are completely uninterested. "Service?" They might be thinking. "SERVICE like when I order a meal? Or when I call customer service to *complain*? DESIGN? Making things *look* good? Why do I care about this? I have to get it *right*". They should care because we all deliver services – we all do *work which assists others*. And shaping our services well can lead to all kinds of benefits – in core outcomes, in engagement, in staff motivation and retention and on the bottom line. To get their attention, I often start by setting them a challenge:

> "Imagine you work for an airport", I say. "You have lots of older visitors, and your figures show that those older folks use the airport lavatories three times more often than youngsters". They look confused, so I continue. "I'm not sure what 'older' means in this case. But I turned fifty a few years ago, and my Facebook advertising turned overnight from adventure holidays to *continence* products. So I guess it's fifty plus".

This gets the first little laugh, and some of the frowns disappear. "Now, imagine your bosses want to make the airport experience better for those oldies like me. They have put you in charge. What do you do, based on this data? Please talk with your neighbour".

DOI: 10.4324/9781003383161-7

A ripple goes through the audience as a lively conversation breaks out. This is popular. They are being asked to analyse a situation – there is even a little bit of quantitative data – and to make a decision. There is a chance to show their intellectual powers and to be *right*. How hard can it be?

After a minute or less, I quieten them down and ask for their response. Having posed this challenge many times, almost all the answers are familiar. "Build more bathrooms!" – "More signage". – "Make the stalls more accessible". – "Clean!" – "Play 1980s music!" After a few more replies, they are nodding. This simple challenge seems to have been solved. Piece of cake!

> "Nice ideas", I say. "Some will be expensive, disruptive… but they all could lead to a better experience. But hold on. WHY are they entering the lavatories? Are you sure you know? And how would you find out?"

There is some muttering. Waste of time! After all, there are only so many reasons to go into a bathroom.

> "In this real project", I explain, "the service design team used a research method called non-participative observation. In other words, they washed their hands in the lavatories for a really long time. And they found something interesting. Many – even most – of the older folks going into the bathroom were not using the toilets at all. They were in there because… (pause for effect) … in the bathrooms you can *hear the flight announcements* better".

The reaction in the room is always audible. There are gasps, exclamations, a few hollow laughs.

> "Service design is many things and can take us to many places. But one thing it does particularly well is, it stops us wasting resources on *solving the wrong problems*".

By now, my sceptical audience is listening.

What is service design?

I have been working in service design for decades, though I have only used the term since around 2010. I have co-written two books on the subject which are commonly used as textbooks and reference works in firms and universities. I'm not an academic, but I am an educator and teach in many contexts around the world; in design, in tech and most often at the IE University in Madrid and its top-flight business school. I would like to offer my view on what service design is, how it works, and why it is so very relevant to HE.

First, let's get the name out of the way – *service design*. There are many definitions of what "service" is, but I love Lou Downe's (2020) 'a service is something that helps someone do something'. Let's add Merriam Webster's dictionary definition of design as 'to create, fashion, execute or construct [...]'. So, service design might be "creating, fashioning, executing or constructing things that help people do something". In our case, when we apply service design to HE, we might say we are shaping the means to help people learn and become educated and to advance knowledge.

By the way, I use the terms "service design" and "design thinking" completely interchangeably in most contexts. Yes, they have different histories, and some design thinkers will point out that they work on wider problems than just "services", while some service designers counter that "everything is a service". But if you look at what "design thinkers" and "service designers" do day-to-day, they are doing the same things. One reason to prefer the term "service design" is because the phrase "design thinking" has been burned by folks selling short ideation workshops (lots of sticky note miracles) and calling it design thinking. That's a pity because it badly misrepresents a robust practice. So go ahead and use both terms, but if someone says "design thinking", ask them carefully what they mean.

Service design (or design thinking, if you prefer) is a human-centred design approach that focuses on understanding the needs of users, employees and organisations and fashioning offerings that meet those needs in a holistic and integrated way. Service design usually tries to understand stakeholders' needs – and indeed meet them – via a strong focus on their *experience* of the situation. While it considers the classic design triad of *desirability, feasibility and viability,* the starting point is the users' and employees' perceptions and whether they feel their needs are met. Many studies and even more practice have shown that understanding and shaping the experience is crucial for success. It involves investigating needs, finding pain points or missed opportunities, ideating possible offerings, prototyping to evolve and test those ideas, and implementing and evaluating the resulting service – all of this in iterative, experimental learning loops (Stickdorn & Schneider, 2010)

Service design has been applied in many contexts, including healthcare, banking, retail, government services, transportation, and certainly in education (Reason, Løvlie & Flu, 2015). Used well, it brings impressive improvements in user and customer experience, efficiency, innovation, employee engagement and competitive advantage. It can also drive income and reduce costs. It is taught at design colleges, business schools and universities, offered by the big professional services consultancies, used by governments and public servants and adopted by organisations of all sizes.

Back in 2010 Marc Stickdorn and Jakob Schneider offered five principles of service design which became widely referenced. In 2018, when Markus Hormeß and I sat down with Marc and Jakob to write the "sequel", *This is Service Design Doing*, we updated and expanded the list. Service design is:

1   Human-centred: Consider the needs of all the people affected by the service.
2   Collaborative: Stakeholders of various backgrounds and functions should be actively engaged in the service design process.

3   Iterative: Service design is an exploratory, adaptive and experimental approach, iterating towards implementation.
4   Sequential: The service should be visualised and orchestrated as a series of interrelated actions.
5   Real: Needs should be researched in reality, ideas prototyped in reality and intangible values evidenced as physical or digital reality.
6   Holistic: Services should sustainably address the needs of all stakeholders through the entire service and across the organisation.

As you will read in this book, service design already has a strong foothold in HE – but there is a still greater potential to create better experiences for students, staff and other stakeholders, with associated benefits in efficiency and engagement and even competitive advantage. Beyond that, it could improve the quality of education and create more positive outcomes for all involved.

Why (Higher) Education?

Like many organisations, HE institutions face a wide range of challenges, from increasing competition, to changing expectations (of students, employees and other concerned parties), to limited funds. They are being asked to do more, with less, and these challenges require a fresh approach.

Service design can help educational institutions to identify pain points, challenges and opportunities for students and their families, as well as for employees and partners. By reducing these frictions and identifying new opportunities, they can provide better support and be more valued. Service design can also help institutions to create more personalised and tailored experiences that meet the needs and expectations of different types of students, from traditional to non-traditional, from domestic to international, accommodating different abilities and disabilities. It can improve communication, personalise support and create a sense of community and belonging.

This is not about "being nice" or "doing everything students want". Students – especially the increasing number who are the first in their family to attend university – face real struggles in navigating or even accessing the complex world of HE. Enrolment, funding, housing, learning support, pastoral care – a whole spectrum of academic, administrative, and financial processes – are often perceived as bureaucratic and unnecessarily complicated. Students and their families are demoralised or frustrated, while administrative staff are bogged down wasting time by explaining complex processes around simple tasks. The result is disengagement, wasted resources and lost learning opportunities.

By focussing on real needs, service design can help institutions to streamline their operations, reduce costs and create more efficient processes. This effect, which has been clearly observed for example in healthcare, can lead to better outcomes for students, staff and faculty, and a more sustainable institution overall. This book presents rich evidence that the context of HE shows the same potential, reducing waiting times, increasing student independence and freeing staff capacity.

It's not just students and administrative staff who benefit from service design. Teaching staff could benefit from more effective and engaging teaching experiences, increasing job satisfaction – creating clear communication channels, providing professional development opportunities and fostering a culture of collaboration and growth. And for leadership teams, service design can create a more sustainable and effective institution, with a clearer vision and strategy, better training and support and a culture of innovation and continuous improvement.

Service design is not just about improving individual experience; it can also address systemic issues and create social impact. Service design has been used to address issues of social inequality, such as access to education and support for marginalised communities. It can also be used to tackle environmental sustainability, such as reducing carbon footprints and promoting eco-friendly practices. All of these are crucial in today's HE landscape.

All of this reads like a wish list for any organisation – but service design has been used, efficiently and inclusively, to engage a wide spectrum of stakeholders and solve problems just like these, by offering them a shared language, a robust but accessible toolset and a productive, curious mindset.

Service design in practice

I divide service design practice into four chunks (Figure 2.1): research, ideation, prototyping and implementation. Let's call these *activities*, not *phases*, as we *don't*

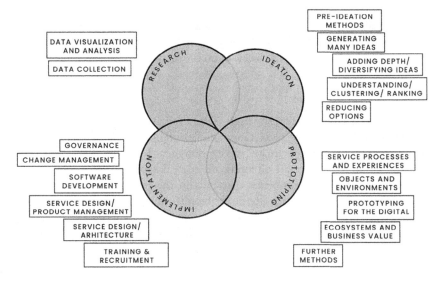

THE WORLD OF SERVICE DESIGN

Figure 2.1 Service design activities

work through them in order but jump between them as needed, always asking "What should we do next to answer the most important questions?"

Research

Before we try to build the world of tomorrow, we service designers spend much of our time trying to understand the world of today. Before we solve the problem right, we make sure we are solving the right problem – like in the toilet example which opened this chapter. We call this *discovery*, or *empathy* or simply *research* – but it is not the same as traditional "market research". Yes, we will do the occasional survey, and we are interested in all those other quantitative tools. But we balance them with a bundle of quick and approachable qualitative methods like contextual and expert interviews, different types of observation, co-creative workshops, auto-ethnography ("try it yourself"), diary studies and so on.

We are trying to build empathy with users and other stakeholders as well as uncover dependencies, understand contexts and get hard data. We triangulate our methods to fight the biases that all methods (and all researchers) carry, and we do *not* do this alone. Service design is co-design, so our lightweight and agile project teams will include people who will one day be building, running and even using the service, and even those who might block it. It saves so much time and misunderstanding later on.

From our research, we hope to get data – qualitative and quantitative, stories, as well as numbers – that are robust, quick and inspirational to our teams. We synthesise and analyse the data as we go, using various simple but powerful visualisations like journey maps, personas, stakeholder maps, as well as simple data formats like key insights or jobs-to-be-done. Some call this "*sensemaking*", and we are seeking patterns or gaps which might suggest a quick pivot in our research questions or methods. We jump back into research any time we need it – *it's not restricted to the start of the project* but is part of a wider process of learning our way forward which includes both observation *and* experimentation.

Ideation

Whenever we have some insights from our data that we think look useful, we might do a spot of ideation: generating and sorting our options. There is a lot of fuss about ideas, but like many service designers I am very convinced that *ideas* are overrated. There are all kinds of ego problems associated with working inside our heads on problems that exist in the real world – especially in those focussed formats people often call "brainstorming". So, we try to handle ideas lightly and get back to more practical things as soon as we can, taking a portfolio of ideas (never just one!) forward. And of course, the best ideas come when you are researching, prototyping and implementing – not when you are straining to "think outside the box".

Prototyping

My favourite service design activity is prototyping, where we try to evolve and (later) test our ideas by building them, at least partially. Now we come to the part of "solving the problem right". People are often puzzled how we can prototype services, which seem largely intangible. But service design has a range of robust methods to prototype pretty much anything, exploring the value, feasibility and even the look-and-feel of our solutions. We might model software on paper, in simple apps or by having humans act it out. We can simulate logistics and other processes by moving tokens around on a map, much as military planners move models on sand-tables. We can mock up devices or spaces using physical or digital models and write first drafts of contracts, handbooks or advertisements, to better understand what we are making and where it might go wrong. Prototyping can look playful – and indeed playfulness offers some very valuable potentials at times – but it is an incredibly powerful and productive process of "researching the future". The principle is always to learn as much as we can, as quickly as we can, failing fast and early – instead of making mistakes in real work with real money and real partner relationships.

Prototyping can throw up new questions, which send us forward into (more) research. Or we might need to generate new ideas at any time or build a thing to understand or test it. So, we move lightly between the different core activities, learning cheaply and quickly until we need to invest more to move forward. Later prototypes might be full scale simulations, and they are followed by pilots where we try to implement our services on a limited scale, but increasingly use real platforms and personnel.

Implementation

Implementation is a key activity of service design, but as the practice varies enormously depending on the type of project we cannot discuss it at length here. It is important, though, *not* so see implementation as something separate from "design". During research, ideation and prototyping activities, people accumulate a huge amount of insight and empathy – and this is lost if they are excluded from implementation. And after all, we discover most when we try to make a thing real. So instead of "handovers", service design projects see a shifting balance of personnel which always involves a diverse core team (including implementers) who are there from start to finish.

The mindset challenge

When I describe these service design activities to people, they are often shocked. "Isn't that expensive? All those different research methods *before you even start*, and all that prototyping?" In fact, this way of working is often cheaper and faster than traditional approaches and produces equal or better results.

But more importantly, this is where the power of service design comes from. "The Business Value of Design" (*McKinsey Quarterly*, 2018) study showed that companies who did design well had 32 per cent higher revenue growth and 56 per cent higher shareholder return than their peers. Those are strange benchmarks for many educators, many of whom are not fans of organisations like McKinsey anyway. Sensibilities aside, the numbers show that this stuff works – *dramatically* well. And the critical behaviours that led to this success? A focus on user experience; an *iterative* process of *research* and *prototyping*; spreading responsibility for design *across* the organisation; and a leadership that *focussed on design* just as much as on revenues and costs.

That's a mindset change for organisations. It means spending time with people outside the immediate working context to understand their lives and struggles. It means being aware of our biases and making decisions based on evidence, not on gut feelings or outdated experience. It also requires us to break down silos and work closely with other functions. And it makes it essential that people around the organisation have the means and the permission to quickly try things, to experiment and to share both successes and failures.

It may sound like chaos, but all this is very manageable, as so many successful projects have shown. It does, though, require culture change. And it needs a new understanding of how we move forward.

The learning loop

You see, we have been taught that the fastest way from A to B is moving in a straight line. We think smart thoughts, we have a plan, and then we execute it. But there is a fundamental problem with that – if we want to dash forward in a straight line, we must aim really well. We need to think everything through and be very sure of each irrevocable decision, validating and testing every option. So, this gets slow, and expensive, and of course there is always something we didn't think of. Service design, like Agile software development, accepts the obvious reality that the future is not wholly predictable; and it doesn't try to predict everything. Instead, it moves forward in *learning loops* (Figure 2.2). In the context of HE, you may notice similarities to experiential learning models (e.g., Kolb, 2014) a widely promoted approach to deep learning. Just as the scientific method works in a loop of hypothesis, experiment design, experiment, data, modified hypothesis and so on, (service) design works in much the same way. We can start, for example, by looking at an existing situation and gathering data. We sift the data for insights, and they give us ideas for what to do next. We might see the need for another research activity. Or perhaps we build a prototype. Or we go ahead and implement some change. Whatever we choose, we will then see what happens… giving us more data and new insights for the next round.

Put like that, it seems a bit of a no-brainer. But it makes people in traditional organisations very nervous. It sounds a lot like not knowing where you are going

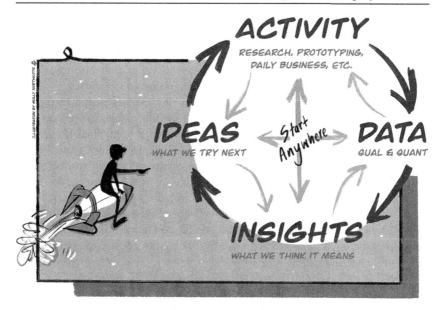

Figure 2.2 Service design learning loop

(quite right!), like making it up as you go along (yup!), and if we go from proto-typing "back" to research, *doesn't that mean we got it wrong before?* Oh, and what about my charismatic leadership style of "I know the way, follow me?" Indeed, the characteristics of a good design leader (and good designer) – curiosity, humility and transparency of results – are not what we usually expect in traditional leaders.

But slow down. There are many situations where traditional linear work practice would still be appropriate. When we are doing a thing that we have done many times before, we work in a more linear way. We focus on quality, minimise variation, and scale or optimise. But that is *exploitation* – getting better at doing what we already know. When it comes to *exploration* – doing a new thing or changing how we do a thing – that behaviour is not helpful and in fact even harmful. We don't know the right thing to do yet, and we need to figure it out safely using learning loops.

Less talking, more doing!

Service design is a hands-on practice, not another approach to sitting in com-mittees and debating change. It means getting out of the building and getting our hands dirty. That's off-putting to many – and indeed the strangeness of service design often makes people reluctant to consider it. So how do we convince them?

Reassurance comes from wrapping service design in more traditional lan-guage that will also resonate with organisations like universities. We might talk about reducing risk and saving cost, say "scoping" or "reality check" instead of research and reframe prototyping as "pre-invest test and refinement". To argue for research triangulation and multiple prototypes of multiple ideas, we use the same language as investors and speak of portfolios. We take care to closely tie our work to existing strategies around increasing value and efficiency.

Still, it's often been said that the only way to "get" service design is to try it (Manhaes, 2017), so we need to invite our colleagues into a safe exploration space where they actually *do* the work, at least for a short time. Some folks like special innovation centres, incubators or skunkworks. Others prefer to designate a small project as a test case. I tend to use short "Jam" events – perhaps two days when we apply service design to a challenge, getting out of the room to do quick research, then ideating and prototyping solutions before going out to test them again (e.g., Global Jams). At the end, we will have a 360-degree view of the problem – *and* solution-space, as well as valuable skills and human connections which will help in the next iterations – and indeed help with other challenges. Most importantly, we understand how service design works on an experiential, emotional level as well as an intellectual one. And that, in a way, is the key.

Conclusion

I hope this chapter has given you some insight into the why and the what of service design, as well as some of the opportunities and challenges it presents. We have seen that service design is a working practice, toolset and mindset that tries to understand the needs of humans and organisations, then develops solutions using lightweight, safe experimentation. As well as improving experiences, it can lead to efficiencies, savings, boosted engagement and improved core outcomes. It has been used successfully in a wide range of contexts and has huge potential in HE, where it can serve not only students and their families, but also staff, leaders and our society.

I have outlined the key activities of service design: research, ideation, prototyping and implementation. They do not form a sequence, but rather a toolbox which we use to explore our way forward, reducing risk by visualisation and by lightweight, robust iteration. We work co-creatively with other stakeholders, so the actual techniques we use must be reliable yet simple and approachable. The non-linear progress in "learning loops" embraces a degree of uncertainty (and indeed expects negative results or "failure") which can feel uncomfortable to people used to linear work, but is safer, more effective in this context and very manageable.

Finally, I have presented some thoughts on how reassurance and exposure can motivate sceptical colleagues to explore this world and the huge potential it offers for HE. The rest of this book will give you the examples, case studies and HE insider-thinking you need next. Enjoy the journey.

Key learning points

1   Service design is a proven and successful approach to change and improvement which can lead to better experiences, efficiencies, more engagement, improved core outcomes and to innovation.
2   Service design is a non-linear practice using "learning loops" of accessible methods which engages diverse stakeholders in identifying and understanding problems, then developing solutions through experimentation. This usually makes it cheaper, faster and as effective as, or more effective than, traditional linear "waterfall" methods. It also reduces risk.
3   As this book shows, service design is eminently applicable to Higher Education and the particular challenges faced there. The most effective way to understand it (or to help colleagues understand its power) is to try it in a protected context such as a specified project or short event.

References

Downe, L. (2020) *Good Services: How to design services that work.* Amsterdam: BIS Publishers.

Global Jams. Available at: http://globaljams.org (Accessed: 10 October 2023).

Kolb, D. A. (2014) *Experiential learning: Experience as the source of learning and development.* Hoboken, NJ: Prentice Hall.

Manhaes, M. (2017) The importance of exposure to service design over its precise definition. LinkedIn. Available at: www.linkedin.com/pulse/importance-exposure-service-design-over-its-precise-manhaes-ph-d- (Accessed: 10 October 2023).

McKinsey Quarterly. (2018) The Business Value of Design. Available at: www.mckinsey.com/capabilities/mckinsey-design/our-insights/the-business-value-of-design# (Accessed: 1 May 2023).

Merriam Webster Dictionary Design Definition & Meaning – Merriam-Webster. Available at: www.merriam-webster.com (Accessed: 1 May 2023).

Reason, B., Løvlie, L. & Flu, M. B. (2015) *Service design for business: A practical guide to optimizing the customer experience.* Hoboken, NJ: John Wiley & Sons.

Stickdorn, M., Hormess, M. E., Lawrence, A. & Schneider, J. (2018) *This is service design doing: applying service design thinking in the real world.* Sebastopol, CA: O'Reilly.

Stickdorn, M. & Schneider, J. (2010) *This is Service Design Thinking.* Amsterdam: BIS Publishers.

Building Capacity, Developing Mindsets

Foreword

Paul Moran and Annette Robinson

As with many industries and service settings, Higher Education (HE) has many different stakeholders with a variety of aims in the context of achieving good positive outcomes. It can be challenging to navigate the complex landscapes that sit behind the delivery of these services and the diverse stakeholder perspectives when trying to deliver change and improvement. As a practitioner and advocate for user-centred design, I'm convinced there is value for HE institutions in exploring and using these approaches or further developing their current use where they are already in place.

The user-centred design mindset and practices can be applied at different levels in the HE environment and enable improvement to student, staff and wider stakeholder experiences and outcomes. Teams tasked with delivering improvements to services will benefit from activities such as end-to-end service mapping and user research. By creating new views of the service setting and extending the perspectives of the service participants and wider stakeholders, these approaches can bring about deeper insights and open the door to new opportunities.

The content of this book includes examples from teams applying some of these techniques and highlighting pathways others can follow. In a sector that has such a strong influence on the future direction of people's lives, I'm convinced that a user-centred approach can play a part in setting up all participants in the system for success.

Paul Moran, Head of User Centred Design, DVSA

This book is critical to HE professionals who are responsible for developing and reviewing process. Universities are large and complex organisations, which can result in siloed thinking and behaviour and the creation of processes that are complex for the actual user to engage with. Service Design puts the users at the heart of the process, enabling us to recognise and develop empathy with their experience and to simplify and develop efficient, human-centric approaches that colleagues will use and appreciate being involved in their development.

This book includes case studies that illustrate the practical application of the different stages of the process and the benefits derived from them. This is pivotal in an age when we face increasing time pressures and need to work more effectively together.

Annette Robinson, Organisational Developer

DOI: 10.4324/9781003383161-9

Chapter 3

Change HEROs

Scaling Service Design as a Core
Competence for Professional Services Staff

Pamela Spokes and Jean Mutton

Introduction

If you started a career in academic administration at any point in the last 30 years you are likely to have had some generic management training. You may have done a master's in business administration, Prince2, Project Management or learned about Lean processes. All very valuable in their own way, but drawn largely from the world of manufacturing, logistics and the shop floor. It was not until we came across service design, with its human-centred focus, that we found a way to make an impact in enhancing the student experience, across the student journey, from prospect to alumnus. All the personal development courses we had been offered were geared towards the 'right first time' culture and 'we know best' mindsets which still prevail across the sector. There was a genuine desire to enhance the student experience, but the view was still very much from a process delivery rather than an end-user perspective. 'One stop shops' and other services were shoehorned into online platforms not fit for purpose. Every department had to have their own webpage and innovations rarely directly or even indirectly involved students in their creation.

Managing many central and school-based administration services covering the student journey - Admissions, Enrolment, Assessment, Progression and student support right through to Graduation - was a great training ground. We were working closely with both academic and professional services colleagues in large, complex organisations which operated in individual silos reinforced by top-down management structures with personal and departmental targets driving much of the agenda and setting priorities. Service design, with its human-centred lens, offered a new way to make real impacts in enhancing systems and processes improving both the student and staff experience by focusing on user need balanced with business strategy. The difference that came with that change in mindset – to be more open, more collaborative, to find the right question rather than look for a ready solution – has reset our approach to change management in Higher Education (HE).

DOI: 10.4324/9781003383161-10

Pamela's story

Originally Canadian, I have lived in Finland for many years. My university student years were filled with international experiences to Finland, Russia and Sweden. These international experiences forged me into the person that I am today. One with an intense passion for the student experience. There were many times during my academic journey that I felt voiceless and at the mercy of administrators who did not understand my needs. Whether this was by design or a by-product of how they worked, I did not know.

It was the 1990s, and systems did not speak "the same language" – both literally and process-wise. This caused me endless problems in trying to transfer some of my credits back to my home institution so I could graduate. My first exchange took about a year to get the credits sorted out. A process that was fraught with frustration and worry as graduation came on the horizon. But it was also *the people* who did not speak the same language – again both literally and process-wise. I missed my very first course in Finland because it was not communicated to me how to register for a course (just showing up on the first day was considered registering). But I came from a system that required you to register before you were allowed to show up.

It was gaps such as these that made me realise that the student experience can be made infinitely better by designing services and experiences purpose-fully. It was when I was employed as a student worker in the international office that I could see the disconnects between the needs of the students and the restrictions of the institutions.

When I discovered service design, all of my HE institution work experience was from the international perspective. This is important to my story because when you are dealing with a system that has been created to serve one kind of student (home or domestic), it can often make those who are different hard to accommodate. Trying to internationalise, as many institutions want to, exposes these difficulties, and there needs to be a will to tackle the real problems. Schedules will need to change whether this is about application dates, admission letter arrivals, acceptance deadlines, graduation dates, alumni activation, etc. Understanding the needs of different groups is essential to understanding the kinds of services that they will require and look for.

Looking to professionalise deeper into the student experience, in 2014 I enrolled in Laurea University of Applied Sciences' MBA in Service Innovation and Design. This was the world's first master's programme in service design. Here I found others who approached things similarly and learned the mindset, the process and the methods and tools of service design. At last, I had found a repeatable, reliable process to address these concerns and to have a conversation about what I was seeing and how I thought we could tackle it. It gave me a process and a language to help move the problem forward in a predictable way that was learnable by others – how service design democratises change and gives all stakeholders a voice.

Jean's story

I began my career in HE administration in 1982 – before we had personal computers, not even the internet, and much that we take for granted now, especially around communications. If we wanted to send a paper to a colleague on another site, we used an internal postage system. We all worked hard on being clear about policies and procedures because everybody had to know what else was happening across the academic calendar and at different university sites. There was not much room for experimenting, creativity or innovation in that scenario.

In 2009 I began working with an innovative student experience team, which included students working as interns. We talked about 'the felt student experience'...but what was that exactly? I did a course on Systems Thinking and led a major review of enrolment and registration. The work was sponsored by the Joint Information and Systems Committee, which funds universities mainly for IT developments, but they asked us to look at both the 'hard' (IT) and 'soft' (process) systems, using service design methods. This led us into new territory – collaborating and working with students directly to find out what they wanted and needed rather than what we managers thought. We observed students going through the enrolment process; we asked them to make short recordings at the end of each day during their Welcome Week: what went well, what would they have liked more of? During enrolment week we sat in the Atrium with a box of chocolates and a sign that read 'If you could change one thing about your day today, what would it be?' We worked on a student journey map and came away with a 40-point action plan. We made sure that all staff involved walked through what the students would themselves be experiencing. The response was great – feedback from both staff and students was positive and we had some encouraging metrics: 68% of students rated their overall enrolment experience 'better than last year' – up from 36% the previous year and quotes from students like 'Enrolment was spot on in terms of speed and reliability' meant we were on the right track.

However, there were still a lot of legacy systems and processes such as poorly designed forms which must be filled in manually and touted around several staff members to be signed off because 'it's always been done that way'. For example, we recently found that when a student wanted to take a break or withdraw from their studies, the process had changed little over the years. Students came to an enquiry desk, asked the receptionist to print off a form which they had to get signed by three different staff members and then return the form to the desk. If the right staff members were not available this could take weeks, at a time when the student was under a lot of stress and potentially walking away from their studies.

Trying to bring staff on board with this new approach we would ask – what themes have you got coming out of your student surveys and are these being echoed in your complaints and appeals? How are you tackling and monitoring issues the students are surfacing in a programme committee, and what is the staff survey telling you? What are you hearing from your external examiners? How are you collating all that rich information, the qualitative and the quantitative data, about what is effective within your programmes and what is not? How are you joining all those dots together? And the crunch question, 'how did you involve students in this review?', the answer was usually 'no'.

Building a shared understanding

Our lived experience of working in HE administration and management coupled with the impact we were seeing from this new collaborative approach infused us with a desire to share the good news but we knew it would be hard for many staff to take their eye off the ball of their personal or departmental targets and reach out for some vague outcomes. We could see how by encouraging co-creation, staff could build relationships outside of their immediate frame of reference. How each organisational silo impacts another and understand that a university is a massive ecosystem – a community that needs to come together to focus on the end user experience. How effective services bring efficiencies, be those monetary or otherwise. Yes, there were challenges. The service design process can be a hard sell. Getting the message across to people – talking to students, professional services staff, teachers, lecturers and managers, bringing the knowledge that all stakeholders need to be involved can be an uphill struggle.

Unless there is an agreed perception of firstly, the need for change (especially when you may think your bit of the service is not actually broken) and secondly, a common vision of how to go about it, impactful service enhancement is hard to come by. So, what have we learned over the years? How is that shared understanding built? We believe it starts with having the right mindset.

Bad services are often created on a foundation of bad design, whether these are services in a private company, a public service or an educational institution. Often this bad design is based on individuals or groups using their own anecdotal experience or knowledge as the basis of creating their services. It is not a malicious desire to create services that do not fulfil the end users' needs, but it can happen often when services are created in a vacuum or only with the people who provide them.

To begin to design better services, we need to start with an open mind and understand that the answer lies with those who use the service. This open approach does not come easily though. It often requires an entirely different way of thinking and doing. How do you begin to address this mindset shift on a bigger scale in a HE organisation? So, we set ourselves a challenge – how might we evangelise the service design methodology and build a bridge of understanding which would be bespoke and accessible to professional services staff working in HE? How might we set the framework of service design squarely in the context of the systems and processes of their day-to-day operations?

We decided to face the challenge head on and developed an online course specifically designed for university administrators which we called Change HEROs (Higher Education Re-Organisation for Students and Staff). In choosing this name, we wanted to reflect what is happening in HE. There are often change processes happening and we know from experience that service design is a necessary tool to have in a toolbox. Successful transitions happen when there are understandable processes that everyone buys into. We want to provide the right tools so that anyone can participate and have an impact. To do this, we needed to figure out how to teach service design to enough professional services staff. Our overview of how we went about this is divided into four sections adapted from the Double Diamond Design framework developed by the Design Council UK.

Case study: Change HEROs – development of an online course

Discover: We asked ourselves "what would we have wanted when we first learned about service design?" From there we began to work together to create an overall structure of the topics that we would have liked to learn more about and how it related to university administration. While service design is a process that is applicable to any industry that provides services, it is helpful to hear how it applies to the one that you work in and to hear how others are using it. Educational institutions are sometimes not entirely used to thinking about what they do as "services". And especially not used to talking about customers – terminology that is often used in service design. We believe that anyone working in a university can learn the mindset and skills of service design. Student experience managers may be the most the most obvious, but anyone working in professional services – from Admissions right through to Alumni – as well those working on the academic side of things, can become a changemaker.

Finding the right title was tricky. We tried out several options but settled on Change HEROs (which stands for Higher Education Re-organisation for Staff and Students) as we the feedback we had was that this was snappy, appropriate and would appeal to staff – as they are the 'heroes', bringing change to their organisation.

Define: *How might we* provide education in service design to university administrators and managers at a reasonable price? In-person training takes a lot of time and cost to put together – trainer time, venues, food, etc. They also require staff to relocate themselves away from their offices/homes for extended periods of time which add to the costs for the learner – both financial costs and opportunity costs.

It's our view that we need as many staff as possible to learn the service design approach because redesigning services in universities needs to be a collective endeavour. This is why we created a course that is both flexible, to meet the needs of busy staff, and affordable.

By the end of the course, we wanted learners to:

- understand how to create real value and change in their student services
- be able to work with their team and others to achieve greater student satisfaction, which in turn can:
  a improve student retention
  b enhance their organisation's reputation
  c help them attract talented students
  d improve staff satisfaction too

- become a change ambassador at their university
- do work that's more impactful and therefore more rewarding.

Develop: Once we had defined how we would create this course and who for, we began to build a framework for the structure – adjusting as we went along, allowing ourselves to try different options. We wanted to make sure that the students could begin to understand the true value of service design and especially the service design mindset. In order to fully embrace the service design mindset, we needed to make sure that the students embraced the four main elements that are required to start any project. These are focusing on the problem and not the solution, that assumptions are not equal to knowledge, that inclusion matters and that having the right mindset in leading the process is vital. We open these more below.

We had made the decision to create an online course, because of the flexibility it would allow. The course began to shape up: six modules, 20 lessons and six one-on-one interviews of HE experts talking about how they have used service design in their work.

Deliver: We partnered with a British university located in London to pilot the course. Included in this agreement was a module-by-module feedback form to be filled in. There was also another overall form that was sent out to the participants about a month after completing the course to see how it had stayed with them. With this feedback we were able to make improvements to the course to make it even more impactful and user-friendly.

Participants said:

> "The whole concept of service design was not one I had remotely considered before doing the course. It was really useful to go through this all and break it down".
>
> "It's such an enlightening process when you break down the complex web we often weave ourselves in HE to what a student actually sees, experiences and has to negotiate their way through".
>
> "This course has given me very practical and solid steps on how to approach it [service design]".

We were reassured that we were on the right track at last.

Key principles that informed our pedagogy

Focus on the problem and not the solution

An underlying foundation of service design is "Love the Problem, Not the Solution". This means you do not fall in love with a particular solution because it may not be the right one. If you focus on solving the problem you will be successful, as success comes in the form of solving a real problem that the user has.

A lot of time in the service design process is used for learning about the users, their lives and finding the right questions. It is only once the real problem is correctly identified that any ideation around a solution should be started. A great deal of effort by those leading a service design process is spent on holding participants back from trying to create solutions too early in the process.

In this way, the problem gets thoroughly explored and identified through active research. This will either confirm previous assumptions or refute them: both are acceptable outcomes of this beginning part of the process. Service deliverers may know where the problem is but are not at all sure as to the *why*. Without proper research, the why is only ever a guess. Spending a lot of time on the solution without understanding the problem will not solve real problems.

The wrong path (Assumptions ≠ Knowledge)

It is human nature to think that, through our long experience, we "know" what is wrong. These are what can be called informed assumptions.

Assumptions can be used as a starting point in a process, but they must always be tested through research. Assumptions require the provider to understand that these are not verified problems and must be open to being wrong. Unverified assumptions should be considered guessing and can hinder the process and will lead you down the wrong path if not properly acknowledged and tested.

Unfortunately, many professional experts succumb to informed assumptions. Dan and Chip Heath refer to this as The Curse of Knowledge (Heath & Heath, 2008), where the expert can no longer look at issues objectively. These are almost always a form of informed assumptions and include recognisable examples such as:

- "We know who our users are".
- "We know what 'they' want from our service or product".
- "My part of this process is not broken, it's others in the process that need to change".
- and the *Ultimate Shutdown* – "This is how we do things around here".

It is important to change your mindset from "I know what the problem is and how we can solve it" to "I have a general idea of what or where the

Figure 3.1 Legacy Systems

problem might be but let's test it and verify the real problem". These are two very different mindsets.

In addition to mindset, this shift can be hindered for other reasons:

- Staff could be working to specific targets, which can often force them to focus on something that will be measured, rather than what will provide quality and value to the user.
- People may be nervous to show vulnerability – 'I don't know' is a difficult sentence in an organisation that encourages a competitive leadership environment.
- Prioritises inclusion.

Determining who the stakeholders are in a service is important. Making sure that representatives of those stakeholders participate in the process is crucial. If users and other stakeholders are not a part of the process, then the outcome will not be robust. By using processes that prioritise 'knowing' over 'following the research to find out', it often means the loudest voice gets heard or the highest rank gets to decide. This has the effect of excluding real users, their lived experiences and any kind of diversity from very early on in the process.

It matters who is included and who leads

Because services are everywhere, it matters who is included in creating them and leads them. Early on in her own service design journey, Jean was invited to take part in a project led by the Equality, Diversity and Inclusion Strategic Advisory Group of Advance HE, to explore how students with disabilities could have a stronger voice in the design of their university environment. Initially it was a challenge to get any engagement from the managers who ran the Estates Department and the invitation to join the project was passed from one person to the next. Eventually, one of the senior managers joined the group and after a while working directly with a range of students with disabilities, they admitted that they had a fresh perspective and an understanding of how and why the needs of the end user should be sought from the very beginning of any Estates project, be it a new build or other changes to the campus environment. From then on, the need to include end users right from the start of the design or re-design of buildings and campus layouts was sustainably embedded in their policies and procedures.

Just as it matters who is included, it matters who leads. Leaders set the goals and targets for the work that teams do. How they see the value in co-creation and how they set key performance indicators will have an impact. As one form of the saying goes "we measure what we value" but that becomes more difficult when what we value cannot be measured in traditional terms. Can we measure the joy our service brings to someone? Maybe if you can dilute that into a happiness score or a return user score – but is it really measuring joy? How about inclusion? We can measure who was there. We can even dig down and measure how often different people speak in a meeting if we really want to. But can we really measure inclusion with the tools we now use? Not really.

It leads to efficiencies

Being efficient is important to any organisation. When a service design process is properly engaged, it will naturally lead to efficiency. This is because the outcomes should not include elements that are not needed. Unnecessary elements should naturally be eliminated with proper research, prototyping, testing and solving the right problem.

When you try to solve the wrong problem, you can create waste. Even with the most efficient or paired back bad service, there will always be waste because it does not address the underlying issues. Professor John Seddon calls it "doing the wrong thing righter" (Seddon, 2016) – the goal is to have a service that helps the user get the required job done, not to make a less useful service more efficient.

As we have seen, at its very heart, service design is a mindset. This mindset, the way in which we approach problems from the moment they are suspected, is very important to the success rate of solutions as it moves the focus:

- from solutions to the problem
- from organisation to the user
- from failure to learning
- and from efficiency to impact.

For optimal impact, this change in approach has to be embedded throughout the organisation. If only a few people are shifting their mindset in the long run, this new way of working cannot solidly take hold. This will result in developments within the organisation being uneven and disjointed. Service design needs to work holistically, using the mindset, the process and the toolkit. This is important for organisations to design a future where they are being inclusive, their objectives are being met and the right problems are being solved. Everyone in the organisation has a part to play in it.

Conclusion

We believe that having access to service design training is a vital part of creating the right mindset in every organisation. This learning will help to transform HE institutions and give professional services staff the tools that they need to do their work with greater impact. For us, it was very important to understand the challenges these staff members have in taking on service design. Where did our training not meet expectations? What did we learn about the participants and how they interacted with the course? In the DELIVER phase we found out as feedback came in, in two ways – feedback regarding the course and feedback regarding service design and its relevance. Both are highly important to us. It helps us to hear different perspectives from people who are new to the topic or who view its relevance differently. Additionally, in the participants, there was a diversity of experience with online courses and this variety helped us to see a broader experience of the online course format.

When it comes to our course specifically, we were asked to add captions/ subtitles as one person was hard of hearing. We had not considered this since neither of us have that challenge, but that it will help all people who take the course in the end was a great insight for us. We found that those people who volunteered to take the course (rather than it being a requirement from their supervisor) had a much higher completion rate. As did those who had some prior knowledge or experience of service design, unsurprisingly. We thought long and hard about timing (when is the 'best' time to start across the academic year), concluding that there is no 'right' time. We also learned about the time challenges that many professional services staff have and we are able to reset our own expectations on how long the course might take to complete.

With the wrong mindset, these could be seen as failures but with the service design mindset, these are the next steps of improvement. We will help more people, in a more appropriate way, in the future.

And so, we continue our own learning journeys and our quest to bring service design via accessible and affordable training specially designed for the needs of university professional services staff. We know that there is an appetite for sustainable change but people working in HE do not always know where or how to access the right information. We aim to address that need.

Key learning points

1   The right mindset for sustainable change is vital.
2   No matter how passionately you believe that service design is the right way to go, you must find a way to bring others along with you; this begins with understanding their needs and motivations.

3   Launching any new service (such as this online course) requires an open mindset that embraces failure and understands it is integral to the learning journey and future revisions.

References

Advance HE. (n.d.) Equality, Diversity and Inclusion Strategic Advisory Board. Available at: www.advance-he.ac.uk/about-us/strategic-advisory-groups/equality-diversity-and-inclusion-strategic-advisory-group (Accessed: 13 August 2023).

Design Council. (n.d.) The Double Diamond. Available at: www.designcouncil.org.uk/our-resources/the-double-diamond (Accessed: 13 August 2023).

Heath, C. & Heath, D. (2008) *Made to Stick: Why some ideas take hold and others come unstuck*. London: Arrow Books.

Joint Information Systems Committee. Available at: www.jisc.ac.uk (Accessed: 13 August 2023).

Perez, C. (2019) *Invisible Women: Data Bias in A World Designed for Men*. New York: Abrams.

Seddon, J. (2016) '*Keynote Speech*', Vanguard 12th Annual Health Conference. Available at: https://beyondcommandandcontrol.com/john-seddons-keynote-speech-at-the-12th-annual-health-conference (Accessed: 13 August 2023).

Chapter 4

Inspiring change at all levels

The personal and professional impact of service design training

Sonia Virdi and Katie Murrie

Introduction

Sonia Virdi and Katie Murrie met at the Service Design Academy (SDA), which is an accredited qualification and training provider operating as part of Dundee and Angus College, Scotland. This is where Katie was the lecturer and lead service design consultant, and Sonia was the student, absorbing every ounce of knowledge and inspiration. This chapter highlights the impact of service design education from both a learner/practitioner's and a lecturer's perspective.

The narrative begins by following Sonia's journey to service design education by exploring the motivations that influenced her move to follow a Professional Development Award (PDA) in this field. It explores her background as a graphic designer and her involvement in professional services at the University of Edinburgh, leading to her enrolment in the course. Sonia's case study details how she implemented service design within a real work-based project for the final unit of the PDA, the portfolio project. Throughout the portfolio project, Sonia utilised the training to showcase collaboration with University of Edinburgh staff on the creation of design principles employing various techniques and methods. The chapter highlights the benefits derived from this collaborative approach.

Finally, we explore how the PDA transformed Sonia's role as a manager and product owner and share Katie's insights, through the lens of SDA, as a service design educator and facilitator. Overall, the chapter shares the most important lessons and takeaways gained during Sonia's training, providing insight and inspiration to other's beginning their service design journey.

Context and Background

What is a design system?

Think of a design system like a box of Lego®. Just as a Lego® set provides various bricks for building objects in different configurations, a design system

DOI: 10.4324/9781003383161-11

offers reusable components and patterns that facilitate design at scale. In Higher Education (HE), this ensures effective, consistent and efficient digital experiences, reducing the need to reinvent the wheel, allowing people to focus on more complex challenges.

Usually, a design system is presented as a website, serving as the central hub for accessible and usable resources. These resources encompass editorial style guides, brand assets, coded components and patterns, empowering teams to design and develop digital products consistently. Standards, guidelines and principles underpin the system, ensuring a uniform approach. This is useful when design responsibility is distributed across schools, colleges and departments.

A key objective of the design system is to prioritise the needs of internal staff involved in designing digital products and services in HE, including project sponsors, project managers, product owners, software developers, graphic, content and user experience designers and specialists in communications and marketing.

But a design system is more than just a standalone tool, it is also a service. Since it is something to be used by people in various contexts, it needs to consider these perspectives during its creation and evolve based on their usage. It is not designed for a specific output; it is designed to be flexible, to accommodate many use cases brought by many people with different technical skills. Therefore, the content of the design system should be accessible to anyone without technical expertise, while still catering for those who are more experienced.

The service supports this by:

- encouraging a community of people who use it to suggest changes, contribute new elements or make improvements.
- providing support and documentation to help users understand how to use the items in the system and promote its continued improvement and growth.
- implementing a valid process to accept elements into the design system, including consideration by a change advisory board and incorporating input from stakeholders.

The Double Diamond

On the PDA, Sonia began her learning journey by referencing and using the UK Design Council's Double Diamond which was created in 2004 (Design Council, 2023b). It is a powerful framework because it provides a clear roadmap for the service design process. It encompasses all the key stages of design: problem discovery and exploration, analysis, co-creation, prototyping, testing, implementation and evaluation.

As well as giving a clear overview of the practical application of the service design process, the Double Diamond is also valuable in the academic space for sharing complex concepts about service design. It highlights the tools and methods that can be used to support the design journey, within the stages of

Discover, Define, Develop and Deliver. Here Sonia learnt how divergent and convergent thinking can be aligned to the nature and practicalities of change and innovation.

Although the Double Diamond represents the process in a linear format, Sonia was taught to iterate continuously, returning to research (the Discovery phase) throughout, recognising that it is common to uncover underlying problems or opportunities that may require a return to the beginning of the process. Perpetual learning and data-driven evidence support impactful and sustainable change in our ever-evolving world. This iterative approach propels us to continually strive for improvement, demonstrating that the design process never stops.

The Service Design Academy

Service Design Academy (SDA) delivers the Professional Development Award (PDA) in Service Design. It is designed to transform the way individuals approach their work through four comprehensive units: a) tools and methods; b) user research; c) co-design through a learning journey; culminating with d) the final unit which brings together all the units within a portfolio project. The capstone portfolio project is where learners apply key concepts in a real work-based context. It is an opportunity for students to practice service design by taking a holistic view, involving service users and learning from them. This is demonstrated through the practice of user research, co-design, prototyping and iteration. The final portfolio project allows the learner to put theory into practice, refining their service design skills with on-hand support from tutors and mentors. The SDA programme is unique in its twofold approach, which not only meets academic requirements, but also drives meaningful change within the learners' workplace.

Case study

This case study centres around Sonia's final portfolio project, offering insight into how service design approaches were implemented within the framework of developing design principles for the University of Edinburgh's design system project. The case study highlights the impact of service design on Sonia's colleagues and how the training serves as the foundation for her continued engagement in the practice of service design post-course completion.

A Journey into Service Design Education

Sonia's story: Ask for forgiveness, rather than seek permission

The pivotal moment of my transformation occurred in 2017 when I encountered Design Thinking at the 'Design It Build It' conference. This revelation ignited my passion, as it offered a discipline and process not limited to aesthetics, but capable of enhancing experiences, systems and services. With over twenty years of experience as a graphic designer in HE, I recognised the imperative of placing human-centred methodologies at the heart of my work, to effect real change by improving people's lives.

Having recognised the desire to influence change and make meaningful impact in my role, the first step was to acknowledge my current position. As a graphic design manager, at the University of Edinburgh, I often found the graphic design process to be one where you do what the customer asks. The look and feel were prioritised over the purpose, value and effectiveness of the output. This method of working contradicted my design education, where I had learnt how essential it was to understand the problem before creating solutions. Making the case to internal customers using the graphic design service, to value the user's needs, pains and challenges felt like a difficult battle.

I also recognised that I had developed a broad range of skills during my time at the university that was not being effectively utilised. These included strategic thinking, aligning business and user needs and working with various university users, including academics, researchers, students, visitors and professional services teams. Recognising the alignment between my skills and that of human-centred design, I was on a mission to teach myself how to do this work.

In this initial phase of my journey towards service design education, I often started using human-centred techniques in my work before I had permission. I learned by making friends with user experience experts, shadowing them on projects and experimenting with techniques like personas, interviews, sketching, prototyping and user testing within my graphic and digital design projects. I also practiced using collaborative approaches such as co-design to learn from people and involve them in my work.

This gave me the confidence to collaborate with professional services staff in a change project, focused on improving the brand experience of my department Information Services Group (ISG). This project gave me valuable insights into ISG's services, bringing to light complex issues related to a siloed culture and fragmented end-to-end service delivery. These problems became a recurring theme in various other digital projects and I became curious to know how service design could be leveraged to drive change, address complex cultural problems and improve service provision organisationally.

In service design, I felt an affinity as it aligned deeply with my existing design skills and values. Yet, as a newcomer in this field, doubts crept in about whether I was approaching it correctly. Recognising the importance of a deeper understanding of service design principles and methods, I acknowledged the need to enhance my knowledge to confidently apply this design mindset. This need led me to undertake the PDA, where I hoped to develop and build on what I had been learning on my own.

Katie's story: Professional Development Award at the SDA

The pivotal moment in my journey happened during a Global Gov Jam. This is an annual event held globally, in multiple locations, that offers participants the opportunity to learn, design and network. Volunteering as a Jam organiser and facilitator at Dundee and Angus College, despite having only led service design workshops as part of my Master's in Leadership and Innovation, was a revelation that challenged and inspired me. This led to co-designing a curriculum that has become the hallmark of SDA's courses. We see introducing others to service design as a powerful opportunity to energise, motivate and refocus them on the human impact of their work, amid the daily chaos of work and life.

At the SDA we have found that people join the PDA for a variety of reasons, but they often fall into four categories:

- Proof gatherers: seeking accreditation to add credibility to their experience.
- Career changers: wanting to use service design to start a new career.
- Skills developers: learning to do their work better.
- Participants: joining the training for the benefit of their organisation.

Thinking about this in relation to Sonia's journey, she wanted to broaden her experience as a graphic designer. Although she initially became a participant in the PDA to find new ways to bring positive change to her work at the University of Edinburgh, she soon realised that this new approach and methodology could lead to sustainable professional and personal development.

SDA's work-based assessments and focus on individual student needs motivated Sonia to take up this learning opportunity allowing her to practice applying service design concepts in real-world scenarios. It not only accelerated the embedding of her knowledge in this field but also enhanced her ability to perform tasks effectively and confidently as demonstrated in her final portfolio project.

Case Study

Creating design principles: Trusting in the process

This case study focuses on my final PDA portfolio project, where I aimed to craft design principles for the University of Edinburgh's design system. My role in the design system was product owner. The emphasis of the final portfolio project is on trusting in the processes learnt to navigate complex problems with a creative mindset, to embrace challenges and question assumptions. By looking at design principles within the scope of the design system project, I saw the opportunity to employ service design methods and approaches across the

Double Diamond phases, involving university staff in my user research, co-design and prototyping activities.

The decision to create a design system stemmed from an audit of the University of Edinburgh's web estate. This revealed an overgrown and inconsistent digital landscape resulting in disjointed end-to-end user experiences. While a digital pattern library, Edinburgh Global Experience Language (EdGEL), was developed to aid the production of effective digital experiences by providing digital experience standards, including a set of design principles, its implementation by internal staff was inconsistent. This was first because the central website platform mainly drove its use, restricting its application to website-driven scenarios rather than encompassing broader digital use-cases. Second, it was primarily aimed at technical developers, neglecting other specialists like designers and marketers, who accessed resources from alternative online locations. This accelerated the need for a central design system where the essential building blocks for the creation of effective, accessible and user-driven digital experiences were consolidated in one place.

Discovering the challenges faced by internal staff using EdGEL and recognising the necessity of shared design principles to aid the development of effective digital experiences prompted a re-evaluation of the existing principles. Design principles serve as a cohesive guide, promoting consistency, transparency, efficiency and user-centredness during product, service and interaction development. Notably, Gov.uk's design principles stand out for clearly stating their purpose, use and outlining the benefits for end-users, as seen in the principle 'Do the hard work to make it simple' (Gov.uk, 2019). Given the site's extensive use for complex tasks, prioritising simplicity for users is crucial. Inspired by this, I aimed to explore how design principles could go beyond being words on a webpage, becoming actionable elements in our design and development processes.

Applying the Double Diamond

Pre-discovery

I initiated the planning process for my final portfolio project by mapping out the Double Diamond in a collaborative online workspace, providing a visual guide for navigating the 'what,' 'how,' and 'why' within each phase. This visualisation assisted in helping me select the most appropriate techniques and approaches that would allow me to zoom in and zoom out of each phase and focus on intended outcomes. Engaging key stakeholders early on ensured alignment with crucial business requirements and incorporated their valuable insights into the existing design principles.

Utilising the online workspace not only offered an effective means to communicate my design plan to the entire team, but also fostered engagement in my learning journey. It facilitated productive discussions about objectives enabling the team to progress or adapt strategies based on insights gathered. Flexibility in adjusting the plan, despite having an initial outline, remained integral to the learning process.

During my pre-discovery research, I also encountered the concept of emergent principles, elucidated by user experience researcher, Jared Spool. Drawing on his work with product teams, Spool explained how emergent principles arise from teams observing real user problems during the development of products, services or projects. In contrast to general principles, that may be created but never revisited, emergent principles become influential in design discussions. They assist teams in identifying and addressing authentic user problems, understanding the essence of good design and striving for improvements that benefit the intended user. An example provided by Spool is the "Polish before new features" (Spool, 2017) principle, emphasising the importance of addressing existing software problems before introducing new features. This approach reduces the risk of technical debt and ensures that existing features work effectively for users.

Exploring the advantages of emergent principles in enhancing the design and development process, positively influencing team collaboration and building more effective digital experiences, sparked my interest in generating such principles for the design system. However, before I could do this, I needed to comprehend the specific problems and challenges encountered during digital project development across the university. It was also crucial to understand how existing principles were referenced and applied in those projects, if at all. This formed the basis of my Discovery exploration.

SDA insight

As learners make their way through the PDA journey and approach the final portfolio project, the learning experience very much depends on the dedication and determination of the individual. As educators, we move from guiding to following, ensuring learners are on the right path and assisting with direction where appropriate and requested. It is up to the learner to apply the theoretical and practical learning they have acquired to demonstrate how to approach solving complex problems through to implementing change. Pre-discovery is a crucial element often undermined by those without experience. As acknowledged by Lou Downe, setting the right conditions for design to happen successfully can be more than half the battle, when convincing people that change is needed (Downe, 2022).

For Sonia, there were a few essential elements that were in place at the start of this project that helped to set the scene for success. Sonia had support for the project, following an audit and strategic decision to create a design system, her colleagues were open to collaboration, and she made sure she invited those who had expertise required to implement change.

Discovery

As the focus for the design system was internal staff, I invited nine professional services staff, to ensure a range of university projects were exposed. This included content designers, user interface and user experience designers, web and application developers, project managers and communications and marketing specialists, each bringing their varied experiences of EdGEL to enrich my research efforts. I employed user journey mapping followed by user interviews and empathy mapping to get a well-rounded understanding of the challenges and problems that occurred during project development and the impact on the intended user of those products or services.

Developing a user journey map was key in helping me understand the activities of internal staff in their digital projects and their approach to these tasks. The map visually represented the steps in their process, identifying where problems came up and if the design principles played a part in helping to resolve them. To gain a more comprehensive understanding of the challenges and problems encountered, I asked participants to add what they were thinking, doing and feeling at each step, adding depth to the insights gathered.

Overall, I discovered that research does not have to be time consuming, and when time is limited, methods such as observational and guerrilla research can be adopted to learn something in a brief period while still producing reliable results. To add depth and colour to my research, I incorporated short video clips showing users' actions and thoughts. These approaches were essential in bringing problems to life, which became important when playing back research findings to the team and stakeholders.

SDA insight

"If you can only do one thing in design, do research".

(Adam Lawrence, Service Design Show, 2016)

Within the final portfolio project, Sonia learned how user research is the foundation of service design and a human-centred approach. To create services that meet the needs of users, it is essential to understand their experiences, emotions, feelings, challenges and pain. This can be done through immersive user research, which involves collecting qualitative data based on lived experiences, supplemented by quantitative data.

Sonia was able to explore the different types and methods of user research, as well as ethical considerations, human behaviour and biases, insight collection and data analysis. She began to understand when and how to collect insights, based on the users and the project at hand, and how to do so safely. By developing a deep understanding of users, Sonia could see how to create services that are truly human centred and make a positive impact on people's lives.

Define

The user journey map highlighted on the one hand that existing design principles offered guidance into good design, however it lacked practical application guidance and failed to show the benefit to the user of the product or service. The research helped to validate the emergent principles concept in playing a significant role in making principles a more conscious and actionable part of the design process.

This evidence suggested framing the problem statement as "How might we unify our community under a design system through actionable principles that guide our design, development and creative processes?" I saw the potential of emergent principles in shaping the way we work as I entered the co-design phase.

SDA insight

The aftermath of Discovery can be overwhelming, with masses of data and insights. Sonia learned the importance of taking the time to constantly analyse data. The define phase provides space to identify and build up an understanding of the patterns and themes in the findings to inform further research, keep a check on cognitive biases, fish-boning the integral information that provides a true and accurate representation of the insights gathered. This is a skill within itself, and it is extremely important for the data to drive next steps and for Sonia to truly understand the problem area before diving into the second diamond.

Develop

In the co-design event, I aimed to put the emergent principles concept into action, creating some new emergent principles and prototyping them to assess their value. I utilised SDA specific planning tools, including the Stakeholder Wheel, a tool to help ensure diverse voices were involved, and the Session Builder to aid logistics and effective delivery. Re-engaging with the same participants from the user research allowed them to experience ideation techniques and revisit the user journey maps from Discovery within this collaborative session.

To maximise rapid idea generation, I first used SDA's ABC Avalanche tool, to get the brain thinking creatively using the letters of the alphabet. This enabled participants to collectively identify known problems and their impact on product or service users. The SDA's Sunflowers technique – based on the Lotus Blossom method by Phil Delalande (Delalande, 2019) – followed to generate multiple ideas for new principles which could address these problems. Finally, dot voting helped prioritise the most valuable principles created, resulting in the formulation of two new principles, "open processes" and "validate and test regularly".

To prototype testing these new principles in action, participants were asked to look at the original user journey maps created in the Discovery phase to assess how the journey would change with the new principles, "open processes" and "validate and test regularly" applied. Therefore, the participants were iterating on the original journeys. Participants had the opportunity to select from a broad range of projects ranging from the development of a website to guidance on the university website for applicants affected by exam cancellations.

Seeing the application of the user journey map used for prototyping within the co-design session was, as one participant expressed, "enlightening" as it gave them a unique perspective on different roles and processes, which they may otherwise not have insight into, raising awareness and highlighting challenges. It also helped to show participants how the new principles could guide better design decisions, thus improving the underlying experience of products and services. A participant noted that the implementation of the new principles would "make a massive difference" because expectations would be managed and understanding increased across the board.

The co-design techniques I learned were instrumental in planning and establishing a creative environment for idea development and problem-solving. Testing and refining my co-design session with my team, who acted as 'critical friends', ensured its smooth execution and yielded valuable outcomes. These approaches also demonstrated the potential for rapid idea generation, as a participant remarked, "it was a fantastic platform for uniting our design community and addressing design principles. The workshop format was a fun way to quickly generate creative ideas, and the results were incredible".

Overall, this session highlighted the value of involving real people in the design process, emphasising the effectiveness of the service design approach for all participants.

SDA insight

By immersing herself in the problem space, Sonia began to appreciate how to use insights gathered to guide innovation. Sonia explored creativity, collaboration, facilitation and co-design approaches to problem-solving. This experimental play guided strategic direction, allowing her to develop knowledge, experience of organising and facilitating co-design and prototyping for mixed audiences.

Sonia could appreciate how co-designing principles ensured an open, equitable and collaborative space for people to contribute to shaping solutions. Learning to facilitate different types and methods of prototypes using low-fi, cheap and playful resources to explore how a service will look and feel in a wider organisation, provides focus on turning ideas into implementable solutions. Co-design also emphasises the need to harness everyone's differences, experiences and skillsets to create innovative solutions.

Deliver

This portfolio project provided a comprehensive perspective on developing and applying design principles throughout an entire project, demonstrating their efficacy in aiding internal staff when addressing user-related challenges in product and service development. Through problem-solving, collaboration and knowledge exchange, two emergent design principles were created, "open processes" and "validate and test regularly". This facilitated a greater awareness among participants as one aptly noted, "Recognising that others face similar challenges is crucial. Bringing this community together helps us refocus on our processes, generate ideas and provide immediate solutions for our projects".

Compiling the final portfolio presentation allowed me to reflect on the service design approaches employed and articulate key takeaways, with my manager, product team and stakeholders. This work highlighted:

- The design process used and the project types undertaken by teams and the challenges encountered by them.
- Instances where existing design principles were not referenced or found to be difficult to use.
- The value of emergent principles in crafting comprehensive guidelines to enhance the design system and serve as the foundation for our product and service development processes.

The impact from this work remains ongoing, however we intend to continue building from what we have developed, using the outputs to contribute to future endeavours in the development of our design principles. Success will be measured by the practical application of these principles in future projects undertaken by our internal staff, as well as by teams sharing their experiences with fellow design system users. We hope to share future case studies on our design system website, as they begin to be adopted.

One unexpected outcome was that participants recognised that, as a result of a siloed culture and the large, decentralised nature of the institution, solutions were often repeated, requiring more effort than necessary. This resulted in the realisation that a change in our ways of working was fundamentally needed, as a participant emphasised, "Collective work has tremendous power, and the more its benefits are known across the university, the better products and services we will design". This resulted in all participants acknowledging the value in collaborating to address problems and discover solutions that contribute to the overall benefit of the organisation.

SDA insight

Sonia's project demonstrates perfectly, that although it may be the end of the process, the hard work is only just beginning, and the design process never ends. It is a constant iterative process within itself, inviting designers to constantly seek out and invite in change and improvements.

Measuring success in service design focuses not only on the output of the project, in Sonia's case the co-creation of emergent design principles, but also on the power fostered through meaningful and impactful outcomes. By adopting a service design approach, inviting the relevant people in at the start of the project and elevating their lived experience and expertise, Sonia was able to positively agitate ways of working, acting as a catalyst for a shift in organisational culture.

Case study: final reflections

In my final portfolio project for SDA, I aimed to infuse a service design mindset into the formulation of design principles, crafting a framework that guides decision-making and action within our university. Fostering discussion, promoting collaboration and engaging diverse voices in all parts of the process, transforms learning into a collaborative effort that enriches perspectives and contributes significantly to shaping projects and effective problem-solving. This experience has given me the confidence to ask tough questions and facilitate collaboration in creating a design system that brings university staff on that journey.

The PDA is a testament to the significance of trusting in the process, as Katie encouraged us to develop unique approaches, focus on value and develop skills that complemented the design process. These included, empathy, curiosity, recognising biases, creating conducive environments for co-creativity and storytelling. I completed the training with the skills, capabilities and confidence to transition these practices into my workplace. This set me on the path to continue applying service design within the design system project and seeking ways to foster a service design mindset within my organisation.

The Impact of the Training

Sonia's experience

"Good design must serve people."

(www-03.ibm.com, 2012)

The experience with SDA gave me confidence to develop my approach to service design, blending my visual design strengths with a heightened focus on user needs. I learnt that human-centred design is flexible and iterative. There is no one-size-fits-all approach and constant learning, and adaptation is essential.

The impact of the training encouraged me to delve deeper into our design system project, prompting me to investigate a critical service component – the contribution process. This process is essential in supporting internal staff when requesting changes and contributing new elements to the design system. Collaborating with stakeholders in the creation of the contribution process, then iterating with service teams, ensured its clarity and effectiveness across different use cases. This engagement fostered buy-in with internal staff using the design system, by instilling confidence in the product and service we were developing.

Co-design allowed me to extend the practices and principles of service design beyond my immediate team, promoting the adoption of this mindset and breaking down the misconception that this work is 'niche' or specialist. A colleague from the Edinburgh Research Office highlighted the impact on participants during a session stating, "it facilitated a process which enabled us to co-create and iterate, which unlocked our creativity and enabled us to share ideas". The project resulted with the research team having a clearer definition and understanding of their audience, as customers and elevating the recognition of their service among researchers.

The personal impact of the training was felt through the confidence it instilled in me which reframed my approach to work. Before the training, I did not feel confident to share my ideas and opinions in relation to service design in the way that I do now. It is important as a designer to do this, so people understand your product, service or project and see the importance of it in the way that you do. This has helped me to share the knowledge gained with students within the School of Design, educating them on human-centred methods to enrich their design practice. I have also sought opportunities to connect with like-minded individuals through participation in collaborative, education-focused events like EduJam and joining HE user experience networks and groups.

At its core, this mindset requires collective responsibility to deepen our understanding of the people our organisation serves. By nurturing an open and inclusive culture, universities can transcend institutional boundaries and collaborate across the broader educational landscape. Sharing insights and best practices across institutions helps us avoid common pitfalls, inspiring others to create impact by putting ideas out into the world.

Katie's perspective

Once people experience service design and see its positive impact, they become more eager to get involved. This facilitates a cycle of learning that goes far beyond the realms of the PDA, transcending to the workplace and beyond. Service design education can empower learners to find fulfilment and positively influence others' lives. It can also help to develop the skills and mindset needed to overcome challenges, such as pushbacks, denial, cognitive biases and assumptions. The Double Diamond process is a valuable framework, but it is important to also develop empathy and iteration skills. One of the best ways to develop these skills is by trying, failing and learning from mistakes.

The PDA provides learners with experiences to develop the skills and mindset needed to make a positive impact. It aims to empower learners to become agents of positive transformation in their communities and beyond. As the service design industry grows, there is a clear need for a learner pathway that supports the embedding of service design into organisations. It is a discipline that is not exclusive to experts. It is accessible to anyone interested in creating positive change. By providing a common language and tools, it enables individuals from all walks of life to actively participate in shaping the world around them.

Figure 4.1 Sonia and Katie's takeaways

Key takeaways

Here are our key insights and resources to inspire you to experience service design education for yourself.

1   Ask for forgiveness, rather than seek permission.: Learn by doing
    It's a mantra you will hear from the Global Jams community; learn by doing. Start small with projects that give you freedom to learn and experiment with mindset, process and tools. Play, learn, experiment and do not be afraid to fail. If it feels a little wild, you are doing it right. Jams are a fun and immersive way to learn and make friends for life, in 48 hours! You will not regret participating, you will leave with new ways of thinking, working and sharing.
2   Trust the process: Build your confidence
    As you learn to trust the process, you gain a deeper understanding of the holistic nature of service design, which requires you to weave back and forth across the different phases. This was recognised when the UK Design Council's Innovation Framework (Design Council, 2023a) was released in 2019, to respond to and reflect how service design has evolved, aligning to how the process is used in practice, including encompassing key principles and methods.
3   Good Design Serves People: Share your learning experiences
    As you find your tribe, learn, build confidence, get used to telling stories and sharing your experiences. Being able to communicate in diverse ways, bringing data, processes and systems to life through people and stories will be invaluable. The community is naturally empathic and open to sharing stories and experiences, providing connections locally and globally. Communicate, share and bring others on your journey through the power of storytelling. The online Service Design Show is an excellent place to start listening to designers in the industry sharing their stories.

References

Design Council. (2023a) Framework for Innovation. Available at: www.designcouncil.org.uk/our-resources/framework-for-innovation (Accessed: 30 September 2023).

Design Council. (2023b) History of the Double Diamond – Design Council. Available at: www.designcouncil.org.uk/our-resources/the-double-diamond/history-of-the-double-diamond (Accessed: 30 September 2023).

Delalande, P. (2019) The Lotus Blossom method: ideation on steroids. Medium. Available at: https://uxdesign.cc/the-lotus-blossom-method-ideation-on-steroids-100adb26a0c2 (Accessed: 13 December 2023).

Downe, L. (2022) Launching the School of Good Services. Available at: https://good.services/blog/launching-the-school-of-good-services (Accessed: 12 December 2023).

Gov.uk. (2019) Government Design Principles. Available at: www.gov.uk/guidance/government-design-principles#do-the-hard-work-to-make-it-simple (Accessed: 12 December 2023).

Service Design Show. (2016) Getting your boss to prototype customer experience (and have fun) / Adam Lawrence / Episode #7. Available at: www.youtube.com/watch?v=8YfVoeo3I4M (Accessed: 2 July 2023).

Spool, J. M. (2012) IBM100 – Good Design Is Good Business. Available at: www.ibm.com/ibm/history/ibm100/us/en/icons/gooddesign/team (Accessed: 12 December 2023).

Spool, J. M. (2017) Emergent Principles: A Rebel Leader's Secret to Better Team Design Decisions. UX Articles by Center Centre. Available at: https://articles.centercentre.com/emergent-principles-a-rebel-leaders-secret-to-better-team-design-decisions (Accessed: 12 December 2023). www-03.ibm.com.

Chapter 5

Untangling networks

Using design methods to grow collaborative innovation beyond the classroom

Dr Lara Salinas

Introduction

Universities have three main missions: *Teaching* focuses on education, *research* involves creating new knowledge, and *outreach* or *knowledge exchange* aims to have a wide societal impact. Knowledge exchange, or the third mission, has traditionally been dominated by the transfer of knowledge from academia to industry, however in the last decades the paradigm of collaboration within universities has changed to incorporate a wide range of mechanisms to facilitate positive societal change. Higher education institutions have multilevel and complex structures, and each mission (teaching, research, outreach) has its own set of systems, rules, values and protocols. The dynamic of engagement between academics and external stakeholders also depends on their activity: when doing research staff typically operate at national and international scales, while teaching and outreach activities often operate at a local level (Pflitsch & Radinger-Peer, 2017).

As a design practice researcher and educator, I am interested in exploring how designers in academia can sustain place-based innovation ecosystems to create value for people and the planet. In my role at the University of the Arts London, I have been dedicated to nurturing a culture of knowledge exchange, driving organisational change using service design approaches (Junginger & Sangiorgi, 2009). In this chapter, I provide an illustrative example of how service design is well equipped to support organisational change. I have explored this through the process of designing and deploying an online canvas that facilitates visual conversations with course teams, untangling complex networks of collaborative activities and evidencing the relational value of project-based learning as a greenhouse for collaborative innovation. Service design, understood as 'designing for service', is employed here to design the context and platform where activities of value co-creation take place (Sangiorgi & Prendiville, 2017). Hence, the canvas is not the end result but a platform for facilitating conversations, questioning the norms and values of the organisation and contributing to a deep organisational change.

I hope that my journey can provide useful insights to readers and inform how they can use service design approaches to tackle similar challenges in their institutions. In the following section, I share an example of how I used service

DOI: 10.4324/9781003383161-12

design approaches to support organisational change in my institution. I structure my journey into the following stages: the challenge, preliminary research, designing the canvas, deploying the canvas, the canvas as an output.

The challenge context

Having three missions in practice means that as an academic I am expected to perform on three fronts: I *teach* design to prepare new generations of service designers, conduct *research* to co-create new knowledge on designing better public policies and services and engage with external organisations to *exchange knowledge* and generate social impact building on my teaching and research practices. This is the case of project-based learning, a student-centred approach to learning and teaching in which students learn through hands-on experiences and real-world challenges (Figure 5.1). Project-based learning is mostly studied from a pedagogical standpoint, focusing on the key features such as learning by doing, tackling real world problems, engaging with interdisciplinarity, advantages and challenges versus other pedagogical approaches or its potential for effectively incorporate sustainability in the curriculum (Harmer & Stokes, 2014; Stokes & Harmer, 2018; Kokotsaki, Menzies & Wiggins, 2016). However, in addition to providing an excellent learning experience, project-based learning offers opportunities to establish collaboration with external stakeholders. Recognising the potential of project-based education to scale and lead to collaboration with businesses, non-profit organisations and other groups will go a long way to achieve shared goals and drive social, environmental and economic benefits. However, when we are in a teaching context, fully dedicated to offer the best possible learning opportunity, we often struggle to also articulate the impact of these collaborative activities beyond the classroom. What if we approached project-based education as a seed for collaborative innovation beyond the classroom?

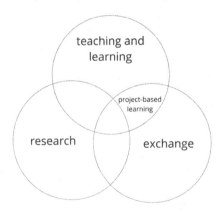

Figure 5.1 The three missions of universities converge

Preliminary research

I am based at London College of Communication, one of the six colleges that make up University of the Arts London, where I lecture on service design and co-lead Service Futures Lab. From 2019 until 2021 I also held a leadership role with the aim of supporting the development of knowledge exchange in line with the university's strategic vision and mission. In this role, I advised the Dean and Senior Management Team on school-level changes to better support knowledge exchange activities. I viewed my role as being concerned with design-led organisational change, as developing better support for knowledge exchange requires examining and challenging existing assumptions, ways of working and structures. I took on this role because I felt it presented an opportunity to build on my service design knowledge to apply the insights that I had gained from extensive research on knowledge exchange in creative disciplines.

My initial task was to devise a plan of action to maximise the impact of knowledge exchange (KE) activities. This involved conducting a comprehensive overview of the state of the art of knowledge exchange across the school. The starting point of my brief was something like: "How might we create a repository of KE activity that allows us to gain the knowledge to better support our colleagues to do excellent KE?" I must admit that as a participatory designer, the idea of conducting research on my colleagues unsettled me, and from the offset I was determined to transform the brief into something more like "How might we support colleagues to recognise and maximise the impact of their collaborative activities?"

I started my journey conducting some preparatory research to better understand and frame the problem space. I built on previous research on knowledge exchange at University of the Arts London (Salinas, 2019) and progressed to conduct ad-hoc contextual interviews with my colleagues to dive deeper into how knowledge exchange was understood and practiced in the college, with particular attention to course team's approach to project-based learning. This led me to build a better picture of the challenge that the Senior Management Team was facing.

The Design School has about 100 members of staff, distributed in approximately 20 course teams that teach diverse creative disciplines such as service design, user experience, illustration, design management and graphic design at undergraduate and postgraduate levels. Each of these course teams typically organises about five collaborative activities with external organisations per academic year. This amounts to about 100 collaborative activities per academic year, constituting a long tail of activities that lecturers arrange with the purpose of creating learning opportunities for their cohorts of students. These collaborations are wide-ranging in scope and scale, contextual to the creative discipline. Furthermore, many of these activities are initiated through informal and relational mechanisms that may not require contractual and transactional services offered by universities' administrative offices (Hughes *et al.*, 2016). The activities, therefore, are known to the core academic team involved in the delivery but are often invisible to the institution. Over time, these knowledge exchange activities result in an almost intractable network of collaborations across courses and years of study. Managing the complex networks of project-based learning can be overwhelming for academic and support teams. Understandably, Senior Management Teams needed to gain a better sense of activities and ensure a strategic approach to the allocation of resources.

As part of my primary research, I approached colleagues rather ad-hoc, over lunch or a coffee to gain a better understanding about their course level collaborative activities. I found out that in the past the school had used questionnaires to create a repository of project-based learning activities in a simple and efficient manner. The answers were collected in a comprehensive spreadsheet, each single activity captured in a row. However, upon reviewing the spreadsheet its many limitations became obvious. Firstly, there seemed to be a strong emphasis on quantity rather than quality. The spreadsheet provided a quick overview of the volume and scale of collaborative activities across the school, but it did not provide any indication of the quality of these activities. It was assumed that if a course had many collaborative activities involving many students, it must be good. Unfortunately, the data in the spreadsheet only provided information on volume and did not offer any insights into other aspects. The data collection process was aligned with the requirements of HE-BCI, the Higher Education Business Community and Interaction survey, which is the main method for measuring the volume and direction of interactions between British Higher Education providers and businesses and the wider community (HESA, n. d.). Secondly, the spreadsheet confirmed that there was an overwhelming volume of activities throughout the college. I began to question the value of recording all these activities. Instead, I thought that it would be more enlightening to understand the motivation behind these activities, and how they aligned with the strategic priorities of the university.

With a better understanding of the challenges and a clearer definition of the task at hand, I conducted semi-structured interviews with colleagues that had faced similar tasks across the university, seeking to learn from their approaches. This led me to confirm that the data that I sought was not collected systematically and that I had to devise a new data gathering exercise involving lecturers.

I wanted to understand the relationships between teaching, research and knowledge exchange, and the spreadsheet did not provide any insights into these connections! So, I really had to do some data gathering. I recognised that data collection processes could be extractive and potentially burdensome for my colleagues. In line with my commitment to responsible and non-extractive approaches in my practice (Freire, 1970; Costanza-Chock, 2020) I believed that it was crucial to support my fellow lecturers in developing their own analyses of the collaborative activities that were relevant to them. Taking an asset-based approach, I wanted my intervention to feel more like an empowering conversation than an audit or training session and to build upon my colleagues' experiences so that any recommendations I would make to the Senior Management Team would be co-created with my colleagues and grounded in solid evidence. This was a radically different way of going about creating an action plan and an opportunity to impulse change in the organisational culture. Furthermore, I was rather aware of the resource limitations, owing both to the heavy workload of academics, particularly during the pandemic, and to my very fractional time to the role. On the one hand, it was important to ensure that I was not burdening my colleagues with my task. On the other, it was not feasible to involve all 100 individuals that make up the school. Therefore, I had to devise a way of engaging meaningfully a representative sample.

I synthesised the insights gained through my preliminary research into some guiding principles to define the problem and solution space:

Table 5.1 Guiding principles to define the problem and solution space

Principle	Action
A repository does not have to be comprehensive; it must be meaningful and representative of the school's knowledge exchange landscape.	Capture qualitative and contextual data. Ask participants to add only activities that are illustrative and representative of their collaboration with external organisations.
Gathering data for the repository should not be a burdensome and extractive exercise.	Create a positive and generative environment, ensuring that colleagues are heard, empowered and that can benefit from their participation.
A cross school activity is an opportunity to initiate a change of organisational culture.	Include colleagues more actively into making recommendations for a plan of action.
Limited resources.	Light touch, aiming for a third of the school about eight participants, no more than 1 hour.
Since data cannot be anonymised, participants should be in control of data input.	Input data with participants.

Development of the canvas

In response to these principles, I created a canvas on Miro, a platform that was increasingly popular among academics working remotely. This platform offered a more flexible approach to data collection that a questionnaire and spreadsheet, and the visual format was much more accessible and familiar to the creative disciplines. My objective was to create a canvas, which is a template with a structured approach to data input, that allowed participants to articulate their own impact narratives in relation to the university's strategic priorities. I would then analyse and synthesise this data to create a system map of the school's knowledge exchange ecosystem, identifying strengths and opportunities of growth.

I went through an intensive phase of prototyping and testing the canvas, in which I would roleplay as an interviewee based on my experience as a lecturer. I also used dummy data to prototype the data analysis and ensure that the canvas was useful in collecting the right data and drawing insights. Of course, this approach to prototyping had limitations, so once I had a stable version of the canvas, I invited my course team to provide critical feedback. I carefully noted every question, hesitation or misunderstanding as a point of improvement in the canvas.

After another iteration of the canvas, I invited all 20 course team members to participate in a 30-minute online visual interview focused on collaborative activities led by their teams, hoping to get at least representation from a third of the course teams, which I did. I made sure to start the round of interviews with the team whose work I was most familiar with, as I anticipated that the canvas would possibly need to be iterated to incorporate some minor changes once again after first run.

Deploying the canvas

For a successful workshop it was important to build rapport with the participants. I began each workshop by thanking my colleagues for accepting my invitation, promising to keep the workshop under schedule and very briefly explaining once again the objective, motivation and dynamic of the workshop for transparency. I invited them to take the following 30 minutes as an opportunity to reflect on their course, on their approach to project-based education and to knowledge exchange. It was important for me to clarify that this was not a training event and that I was actually there to learn from them and ensure that their approach to knowledge exchange, their strengths and opportunities for improvement were understood by the school. I believe that it helped that I was a colleague who shared their challenges and had acquired a reputation as an expert in knowledge exchange in creative disciplines.

We began to explore the canvas together. The online canvas consisted of four stages, each of them containing a brief introduction; a) *Let's look at what we do already* focused on visualising the areas of impact of knowledge exchange activities; b) *Building a narrative* focused on surfacing thematic expertise and alignment with strategic priorities; c) *Amplifying impact* aimed at building a shared understanding of how project-based learning can be supported to maximise impact; and d) *Some facts* aimed at surfacing the resources and enablers of knowledge exchange activities. In the following section I outline each of them and provide an overview of the key insights that can be drawn from using the canvas, focusing on the first and second sections as these addressed untangling the complex networks of project-based learning and potential to initiate collaborative innovation.

The canvas

The online canvas consists of four stages:

*(1) **Look at what we do*** asked participants to outline their most significant knowledge exchange activities and situate them spatially against a Venn diagram to signify the main orientation of the activity as teaching, research or outreach. They then colour-coded the activity according to whether it involves the participation of students or not and drew lines connecting the activities if they were related, such as one activity leading to the next. This first activity revealed at a glance the typical collaborative activities of each course, and the role project-based learning activities played in relation to other type of activities. The posterior analysis suggested that best practice was found in course teams with a mature and focused practice, that was well-aligned with the course discipline and who approached project-based learning with the conviction that it represented an opportunity to enrich the course offering to students, as much as an opportunity to further their professional practice and research.

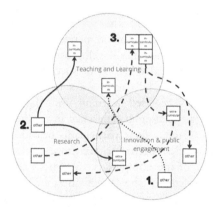

Figure 5.2 Look at what we do

*(2) **Building a narrative*** followed on from the previous exercise to create impact narratives. Participants were asked to add keywords that describe the focus of each one of the activities included in the previous step, and then match it to one of the four strategic priorities of the university (University of the Arts London, 2021). This activity revealed the areas of interest and expertise of each member of the course team and how their unique profile contributes to the course. Although most participants were not familiar with the strategic priorities of the university, it was rather easy to find an alignment (not surprisingly, since the strategy drew on extensive consultation). This section concluded with two open questions to shed light on how academic teams perceive and evidence the impact of project-based learning: "why do you do

this type of work?" and "share one memorable moment". The responses varied and related to the development of professional practice, the development of research, the desire to have a positive impact in the world and the recognition of the wider value of creative practices. This section plays a crucial role in supporting course teams to having a clear understanding of the university's strategic priorities, think about the alignment of their practice and evidence of impact. Similarly, it provides rich insights into lecturers' motivations to go the extra mile in their teaching. Participants felt passionate about their project-based learning activities, which allowed them to give the best possible learning experience to students because it also had an impact in the real world.

At the *(3) amplify impact* section, participants reflected on how they can maximise the impact of their project-based learning. The prompt is "What three things would make a difference?", with a focus on identify opportunities rather than challenges. Responses were varied, but all successful avoided an antagonistic response. One participant pointed out that a more comprehensive training program would help academics better understand how to incorporate project-based learning into their curricula; another suggested that having more opportunities to collaborate with other academics would help them learn from each other's experiences while also expanding their network. Another participant recommended that more expert support should be available to help academics develop their project proposals, such as online guides and a centralised database of successful projects. Overall, the participants agreed that there are many ways to improve support for academics interested in project-based learning and that by amplifying their impact, they can make a meaningful difference in the field of education.

In the final section, *(4) some facts*, participants provided an overview of the enablers of their knowledge exchange activities, outlining a detailed and nuanced understanding of the complex ecosystem of resources and enablers that underpin their knowledge exchange activities.

The 30-minute online visual interviews were praised by participants, appreciative of having the opportunity of reflecting about the course from an unusual perspective, beyond learning and teaching. The exercise was particularly valued by a course team that joined in full and who exchanged different perspectives on how to amplify the impact of their teaching and learning beyond the classroom.

Summary of learnings

I began this journey with the hypothesis that framing project-based learning activities solely for their pedagogic value is a missed opportunity. These activities are one of the mechanisms used by universities to collaborate with external organisations and have the potential to drive societal, environmental and economic benefits. Additionally, I have suggested that over time, course-led collaborative activities create a complex network of collaborations across units of study and student cohorts that is not fully visible at the institutional level. Therefore, the role of project-based learning in universities' knowledge change ecosystem is not fully articulated.

I have approached the challenge of supporting a growing culture of knowledge exchange as a service designer, in a participatory manner, with the creation of a canvas to enable meaningful conversations around knowledge exchange in course teams and untangle complex networks of project-based learning and other collaborative activities. I have also accounted for how this canvas was developed and deployed at University of the Arts London to support the development of the university's knowledge exchange strategic priorities.

Overall, the canvas serves as a catalyst to support collaborative innovation. At a macro level, the canvas provides a comprehensive overview of the complex ecosystem of collaborations, providing a platform to compare different approaches to project-based learning in a unified format. The canvas provides evidence of the connections between different types of scholarly activities, making explicit the key role of project-based learning in building capability for follow up collaborations that have a wider impact on society. At a micro level, the canvas helps individuals to develop a better understanding of their collaborative activities as a team, and in relationship to their university's strategic priorities. By visually mapping out collaborative activities on the canvas with the guidance of an expert facilitator, course teams have an opportunity to discuss and revisit their individual and collective goals, resource allocation, leading teams to adopt a more strategic approach to collaboration with an enhanced understanding the role that project-based learning can play in building knowledge exchange capability. Furthermore, the canvas has been successful in supporting academic teams articulate the value of their teaching and learning beyond the classroom. At the workshop, participants were able to build a narrative of impact that was unique to their discipline and ethos and yet aligned with the university's strategic priorities. The canvas has, therefore, contributed to embed a system perspective into course teams and facilitated communication between course teams and senior management, working as key steps towards changing the culture of knowledge exchange in the organisation. The canvas was never intended as a tool for auditing and will not replace other reporting mechanisms, such as HEB-CI return. Yet, I firmly believe that it has the potential to facilitate timely reporting and strategising if completed, for example, at the beginning and towards the end of the academic year. Additionally, involving students, particularly postgraduate students, in the exercise can help them understand how their journey of project-based learning fits within their career development.

I had secretly hoped that the canvas would be able to work without expert facilitation. However, as I provided guidance and engaged in conversation with the participants, it became apparent that my expert knowledge and facilitation were greatly valued. It made me realise that our encounter was much more than just a visual interview; it involved a strong element of training and guided reflection, which I had not initially anticipated. In fact, participants reported that they viewed the interview as a sought-after moment of peer mentoring and shared reflection, which proved to be an informative and productive exercise in articulating their own approach to project-based learning. This realisation prompted me to let the participants progress through the canvas at their own pace, focusing on the areas that interested them the most.

This canvas continues to be used by course teams to plan and reflect on their activities. Versions of this canvas are used with students to contextualise their project-based learning (Salinas, 2022) Additionally, this and other successful design-led activities have led to an increased adoption of design methods, such as visual mapping, throughout my HE institution, tapping into the design expertise of colleagues.

Key learning points

1 Principles and values in service design: For me being human-centred means being committing to ethical and just practices, and that involved bringing my colleagues' voices into decision making, creating a safe space where they could express their opinions freely, and including hourly paid members of staff.

2 Reframing challenges into opportunities: Designers are excellent at turning challenges into chances. In the process of devising the canvas I transformed the onerous and unrewarding task of building a data base into an opportunity to gain a deeper understanding of our knowledge exchange activities and get colleagues excited about it.

3 Good design looks deceptively simple: In just 30 minutes, the canvas provides a rather comprehensive picture of the knowledge exchange ecosystem at college, at a glance. The visualisation is legible and that makes it seem simple, but it is not. The canvas bridges theory and practice and tells many stories; about how the three missions of universities are interrelated, about how project-based learning activities are seeds that grow into other activities, about the motivation of academic teams, about how to grow impact or about what motivates academic staff.

References

Costanza-Chock, S. (2020) *Design Justice: Community-Led Practices to Build the Worlds We Need.* Cambridge, MA: MIT Press.

Freire, P. (1970) *Pedagogy of the oppressed* (30th anniversary ed.). New York: Continuum.

Harmer, N. & Stokes, A. (2014). The benefits and challenges of project-based learning. Available at: https://gmitchangelab.files.wordpress.com/2016/01/pedrio-paper-6-p bl.pdf (Accessed: 14 December 2023).

Hedge, T. (1993) Key concepts in ELT. *ELT Journal*, 47(3), 275–277.

HESA. (n.d.) Definitions: HE – Business and Community Interaction. Available at www.hesa.ac.uk/support/definitions/hebci (Accessed 14 December 2023).

Hughes, A., Lawson, C., Salter, A. & Kitson, M., with Bullock, A. & Hughes, R. B. (2016) *The Changing State of Knowledge Exchange: UK Academic Interactions with External Organisations 2005–2015*. London: NCUB.

Junginger, S. & Sangiorgi, D. (2009) Service Design and Organisational Change. Bridging the gap between rigour and relevance. Available at https://core.ac.uk/download/pdf/55253543.pdf (Accessed. 14 December 2023).

Kokotsaki, D., Menzies, V. & Wiggins, A. (2016) Project-based learning: A review of the literature. *Improving Schools*, 19(3), 267–277. Available at: https://doi.org/10.1177/1365480216659733 (Accessed: 14 December 2023).

Law, J. (2003) Making a Mess with Method. Centre for Science Studies, Lancaster University. Available at www.comp.lancs.ac.uk/sociology/papers/Law-Making-a-Mess-with-Method.pdf (Accessed: 14 December 2023).

Malpass, M. & Salinas, L. (2020) AHRC Challenges of the Future: Public Services. AHRC. Available at: https://ualresearchonline.arts.ac.uk/id/eprint/15838 (Accessed: 14 December 2023).

Pflitsch, G. & Radinger-Peer, V. (2018) Developing boundary-spanning capacity for regional sustainability transitions – a comparative case study of the Universities of Augsburg (Germany) and Linz (Austria). *Sustainability*, 10(918), 1–26.

Salinas, L. (2019) Understanding Knowledge Exchange at the University of the Arts London. London: University of the Arts London. Available at: https://ualresearchonline.arts.ac.uk/id/eprint/15037/7/salinas2019-understandingKEUALb.pdf (Accessed: 10 December 2023).

Salinas, L. (2021) *Design School KE Master Plan*. London: University of the Arts London.

Salinas L. (2022) *"I am not cheap labour". A visual conversation to unpack the ethics of involving students in knowledge exchange*. UIIN Conference, Amsterdam, 13–15 June 2022. Available at https://ualresearchonline.arts.ac.uk/id/eprint/18771 (Accessed: 14 December 2023).

Salinas, L., Grimaldi, S., Lujan Escalante, M., Ali, H., Lagedemont, M. & Prendiville, A. (2023) Teaching Service Design: Pedagogical Reflections. *ServDes 2023*. Rio de Janeiro: 11–14 July 2023. DAD PUC-Rio Pontificia Universidade Catolica Do Rio de Janeiro. Available at https://ualresearchonline.arts.ac.uk/id/eprint/20075/1/ServDes.2023_teachingSD.pdf (Accessed: 9 December 2023).

Sangiorgi, D. & Prendiville, A. (2017). *Designing for Service: Key Issues and New Directions*. London: Bloomsbury.

Stokes, A. & Harmer, N. (2018) The value of "having a go": Trialling a project-based learning activity to inform curriculum design. *Journal of Geoscience Education*, 66(4), 278–292.

University of the Arts London. (2021) Knowledge Exchange Strategy 2021–2026. Available at www.arts.ac.uk/__data/assets/pdf_file/0028/293545/UAL_KE-Strategy-2021-26_FINAL.pdf (Accessed: 14 December 2023).

Chapter 6

Mindsets Eat Methods

Human-Centred Design for organisational change in Higher Education

Phillippa Rose and Sharon Jones

Introduction

Our working assumption is that universities are potentially uniquely situated to benefit from Human-Centred Design (HCD) because they are networked organisations where members are distributed but work together to achieve common goals. Recent work by Ney and Meinel (2019) suggests that networked organisations provide a good type of ecosystem for design thinking to flourish.

We are writing from the perspective of consultants coming into two universities to support capability building programmes in HCD for professional and organisational development. Our context-specific working knowledge arises from our dual experience as faculty teaching staff (University of the Arts London; and Cork University Business School, the University of Cork, National University of Ireland) and as working practitioners in the field of HCD across the public, private and charitable sectors.

Methodologically, our approach in our case studies is informed by the UK Design Council Double Diamond model and the Design Sprint model espoused by Knapp *et al.* (2016). We undertook a learning-by-doing approach in response to an existing design challenge of value to the organisation and the participants. This approach seeks to provide a form of apprenticeship, on the job training and development in HCD, while also seeking to address a specific organisational challenge in pursuit of wider change.

We support the definition of HCD as 'as a practice where designers focus on four key aspects: people and their context, understanding and solving the right problems (the root problems), understanding that everything is a complex system with interconnected parts, and doing small interventions' (Interaction Design Foundation, n.d.).

Our definition of mindset is taken from the Oxford English Dictionary 'an established set of attitudes of a person or group concerning culture, values, philosophy, frame of mind, outlook and disposition'.

We adopt the term 'participant-learner' to describe the model and dual aspects of team members (professional and academic staff) as co-designers and learners.

DOI: 10.4324/9781003383161-13

The deliberate inclusion of students in the case studies recognises the value of end-user input and genuine co-creation in defining both the problem and solution space. Case study 1 includes students as co-designers and interviewers. Case Study 2 includes students in prototype testing and journey mapping.

Case Study 1: PhD Student Experience

Case Study 1 concerns the introduction of HCD to the organisation and participant learners as a completely new concept. The University had invested in training and development in LEAN (Womack & Jones, 1996) methods and business process engineering as part of its change agenda although this investment and other organisational redesign initiatives had not delivered hoped-for benefits for students and their learning experience. Consequently, there was a willingness to test a new method on a pilot basis. The focus of the pilot study was on the PhD Student Experience, seeking to improve time to completion, which was a matter of concern for the Dean of Graduate Studies.

Case Study 2: Design Requirements of a Learning Management System: Joint Initiative

Case Study 2 concerns investment in a joint venture by two universities to develop a joint school in a new, high value, practice-based disciplinary area. Neither university team was familiar with the HCD approach although the senior management sponsor leading the joint initiative had undergone training in design thinking and was a supportive advocate. There was senior management support from both universities for a rapid appraisal of the design requirements for a new learning management system (LMS) to be used by both institutions as both were dissatisfied with existing systems (Moodle and Blackboard). The universities had previously worked together to jointly procure third-party systems therefore there was a history of successful collaboration of this type. The focus of this HCD intervention was to team-build across the two universities and scope the design of a new LMS to address the specific needs of students, staff and placement providers in the new discipline.

Beyond method: Preparing to disrupt

A key reflection in both university case studies is that time spent preparing sponsors, leaders and participant-learners to build trust ahead of a design challenge experience is a prerequisite to enabling the effective application of HCD in organisations. Unfortunately, the practice literature on HCD preparation is scant in this regard. We offer some tools and approaches to help prepare for individual and organisational mindset disruption inherent in application of HCD in real-world design challenges that we have found valuable in our practice.

The Problem/Solution Dance

The problem explored is often ill-defined and the rush to solution is hard to rein in. This is not a new phenomenon and is commonly found in analyses of project failure.

Our case study experiences suggest that greater attention to *readiness* is required to prepare participants for the emotional challenges of practising HCD. The importance of building participants' trust and willingness to embrace ambiguity and uncertainty in the design challenge discovery phase must not be overlooked.

Using HCD tools to explore problem definition proved a powerful way to slow down thinking and surface assumptions and cognitive bias in our participant-learners. Exposing assumptions is an uncomfortable and challenging experience for participants requiring the embrace of honesty and transparency. Collaborating to define a problem immediately challenges individual perceptions of expertise and hierarchy, i.e., who has/assumes the authority or the expertise to define the problem (and by implication the preferred solution) and exposes 'the curse of expertise' (Camerer, Loewenstein and Weber, 1989). This issue is explored in more detail later in the chapter.

In Case Study 1 we used the MIT design-a-wallet 90-minute challenge as an opening exercise. Design-a-wallet is a Stanford d.School immersive activity designed to introduce learner-participants to the full design cycle in 90 minutes. This exercise draws attention to attentive listening, challenging assumptions, designing from the human point of view and going deeper to find unmet needs. Participants were unanimously positive about this experience as an introduction to HCD thinking. We used a Mentimeter evaluation at the end of the intervention. Learner-participant feedback noted increased self-awareness of personal bias, the value of attentive listening and observing and the speed at which insights about user need could be gathered and verified.

In Case Study 2 we did not undertake preparation for learner-participants, owing to time constraints. We assumed support from institutional executives was sufficient incentive to engage participants fully in the design challenge. We also underestimated the level of continuing inter-institutional challenge to the joint initiative despite major financial and reputational investment. In this context more was required to create a psychologically safe space and lay foundations to build trust for the impending joint venture. The desired outcome was to align on a user-centred approach and on next steps for the design of the LMS. This was partially achieved. The main learning for the staff is perhaps best represented by a student comment made during the desk-top walkthrough to test an early prototype of the LMS. The comment was made in response to designer insistence on the inclusion of a user manual embedded in the system:

> "No text, we won't read it. Whatever you create must be intuitive, easy to navigate and enable us to find what we are looking for by clicking around."

The student response demonstrates lack of humility, humble learning and the tyranny of expertise. The student comment also illustrates that understanding the situational design context is key in HCD practice – a factor that is often overlooked.

The value of a Design Challenge Readiness Framework

We propose that a design challenge readiness framework is required to guide these early stages of the design journey enabling situational and personal contexts to be addressed. An introductory session to method is necessary but is not a sufficient readiness action. Three tools emerge from our practice as providing groundwork to help prepare mindsets and ensure team readiness to fully embrace inherent uncertainty during the design challenge journey:

- Assumption mapping
- The Design Brief Challenge checklist (Situational)
- Design Brief Challenge charter (Generated by the Design Team)

A Assumption mapping: Assume nothing

In both design challenges we believed we had a mandate to convene and carry out the design challenge using our tools and methods. This proved an erroneous assumption.

The authors applied Assumption Mapping using the Known/Unknown Matrix tool in Case Study 1 to challenge certainties at the start of the design journey. This exercise resulted in a powerful zooming out moment and significant 'unlearning' and 'relearning' for the participant-learners. We returned to the outputs arising from this first mapping encounter to test emerging solutions and understanding of the problem/solution space in a continuous learning and relearning process within the UK Design Council Double Diamond framework, 'tilling the soil' for entry into the zone of uncertainty. We also applied Assumption Mapping in Case Study 2 in desk-top walk-throughs (rapid prototypes) of proposed LMS design solutions to great effect.

Figure 6.1 provides a visual of the Assumption Mapping Framework developed by Rose and Jones, adapted from the UX Strategy Kit. This is a twenty-minute activity conducted by the team in a rapid, stand up, Post-It sticking exercise with four poster-sized flip charts, one for each outer category.

B The Design Brief Challenge checklist: Embracing failure as a mandate to challenge

Agreeing a design brief with the design challenge sponsor is foundational to any design intervention. However, an undervalued benefit in developing the brief in our case studies was the opportunity to coach the sponsor in the

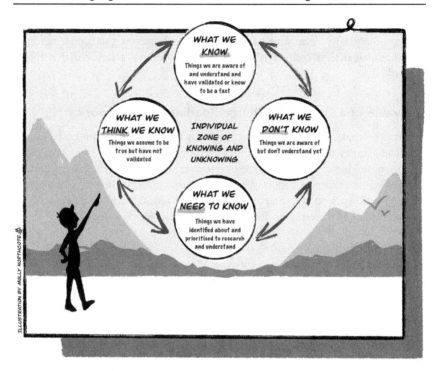

Figure 6.1 Assumptions Mapping

HCD approach. We found the real-world design challenge brief checklist a useful tool to challenge traditional, waterfall approaches to projects and de-risk the uncertainty arising from an HCD approach for sponsors. In each case we tailored the design challenge brief with the sponsor reflecting the situational context, using exploratory language relating to the problem/solution space and to slow down thinking and to avoid solutionising too early.

Design Brief Challenge checklist

Title: [The Design Challenge]

Background: Why is the topic perceived to be a challenge and what evidence is there to support this perception?

Problem Space: Describe the scope of the problem space. There will always be more than one solution. If there is only one solution the problem is not amenable to an HCD approach.

Assumptions: What are our baseline assumptions? How will we test them?

Target Audience: Who are we designing for?

Desired Outcomes: What will be different and for whom if we successfully respond to the design challenge?

Design Constraints: Limitations or requirements that must be considered during the design journey.

Time Box: How much time can we allocate to the design challenge and why?

C Design Challenge Charter: Putting HCD to work and empowering Teams

In both case studies, we used a Design Challenge Charter for the design sprints. This was the first call-out at the start of each day promoting equity and humility in the room, reiterating that 'all voices are equal', building trust and shared values among colleagues and positive reinforcement to 'trust the process'. We included IT, service delivery staff, a HR staff nominee, students and relevant academic staff in the design teams in both case studies. Facilitation was undertaken jointly by the authors, with the addition of Mo-Ling Chui in Case Study 1.

The creation of the Charter is a team sport worthy of incorporation in a Design Challenge Readiness framework. Each team should create their charter by consensus at the initiation stage of the Design Challenge to build cohesion and strengthen the power within the team to pursue unplanned and unrequested ideas. It provides a reference point throughout the design journey. It is dynamic and evolves to challenge/create alignment with the Design Challenge Brief, identifying gaps in team membership as the design journey unfolds. It reinforces 'equal voice' and shared values as foundational principles in HCD, informing development of the WREN wheel introduced later in the chapter. The Design Challenge Charter also unleashes creativity and maximises innovation in an empowered Design Challenge Team. The omission of a Charter in Case Study 2 contributed to team dissonance in this design challenge.

Beyond method: Disrupting during the design journey

We found that mindsets, ways of thinking, are often disrupted, shaken or shifted when applying HCD to work through a design challenge; creating conditions either for innovation and new insight and understanding or giving rise to resistance to change. The authors conclude that mindset disruption is the biggest benefit and challenge arising from the HCD approach.

The essence of the design thinking approach embedded in HCD is to engender curiosity and to seek opportunities for innovation beyond our own assumptions and experiences in multidisciplinary teams. In our experience some participants find designing a liberating experience, unleashing creativity to explore the art of the possible. For others the experience is disruptive, unstructured (iterative) and therefore hard to plan resulting in a feeling of disorientation about 'where we are in the process' or 'what tool should I use now?'

HCD implicitly challenges professional identity and expertise, organisation hierarchies and related power dynamics. HCD practitioners have a professional duty to make explicit these challenges at the outset through engagement in the design challenge brief. The brief also provides the opportunity to call out the paradox of the 'learning-by-doing' approach.

A Mindsets and identities in a time of uncertainty

Universities are professed open communities of scholars and professional services staff. In our experience such institutions are typically hierarchical, disciplinary-specific and professionally siloed between – and across – professional and academic practices.

We identify 'mindset disruption' as a significant advantage and a considerable hurdle for both participants and organisations seeking to adopt an HCD approach to instigate organisational change. Mindset disruption exposes the emotional and intuitive aspects of the practical application of HCD and more holistic and context-specific thinking, which are also often overlooked in the dominant design practitioner 'doing' manuals and training methods.

We find that current HCD and design thinking models developed by leaders in the field such as IDEO and Stanford d.School are also insufficient to prepare and manage the impact of HCD thinking disruption potentially resulting in non-adoption of HCD by organisations. However, the Design Council has made efforts in 2019 to evolve the Double Diamond model more holistically to encompass contextual, cultural considerations and mindsets needed to achieve positive change and in 2021 towards more systemic change.

We particularly experienced institutional power dynamics and internal politics in Case Study 2. Using the tools noted above with participant-learners demonstrated we learned that early questioning, reflecting and visible/relational thinking around a common purpose throughout the design journey is essential to expose power and hierarchy. Therefore, we support Drew's view that more is required to recognise the importance of the 'invisible activities' that sit around the design journey: orientation and value setting, continuing the journey, collaboration and connection and leadership and storytelling (Drew, 2021) or what Jones (2021, p. 43) terms 'design the designing as well as design the output of the designing'.

We observed from our case studies that working with sponsors and groups to introduce the metacognition underpinning the designing approach and the thinking dispositions cultivated in the context of the design challenge situation is a foundational first move in HCD. Careful cultivation of the design situation for un-learning and new ways of seeing, knowing and sense-making in times of uncertainty is necessary to avoid failure by understanding the wider context-dependent ecosystem dynamics from the outset. This observation is supported by the fact that while many organisations have initiated interventions involving HCD, scaling across the organisation is uncommon. This situation prevails despite research indicating the commercial return on investment from adopting HCD methods (Elsbach & Stigliani, 2018) and (McKinsey, n.d.).

We hypothesise that lack of HCD scaling in organisations arises directly from a failure to explicate the value of the questioning mode of inquiry and inherent uncertainty in HCD outcomes in contrast to perceived 'certainty' offered by common waterfall project and change management models. Uncertainty, according to Dewey, is the 'distinctive characteristic of practical activity [...] Of it we are compelled to say: Act, but act at your own peril. Judgement and belief regarding actions to be performed can never attain more than precarious probability' (Dewey, 1930, p. 6).

B The Paradox of HCD learning by doing: the tension between individual and organisational learning outcomes

Our 'learning-by-doing' approach on real-world organisational challenges embodies an inherent tension. A critical question arises during the designing period – which is more important, a) the learning and capability building; or b) the outcomes and solutions? Getting the balance right and in context is crucial, e.g. one situation may be (a), while another situation may be (b). It is about agreeing what fits the situation upfront, through shared understanding.

In the model used in our case studies, positive outcomes evolved for participant-learners and organisations. However, we learned that it is imperative for all those involved (sponsors, participant-learners and stakeholders) to be clear on which aspect of the challenge takes precedence. For example, Case Study 1 was clearly defined as a learning opportunity with benefits arising that may be taken forward by the organisation. To aid this outcome in Case Study 1 the design sprint included senior stakeholders with the authority to take forward ideas and solutions identified during the sprint as part of a continuous improvement agenda. However, as the sprint progressed, we uncovered more complex issues than originally identified. This led to an agreement that more reflective practice and a deeper understanding of the student experience was integral in the discovery phase in Case Study 1.

The situation in Case Study 2 by comparison was a management-led initiative seeking a specific outcome – agreement on the design requirements for the LMS to enhance the student and staff experience utilising a major joint initiative as a catalyst for change. As referenced earlier, preparing sponsors and teams is foundational to fulfilling design challenge intentions. As facilitators, this includes managing expectations and 'right sizing' the design challenge as context-dependent and building relational, collective knowledge as part of the groundwork.

Our learning-by-doing model, combining HCD training and coaching embedded in a real-world organisational challenge relevant to participants, has the potential to provide a double win from a professional development and organisational change perspective. However, this approach is challenging both for facilitators and participants.

Beyond Method: Making sense of the disruption

Von Thienen *et al.* (2018) offer an interesting observation that design thinking remains difficult to explicate, owing to a disavowal of theory. This is a downside of the success arising from practitioners losing sight of the 'why and how the design thinking method works on a scientific basis'. Von Thienen *et al.* call for a rebalancing of 'context-dependent' design thinking knowledge and 'context-independent' scientific knowledge.

We propose that humility, humble learning and moves to make thinking visible are key competencies to embrace disrupted thinking when undertaking HCD. These are essential to building trust and keeping thinking visible, to challenge cognitive bias, throughout the design journey. Making sense of the HCD mindset in this context goes beyond method and we suggest educational theory may have valuable insights to offer for the development of HCD practice.

- **Does Human-Centred Design require humility as a competency to succeed?**

Expert: "A person that has made every possible mistake within his or her field".

Niels Bohr (1885–1962), Danish scientist and Nobel laureate

Academic cases have shown the value of humility, humble learning for knowledge leaders in tackling cognitive bias, shifting mindsets and adapting to change (Trinh, 2019; Vera and Rodriguez-Lopez, 2004). Humble learning is particularly relevant in Higher Education (HE) institutions which often define themselves by their specialised knowledge and expertise.

We experienced the *curse of expertise* among participants in both case studies. Experts tend to perform, make decisions and solve problems better than novices; however, research has shown that they are slower in adapting to change. These cognitive biases cause people to fail to fully understand the perspective of those who do not have as much information as them or propels them to convey what they know, over listening. This can make people unable to unlearn things already known or believed, often ignoring context or evidence.

HCD facilitates learning and development, exposing thinking to new ways of seeing and knowing, acknowledging expert limitations and mistakes. It requires failure and gives permission to ask for advice and to develop others to improve performance. In each case study we sought to create a non-hierarchical learning space, fostering empathy and curiosity, deliberately positioning ourselves as subject matter agnostic. We positively reinforced the shared values and shared intelligence in the room, questioning back and forward utilising Assumption Mapping, the Design Challenge Brief and the Charter.

We most effectively overcame the shadow of expertise during Case Study 1. We were aware of potential biases and strong assumptions among staff (the participant-learners) about the students (end-users). Subject matter experts came to the fore, sometimes struggling with objectivity and making strong assertions about approaches and user needs.

"We've tried this before"
"I know exactly what they'll say"

Participant-learners were tasked to interview a single 'end-user' in groups of three with a lead interviewer and two scribes, one listening empathetically, noting emotions and quotes, the other noting the user journey sequence of touchpoints. This required some staff to be 'active listeners and observers', which was effective in challenging their own assumptions, while evoking empathy for student experiences and issues.

We curated all the assumptions before the in-session student interviews. The user interviews in the session were invaluable in exposing the fallacy of the assumptions mapped earlier. Our use of Assumption Mapping in both case studies lead to pivotal movements of understanding and insight for the participant learners. Newfound humility was demonstrated. Participant-learners moved away from closed mindset dispositions of knowing (referencing earlier assumptions) to a more nuanced and open learning disposition.

In Case Study 2 we exposed staff participants to primary user testing sessions with students. In this Case Study participant-learners observed students (end users) navigating virtual learning environment (VLE) software. Again, we curated prior assumptions in advance on how users would interact with the VLE and what issues might emerge before the observations, which proved to be unfounded.

In both cases the first-hand user interviews and observations challenged expert assumptions. These shared learning experiences challenged and displaced individual expertise and disinclination in favour of fresh thinking dispositions. These exercises demonstrate the power of the 'user-in-the-room' shifting mindsets and reframing points of view as key HCD tenets.

- **How far does Human-Centred Design need to make thinking visible?**

Our case studies illustrate the value of HCD as reflection on and in action based on our learning-by-doing design challenge model as outlined in our Key Learnings. Drawing upon our case study experiences we pose the question 'so what is going on in HCD thinking that impacts on participants to change thinking?' We turned to the literature for inspiration and insight.

We discovered substantial writing in academic journals concerning the designerly mindset based primarily on unsubstantiated attributes models or as an ideal type (Dosi, Rosati, Vignolil, 2018; Swcheitzer, Groeger and Sobel, 2016; Chesson, 2017; Clemente, Tschimmel and Vieira, 2018). We reverted to educational theory literature with a reframed question 'can education theory tell us anything about designerly thinking?' In Making Thinking Visible (Richhart & Church, 2011) the authors offer research-based solutions for creating cultures of thinking in classrooms – thinking routines – identifying eight moves:

- Observing closely & describing what's there. What do you see and notice?
- Wondering and asking questions. What's puzzling about this?
- Making connections. How does this fit with what we already know?
- Considering different viewpoints. What's another angle on this?
- Building explanations and interpretations. What's really going on here?
- Reasoning with evidence. What are you basing that on?
- Uncovering evidence and going deep. What lies beneath the surface?
- Capturing the heart and forming conclusions. What's at the core or centre?

We suggest that Richhart and Church's eight moves provide a potential scaffolding upon which to 'Making HCD Thinking Visible' and offers a foundational step toward 'rebalancing' the field by offering a systematic form of questioning that makes HCD thinking visible, repeatable and scalable. In other words, a means to move toward context-independent theory-based practice in HCD by explicating thinking and action in the cyclical process of experiential learning (Kolb, 1983) and overcoming individual disinclination to use thinking dispositions as predicted by Tishman, Jay and Perkins (1993).

HCD practice requires more than training. It requires coaching to unlearn old thinking habits, to build new capabilities and thinking patterns that keeps learning 'sticky' by making thinking visible. We propose that making thinking visible is a core competency in HCD. Furthermore we hypothesise that such an 'HCD thinking disposition model' would enable cultural adoption and adaptation to HCD approaches by organisations to build workforce capabilities for innovation now and into the future.

WREN – a visual framework to expand reflective thinking and make it visible

In the authors' experience there is a lack of consideration for power dynamics, wider situational context and system in the Western dominant design models. The focus on human desirability, balanced against feasibility and viability as the anatomy of successful design has shifted. Over the last decade global events, seismic technological advances, increasingly wicked problems and the effects of climate change have heightened awareness of the fragility of humanity, society, economies and the need for planet-centred design while reversing historical inequities.

"Human-connected design unites forward-looking design, thinking-doing and approaches. It moves from 'design for' to 'design with' and from 'centred' to 'connected'."

(Siodmok, 2023, p. 77)

This shared view is supported by key findings from the case studies, highlighting the value of humility as a competency, mitigating hierarchy, checking bias and making thinking visible, to adopt a more equitable and relational HCD approach in real-world design challenges. The WREN wheel has been developed (Rose and Betton, 2023) as a reflective self-assessment tool promoting shared accountability and more relational eco-system view in response to the case studies, combined with comparative experience in complex healthcare settings.

The WREN wheel (Figure 6.2) provides a visual framework with four lenses to aid critical reflection (of existing states) or prioritisation (of future state ideas or improvement opportunities). WREN is influenced by, but moves beyond, the IDEO design thinking framework combining desirability, feasibility and viability lenses. It is also influenced by Jobs-to-be-Done theory (Christensen et al., 2016), the NASSS Framework (Abimbola et al., 2019), Doughnut Economics (Raworth, 2017) and Framework for Innovation (Design Council, 2019). WREN seeks to move beyond the singular end user or singular expertise, adopting a more relational ecosystem view, promoting shared purpose and accountability, befitting complex organisational contexts demonstrated by both case study universities explored in this chapter.

The WREN wheel is a deliberative tool incorporating the following lenses:

Workable: feasibility, capability and durability aspects;
Responsible: purpose, evidence and environmental sustainability aspects;
Equitable: transparency and fairness; incorporating equitability, diversity and checking bias;
Needs driven: the needs of primary users and stakeholders in the ecosystem.

These four lenses serve as thematic considerations in group settings when reflecting and reviewing an existing service or intervention, or as a prioritisation aid in future-state concept development. Each lens is scored separately and then reviewed in combination in relation to the situational design context. Each of the four lenses is broken down into a subset of three areas of consideration to deepen thinking and focus further. These seek to surface assumptions and make thinking visible and more equitable in the situational design context – to disrupt mindsets from focussing on narrow success metrics such as the singular end user and the bottom line, placing more emphasis on social, holistic and environmental considerations.

WREN has been piloted in wide-ranging contexts including University of the Arts London, two NHS trusts and the Youth Futures Foundation. It has

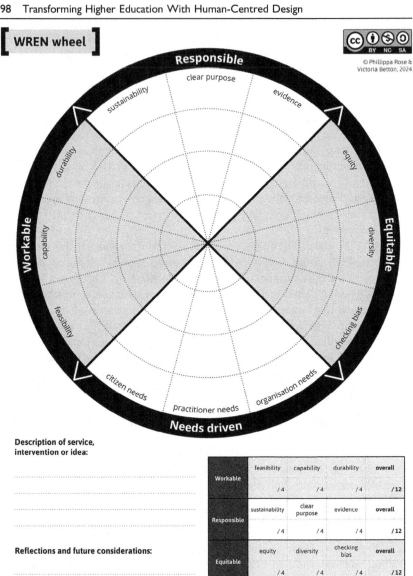

Figure 6.2 WREN model

been demonstrably effective as a boundary object to deepen reflective discussion and review; to level hierarchy, widen frames of reference making thinking more visible and systemic, but without conflict. WREN is offered to the HCD in HE community for further experimentation and development.

For further information and useable templates visit http://current.works/resources/.

Conclusion

This paper recounts shared experiences of introducing HCD interventions using two case studies from different HE live organisational projects. Mindset disruption is identified as inherent in the application of HCD. A selection of key learnings and practical takeaways for practitioners are identified based on evidence from our case studies. Mindset disruption is identified as the most significant challenge and most beneficial outcome for both learner-participants and organisations seeking to adopt an HCD to drive organisational change.

We found that greater attention to 'readiness' as an HCD competency to prepare participants for design challenges is required to ease participants into a state of uncertainty generated before, during and after an HCD challenge. There is also a need to incorporate tools and techniques to foster mindset disruption and active reflection when preparing teams to adopt HCD, while also addressing institutional mindsets as a manifestation of organisational culture.

We conclude that humility, humble learning and making thinking visible are key to understanding and engaging effectively with power relations and hierarchy in real-world organisational design challenges and requisites for the application of HCD as an impactful learning experience. We believe that these competencies are required for HCD to evolve into a more reflective, relational and equitable design practice that is context-independent and thus transferable and scalable from one design context to another. The WREN wheel is offered as an aid to context-specific group reflection and review, with context-independent application.

We call for the HE community to collaborate further to identify context-dependent and context-independent ways of developing HCD to meet the evolving challenges facing universities in the 21st century.

Key Learning points

1   Failure to adequately prepare to disrupt mindsets before applying HCD as part of a change agenda will hamper the process and limit the return on investment.

2   The learning-by-doing approach has the potential to provide a double win from a professional development and organisational change perspective but also embodies an inherent tension. The priority of desired outcomes (individual learning versus organisational change) requires agreement at the outset.

3   Humility, humble learning and making thinking visible emerge as foundational competencies in developing a HCD mindset, enabling deeper cross-functional collaboration, more reflective, disruptive thinking while challenging professional and expert identities evident in organisational culture. The WREN wheel provides a framework to aid context-specific group reflection in this respect by locating equity and sustainability at the heart of design deliberations

References

Abimbola, S., Patel, B., Peiris, D., Patel, A., Harris, M., Usherwood, T. & Greenhalgh, T. (2019) The NASSS framework for ex post theorisation of technology-supported change in healthcare: worked example of the TORPEDO programme. *BMC Medicine*, 17(1). doi:10.1186/s12916-019-1463-x.

Camerer, C., Loewenstein, G. & Weber, M. (1989) The curse of knowledge in economic settings: an experimental analysis. *J. Polit. Econ*, (97), 1232–1254.

Drew, C. (2021) Developing our new Systemic Design Framework. *Medium*. Available at: https://medium.com/design-council/developing-our-new-systemic-design-framework-e0f74fe118f7 (Accessed: 9 November 2023).

Chesson, D. (2017) Design Thinker Profile: Creating and Validating a Scale for Measuring Design Thinking Capabilities. PhD Thesis, Antioch University AURA – Antioch University Repository and Archive.

Clemente, V., Tschimmel, K. & Vieira, R. (2018) A Metaphoric Thinking Styles Taxonomy to Promote Students' Metacognitive Self-reflection in Design Learning. Back to the Future. The future in the past. *ICDHS 10th Conference Proceedings Book*. Barcelona.

Christensen, C. M., Hall, T., Dillon, K. & Duncan, D. S. (2016) Know your customers; jobs to be done. *Harvard Business Review*, 94(9), 14.

Design Council. (2019) Framework for Innovation. Available at: www.designcouncil.org.uk/our-resources/framework-for-innovation (Accessed: 9 November 2023).

Dewey, J. (1930) The Quest for Certainty: A Study of the Relation of Knowledge and Action. *Journal of Philosophy*, 27(1), 14–25.

Dosi, C., Rosati, F. & Vignoli, M. (2018) *Measuring Design Thinking Mindset*. DS 92 Proceedings of the DESIGN 2018 15th International Design Conference.

Elsbach, K. D. & Stigliani, I. (2018) Design Thinking and Organizational Culture: A Review and Framework for Future Research. *Journal of Management*, 44(6), 2274–2306.

Greenhalgh, T. & Seye, A. (2019) The NASSS framework-a synthesis of multiple theories of technology implementation. *Stud Health Technol Inform*, (263), 193–204.

Interaction Design Foundation. (n.d.) What is Human-Centered Design? Available at: www.interaction-design.org/literature/topics/human-centered-design (Accessed: 9 November 2023).

Jones, J. C. (2021) *Designing Designing*. London: Bloomsbury.

Knapp, J., Zeratsky, J. & Kowitz, B. (2016) *Sprint*. New York: Simon & Schuster.

Kolb, D. (1984) Experiential learning: Experience as the Source of Learning and Development. *Journal of Organizational Behavior*, 8(4), 359–360.

McKinsey. (n.d.). Designing out of Difficult Times | McKinsey. Available at: www. mckinsey.com/capabilities/mckinsey-design/our-insights/designing-out-of-diffi cult-times (Accessed: 9 November 2023).

Ney, S. & Meinel, C. (2019) *Putting Design Thinking to Work: How Large Organiza- tions Can Embrace Messy Institutions to Tackle Wicked Problems.* New York: Springer.

Raworth, K. (2017) *Doughnut economics: seven ways to think like a 21st century econo- mist.* White River Junction, VE: Chelsea Green.

Ritchhart, R., Church, M., Morrison, K. & Perkins, D. N. (2011) *Making thinking visible: how to promote engagement, understanding, and independence for all learners.* San Francisco, CA: Jossey-Bass.

Schweitzer, J.Groeger, L. & Sobel, L. (2016) The design thinking mindset: An assess- ment of what we know and what we see in practice. *Journal of Design, Business & Society,* 2(1), 71–94.

Siodmok, A. (2023) What organisations will Flourish in the Future and Why We Need a New Design Culture That Is Fit for the 22nd Century. In *Flourish by design.* London: Routledge.

Tishman, S., Jay, E. & Perkins, D. N. (1993) Teaching thinking dispositions: From transmission to enculturation. *Theory Into Practice,* 32(3), 147–153.

Trinh, M. P. (2019) 'Overcoming the Shadow of Expertise: How Humility and Learning Goal Orientation Help Knowledge Leaders Become More Flexible'. *Frontiers in Psychology,* 10. doi:10.3389/fpsyg.2019.02505 (Accessed: 9 Novem- ber 2023).

Vera, D. & Rodriguez-Lopez, A. (2004) Strategic Virtues. *Organizational Dynamics,* 33(4), 393–408.

Von Thienen, J. P. A., Clancey, W. J., Corazza, G. E. & Meinel, C. (2018) Theoretical Foundations of Design Thinking. In C. Meinel & L. Leifer (2018), *Design Thinking Research: Making Distinctions: Collaboration versus Cooperation.* New York: Springer.

Womack, J. P. & Jones, D. T. (1996) *Lean thinking: banish waste and create wealth in your corporation.* New York: Free Press.

Notes

Hasso Plattner Institute, Shape the Future with Design Thinking. (n.d). Available at: https://hpi.de/en/school-of-design-thinking/design-thinking/what-is-de sign-thinking.html (Accessed: 9 November 2023).

IDEO, Design Thinking. (n.d.). Available at: https://designthinking.ideo.com (Accessed: 9 November 2023).

UK Design Council. (2023) Beyond net zero: a systemic design approach. Available at: www.designcouncil.org.uk/our-work/skills-learning/tools-frameworks/beyond- net-zero-a-systemic-design-approach.

UK Design Council, Framework for Innovation. (n.d.) Available at: www.designcoun cil.org.uk/our-work/skills-learning/tools-frameworks/framework-for-innovation-de sign-councils-evolved-double-diamond (Accessed: 9 November 2023).

UX Strategy Kit: Knowns and Unknowns Framework. (n.d) Available at: https:// uxstrategykit.merck.design/methods/knowns-and-unknowns-framework (Accessed: 9 November 2023).

Chapter 7

Prototyping educational change

Learning from a ten-week service design programme

Sarah Dyer and Ksenija Kuzmina

Introduction

The University of Exeter has a centre called the Education Incubator with the remit to support innovation in education practice across the university. While the Incubator has used service design approaches for a number of years, The Innovation Lab – the subject of this chapter – was an experiment in systematically using service design to support educators and students to run short innovation projects. In five years as Incubator director, Sarah worked with many inspiring educators and students driven to improve education and student experience. At first, Sarah assumed this work would require her to draw upon pedagogic expertise. However, it soon became clear that many – most even – challenges people experienced stemmed from trying to bring about change in complex organisations, in which different people have very different perspectives and competing priorities (Dyer, 2021c). Service design seemed to offer powerful approaches for navigating this complexity.

In early 2021 we – the Incubator – recruited eight project teams to take part in the Lab. These included student-led projects to build an anti-racist university and educator-led projects to enhance research-based or community-engaged education (see Table 7.1). Each project received a small amount of funding, a deadline of three months and a ten-week programme of support. The programme was designed to lead participants through a service design methodology during ten weeks of online synchronous workshops and asynchronous material (see Table 7.2). Designing and running the Lab's programme was far more resource intensive than the support usually offered to Incubator short projects. We committed these resources because of our experience of service design, a curiosity about applying it more systematically and because, as a centre which supports innovation, we believe it is important that we too innovate in our ways of working.

We write as Lab 'insiders' but from idiosyncratic perspectives. As inaugural director of the Education Incubator, Sarah conceived of the Innovation Lab programme, wrote briefs and role descriptions, assembled the Lab team, recruited

DOI: 10.4324/9781003383161-14

Table 7.1 Innovation Lab projects. See Exeter Education Incubator (2021)

Funding call	Project Titles
Student-led Anti-Racism Projects	1 Recommended by who? 2 For the many not the few. 3 Active together
Educator-led, Research-based and community-engaged learning	1 Community partnerships: a policy clinic for social change. 2 Encompass: Decolonising STEM 3 Consent culture. 4 'Let's talk about service learning'.
Additional project	8. Exploring the potential of peer mentoring on online courses.

Table 7.2 The Lab Programme

Stage	Week	Synchronous activity	Asynchronous
Challenge	1	Workshop #1: Welcome; Peer network meeting.	Virtual learning environment forum
Discover	2	Project Management open door: Employing students and e-Claims (optional); Workshop #2: Project context within the University; Social Network Meeting (optional); Project Coaching.	Champions Address list Policy and procedures 'how to'
Define	3	Project Management open door (optional); Workshop #3: Project research synthesis; Peer network meeting.	
	4	Project Management open door (optional); Workshop #4: Project value proposition; Social Network Meeting (optional); Project Coaching.	
Develop	5	Project Management open door (optional); Workshop #5: Generating options for project delivery; Peer network meeting.	
Deliver	6	Project Management open door (optional); Workshop #6: Testing the project delivery options I; Social Network Meeting (optional); Project Coaching.	
	7	Project Management open door (optional); Workshop #7: Testing the project delivery options II; Network Meeting.	

Stage	Week	Synchronous activity	Asynchronous
Review and iterate	8	Project Management open door (optional); Workshop #8: Hero Journey; Social Network Meeting (optional); Project Coaching.	
	9	Project Management open door (optional); Workshop #9: Design Principles – value of design in education projects; Network Meeting/designing badges	
	10	Project Management open door (optional); Workshop #10: Design as a mindset for future project planning; Social Network Meeting (optional); Project Coaching	

participants, created asynchronous learning materials, hosted the workshops and meetings and led the evaluation. Ksenija works at the Institute for Design Innovation, Loughborough University London. She drew on her disciplinary expertise as a design academic to inform discussions about the design of the programme. She then led two of the weekly workshops, acted as a coach to one project teams and supervised the MA dissertation of our embedded researcher.

We undertook this work a year into the Covid pandemic. For Sarah, the Lab was a gesture of hope; springing from a need to work on something which was not dictated by 'managing to make things work'. It was driven by a need to work with people on building a shared vision of inspiring change which creates possibilities. The Innovation Lab was a practice of 'critical hope' as a response to the pandemic, which Jessica Riddell (2020, n.d.) describes as a "narrative (which) offers us a way to be broken open, to occupy the position of learner, to embrace empathy and to relinquish authority in favour of collaboration – with our students, with our colleagues, with our communities". For Ksenija, to be part of the Innovation Lab was a real privilege. She drew on her research interest in how service design can transform education (Kuzmina, 2014) and contribute to innovation in organisations (Kuzmina et al., 2020), as well as personal experience of applying design processes in her own Higher Education (HE) institution (Kuzmina et al., 2016; Loughborough University London, 2022). Several studies reported on adaptation of service design in large organisations (Kurtmollaiev et al., 2018; Aricò, 2018; Junginger, 2015), highlighting the challenges that result from the dominant discourses, practices and norms that pre-exist in organisations, while reflecting on how service design prompts change in organisational mindset and routines over time. Ksenija, following Sarah's vision of hope, sees the Innovation Lab as an intervention that can illuminate, disrupt and heal some of the dominant discourses and practices of marketisation and distrust in HE institutions.

In this chapter, we share our reflections and learning. We draw on our own experiences along with participant feedback. The Lab had an 'embedded researcher' who undertook interviews with participants as part of her MA dissertation research. We requested anonymous feedback from three participants each week during the Lab's ten weeks and from coaches after each coaching session. We received 13 out of a possible 30 points of participant feedback and 21 out of a possible 45 of coach feedback.

The Innovation Lab: Five defining characteristics

In this section, we outline five key characteristics of how the Lab was designed and draw on participant feedback to reflect on how the design played out in practice.

Characteristic one: A structured service design programme

The aim of the Lab was to create a structure which would introduce project teams to service design approaches and provide support while they employed them. As the Lab's call for applications set out:

> Understanding each problem as it looks to others, and experimenting with ways to solve it, will be central to our approach in the Lab. This contrasts with ways of working that assume we can understand a problem from our own perspective and jump to one high-stakes solution. The 'Education Innovation Lab' will ask participants to learn more about the problem they are addressing, framing them in their institutional and individual contexts, as part of a structured process informed by design thinking.
>
> (Dyer, 2021a)

The programme structure broadly followed the design thinking Double Diamond (Design Council, 2023) weaving together a selection of workshops, peer-to-peer learning and coaching sessions. Among other things, project teams were invited to learn service design from expert facilitators, attend individualised feedback sessions and access an online library of resources.

None of our participants was familiar with service design at the beginning of the programme. Participants fed back that they enjoyed the weekly workshops in particular and learnt a lot. They identified learning key service design perspectives: seeking to understand their problem from the perspectives of those involved, holding back on making assumptions based on their own experiences, seeing collaboration across areas of expertise as crucial and the requirement to understand the complexity of the system. Their learning was most pronounced in problem definition. This reflects our own sense that participants were less receptive to ideation and prototyping. We suspect this was due to bandwidth and as the end of the programme loomed, participants were increasingly focused on completing their projects. Some participants suggested that they would like to have undertaken the workshops before starting their project. There was no mention in feedback of the asynchronous resources. At the time this felt disappointing because creating and collating these was time-consuming.

Characteristic two: A real world setting

All participants were running internal innovation projects which addressed institutional priorities. Applicants responded to themed calls, setting out the problem they wanted to address. Applications were judged by a panel of senior university leaders and student representatives. Projects addressed issues such as decolonising curricula, PGR mental health and how to involve law students in a policy clinic run for external organisations. Given the limited timeframe of the Lab, Sarah identified people from across the institution who would be important gatekeepers or enablers of projects. She contacted them before the Lab started to explain what we were doing and described relevant projects. We asked if they would be happy for their details to be shared with participants. We called them 'Innovation Lab champions'. The hope was to use the social capital of the Incubator's visibility and reputation to facilitate the Lab participants. Whether directly or indirectly, this seems to have been a powerful element of the programme.

The real-world context of the Lab enhanced the potential for authentic and transformational learning. By transformational learning, we mean learning which creates possibilities for the learner, such as a new sense of themselves and their place in the world. As early as week two, a participant described the Lab as creating a bridge between students and the university. From then onwards there is a rich thread in the feedback which expresses a new sense of hope and possibility of change in the university. Participants conveyed a new sense of autonomy and ability to affect change. They commented on both how inspiring it was to meet others taking part in the Lab and how they had connected beyond their cohort with others across the university who also wanted change and who were working with them to bring it about.

Participants identified the value of participating in the Lab for their project outcomes. This included some generic aspects, such as providing a structure and momentum, but also service design approaches specifically. The overwhelmingly positive feedback needs to be tempered with one piece of late feedback which described experiencing the time commitment of participating in Lab as detrimental to the 'concrete aspects' of their project. This comment touches on our sense at the time, that many people didn't have the bandwidth nor the time to be fully present. This seemed to be most true for University employees. Regularly, participants would not be able to attend because of other commitments, and there were points when some of those who did attend expressed good-natured frustration about the relevance of service design to 'getting the job done'.

Characteristic three: A cohort made up of both educators and students

The Lab was designed to facilitate social learning (Wenger *et al.*, 2011; Wenger-Trayner & Wenger-Trayner, 2019) between educators and students. Participants were both working on their own projects but undertaking the programme alongside each other. Sarah intentionally designed community building into the Lab. This included creating a sense of hospitality and synchronous social online networking spaces, to create and sustain a learning community. In a blog written at the start of the programme, Sarah rhetorically asked where we could possibly start (Dyer, 2001c). Her answer was, 'Start with the people':

> our first session introduced the digital tools we would be using in a step-by-step low stakes way. Sarah asked participants to post a picture of spring where they were. (We were still all online in UK universities.) The task was a nod to the national Mental Health Awareness week which focused on the value of nature for our wellbeing. In the workshop, people introduced themselves to the group, picking out an image that appealed to them. Despite different roles in the university, ages, and different projects, we started to find common interests and hear each other's stories of family and home, enjoyment and longing.
>
> (Dyer 2021b, n.d.)

Intentionally designing community building was valued by participants and, we think, effective in supporting them as they worked on their projects.

Other people featured heavily as a huge positive in the feedback we received from participants. From the first week of the programme, participants referred to how much they got out of hearing about other projects. This continued across the programme with participants describing their 'passionate' and 'enthusiastic' peers. From the third week participants begin to identify learning from peers. They variously describe their advice, feedback and ideas as relevant and useful. There was also a sense in the feedback and in our experiences during the Lab that educators intensely valued the input from the student participants of the Lab and vice versa. We also suspect that having students and educators participate in the programme together impacted its 'tone'; educators resisted common tropes of disillusionment. It felt that the mixed cohort approach was incredibly important in what the Lab achieved.

Characteristic four: Coaches to support participants to apply service design

Each project team was allocated five sessions with a 'design coach' during the Lab. This recognised that translating the structured exercises from the workshop into practical steps for their own project – and then reviewing how these went – would benefit from conversations with practised designers. The coaches, recruited through LinkedIn, were a mixture of design professionals and

Masters students coming to the end of their degrees. Coaches were briefed and received outline documents, and Sarah ran coach catch-up meetings and sent out feedback forms across the programme to see how things were going, as well as undertaking some one-to-one meetings. From the first week and throughout the project, participants praised their coaches. They were regularly described as amazing. Participants valued their design and project management expertise and the opportunity to focus on their own projects.

Coaches too described meetings that were overwhelmingly positive. Ksenija's experience of coaching included working with a team of two professional service staff members on fixed-term contracts and one permanent academic. Despite the precarity of their work contract – or maybe because of it – Ksenija found the professional staff members to be most passionate and determined to engage with the innovation process provided by the Lab. Coaching sessions worked well from Ksenija's perspective, as they presented an opportunity to dive deep into an individual project with the project team. In the first meeting, the team described the problem they aimed to address. While personal experience was essential for the motivation and drive of the project, the meeting also brought up a set of assumptions about existing resources and activities in the university. After the first meeting, the team decided to undertake initial desk research on stakeholders active in this problem space at the university. The project team defined a set of stakeholders and in the following meeting expressed both surprise and excitement about the breadth of activities that were already underway. Discussion took place on how to access and engage with different stakeholders in which, as a coach, Ksenija provided insights on how to utilise design research tools and activities previously presented in workshops. The team drew on its own network within the university to speak to as many stakeholders as they could in the timeframe, with an aim to understand their activities and challenges.

The last coaching session with the team was in Ksenija's view the most important one. It is a session where the team was able to review its initial proposal in light of the research that they undertook. One of the team members was very clear in stating that they need to revise the aim of the project: 'There is already so much out there, but nobody is aware of it. We need to make it visible.' From Ksenija's perspective, this was a huge leap forward. This finding and re-framing of the problem space did not result in an immediate solution. However, it opened up space for the next iteration of the project focussing the problem space and, on reflection, better aligning it with the initial need that was identified by the project team.

Characteristic five: A pilot itself

The Lab was run in the spirit of experimentation. In retrospect, we could have made better use of low fidelity prototyping in its design. There is of course an irony here: creating a programme which tries to provide an alternative to

Table 7.3 Coaches' schedule

Meeting (45mins)	Suggested theme	Stage
1	Introductions and exploring stakeholder research for the project	Discover
2	Distilling learning from stakeholders and redefine question	Define
3	Review ideation and prepare prototyping	Develop
4	Review prototype test/s	Deliver
5	Review the process and strategise next steps and longer-term goals	Review and iterate

working from our 'informed assumptions' based on one's own informed assumption. Participant feedback expressed hopes that it can run again, and others be able to benefit, although other feedback suggested future iterations should be designed to be more flexible and run over longer time periods. We are sharing our experiences in the hope that others will learn from them.

For the Incubator, the next iteration of our work took almost the opposite approach to the Lab's highly structured and supported approach. We took three 'discover' tools and created off the peg workshop plans for people to use with minimal support and a small grant to pay for catering. We did though retain the authentic setting and reinforced the connection to existing governance structures. We called these 'Discovery Grants' (Dyer & Deacon, forthcoming; Exeter Education Incubator, 2022).

Figure 7.1 Elements of the Innovation Lab

Reflecting on three tensions

In this section we turn to three tensions which we identified in our reflective discussion of the Lab. These were not the only challenges or tensions we encountered but we feel them to be particularly knotty and impactful. We make concrete suggestions to address these tensions for the reader's future deployment of service design for education practice innovation.

Tension one: Service design and business as usual (BAU)

The Lab was intended to support education innovation projects in a way that was fully aligned with service design. Sarah felt that the previous piecemeal use of service design created frustrating friction at the 'edges' between service design and business as usual (BAU). She hypothesised that we couldn't realise service design's potential because of contradictions between design and other aspects of existing policies and structures. For example, previous application forms asked about intended outputs of potential projects. It was hardly surprising then that grant holders were reluctant to redefine their problem, as we prompted them to do once their project was underway. They had committed to delivering certain outputs against a timeline and budget that had been agreed upfront. In contrast to such misalignments, the Lab application asked applicants about the problem they wanted to explore and why it was important (and not what outputs they would produce and when). What we learnt in the Lab was that when policies and procedures are better aligned with service design, it moves, rather than removes, the 'edge'. In part, the new edge between design and BAU is even trickier, as it involves our ingrained ways of working and mental models, therefore it illuminates how big the disconnect is, between service design and business as usual.

Changing mental models is tricky. We hoped that by leading people through a structured design process we would demonstrate service design's value. We didn't want the Lab to be a theoretical introduction to service design. We called this 'service design by stealth' because we didn't want to tell participants about service design – we certainly didn't want a theoretical discussion of its merits or otherwise. Prioritising 'doing' seemed aligned with design's intrinsic practice of inquiry and action (Steen et al., 2011) and ethos of "less talking, more doing" (Stickdorn et al., 2018). Our Lab application process asked participants to come with a challenge to explore rather than a solution. We stressed this in our handouts and workshops. We were, however, working with people who have successfully made careers in institutions which prize knowing the answer and getting things done. How then do these people make sense of our insistence on starting with a challenge rather than a solution, if they even register it at all? With hindsight, we could have anticipated that with the Lab we moved the fault line between service design and BAU a bit further 'out', but we didn't – as we had naively hoped – get to sidestep it.

How might you work productively with the disconnect between service design and 'business as usual'?

It is essential to anticipate, acknowledge and navigate the difference between service design and the taken-for-granted ways of thinking and doing in both your planning and with participants. Your participants may have different understandings of the context and culture of your institution. You might:

1 Create a 'space apart' from business as usual. You could explore the use of rituals for opening and closing sessions (McKercher, 2020, p. 122) or other ways of creating shared understandings and practices for when you are working together.
2 Be clear and positive about the characteristics of your space. Identify what aspects of service design you will lead with. You could, for example, identify transformational pivot points or threshold concepts that will underpin what you do – for example six mind-sets for co-design (McKercher, 2020 p. 164) or particular design tools (Dyer & Deacon, forthcoming). Think about how to demonstrate, as well as explain, what is important.
3 Create a buffer zone that sits between your space and BAU. Think about how to support people to translate their experiences back in to BAU. One way may be through creating buffer zones of a 'small circle' of friendly, professional provocateurs or critical friends to practise on (McKercher, 2020, p. 78).
4 Notice and acknowledge how difficult it can be to think and work in new ways. Changing ingrained habits of thought can be really challenging. Explore how to support people who have very low bandwidth to learn. This could include opportunities to read and hear about working differently, as well as creating low stakes ways to practise.
5 Notice and acknowledge how hard it is to support others. Given how challenging this is, it is hard not to feel downcast when all the hard work of designing and planning doesn't provide easy wins. It is important to support those who create support for others and to have a diverse toolkit of different approaches to draw on.

Tension two: People and projects

The Education Incubator first and foremost supports projects. Applicants are self-selecting individuals or teams wanting to bring about a change in their immediate work or study. Funding is competitively awarded on the strength of the proposed project. All elements of the Lab were designed to support the delivery of those projects. That said, it is people delivering those projects. There were 28 people named on successful applications. In practice, about half to a third engaged in the workshop and coaching aspects of the Lab. However, there is very little in a university that one person or small team can independently change, and service design offers powerful tools to surface and engage with important players. That said, bringing about change is more challenging from some positions and almost impossible from others. If our primary aim is successfully delivering projects, it suggests this should dictate participants of the Lab. If we don't intentionally recruit participants who can facilitate project outcomes, it creates a tension.

However, value can be created for the participants independently of the outcomes of their projects. Recent discussions about embedding sustainable and responsible design in HE, identify the institutional barriers to radical innovation experienced by 'academics activists' whose work on sustainability, decoloniality, responsibility and care, requires critical reflection and change at the institutional and systems levels (Boenhart et al., 2022). The Lab was able to provide an environment of peer support and enrichment which gave some of those involved a renewed sense of hope and possibility. Having the 'right' people in the Lab may mean those who are looking for a space for self-reflection and critical evaluation of their practice and system, those looking for allies and inspiration, and those for whom building capacity for design could support radical innovation. In practice we tried to create value for both people and projects, and these aims were variously aligned and in tension.

How might you value project delivery and individuals' professional development?

Delivering a successful project is likely to develop individuals' capabilities and capacity to build more change. If, as we did, you work with self-selecting change makers, it is important that problem definition includes a cold hard look at what success might mean and the scope of the project given the resources, which must include their institutional positioning. However, the Lab structure could also be used to support an established or institutionally-constituted team to deliver 'top down' change: see for example Grabill et al. (2022)'s discussion of the Hub for Innovation in Learning and Technology at Michigan State University.

To support both delivering projects and developing individuals, you might:

1   Provide other avenues of funding. Ensure there are other ways that changemakers can access funding, so that those who enrol in your programme are actively interested in pursuing service design approaches.
2   Address feasibility as part of problem definition. Ensure the problem definition stage realistically addresses feasibility.
3   Make use of the people who are in the room. All participants in the room bring their organisational subject position, their networks, influence and interests. Make sure that you are making the most of this wealth of resources.

4   Run a Lab or lab-like activity for teams who have organisational responsibility for implementing change. Running a Lab with a cohort of students, self-selecting changemakers and institutional teams is an exciting prospect. It would be an amazing opportunity to learn across silos.

5   Be explicit about the aim of professional development. Be explicit about the development opportunities that participation offers. This could include by sharing alumni experiences. The evaluation framework we used enabled us to capture where such value was created (Wenger et al., 2011; Wenger-Trayner & Wenger-Trayner, 2019).

Tension three: Design and implementation

The Lab used service design to support the design of implementable solutions. Design and implementation entail each other: we design for implementation and implementation creates change and enables us to evaluate our design. The many challenges for implementation, including institutional relationships and capital, current context and priorities, may take time to surface. This is why we expect to iterate. Our time in the Lab was limited and was spent on the upfront design. Most of the projects ended the Lab with an implementable solution, while a couple ended with a redefined problem space. In this we played to the strengths of participants, including those who were well-versed in service delivery (e.g. academics) and those who had an insight on the experience of HE services (students). This meant that early stages of the design process that aim to discover the needs, experiences and opportunities from the participants were enriched by their input. However, the relationship between the propositions of design solutions which tend to emerge in conversation, and what is possible in practice, was less clear. Participants in the group had less understanding and knowledge of the likely dynamics, opportunities and barriers to implementing some of the ideas. The Lab was time limited and service design was new to participants. We also underestimated the time people would need to comfortably take on new ways of working.

A similar tension arises more broadly when using participatory approaches to design. Socially-engaged participatory design projects that promote user-driven innovation tend to be time-bound, with set objectives from outside of the community and oriented towards producing a 'solution'. Participant engagement is viewed as necessary to develop enhanced solutions that align with the needs of the users. Participants are brought in to contribute their knowledge, time and resources, but the credit for the solution development – or primary goal of the project – remains with designers/stakeholders who are facilitating the process. This approach has been criticised for being extractive and some call for consideration of the legacy that such projects leave with, and for, participants. A few researchers look at the capacities, capabilities and transformative learning that a project may leave with participants. Such unintended consequences of a participatory project are also important and can be, some argue, empowering (Santamaria & Kuzmina, 2020). This observation reaffirms the importance of considering value created for the people participating in the Lab, but also poses questions about the wider institutional commitment to the projects funded. If an institution funds projects in this way, what responsibility does it have beyond the funding to support implementation? And if such a responsibility exists, how should it fulfil that responsibility?

How might you ensure the Lab supports implementation and iteration?

In order to create space for implementation and iteration, you will need to think about the time and pace of the support you offer. You might:

1   Explore different models and timeframes. An obvious iteration is to extend your programme to accommodate the life cycle of a project. You might offer follow-up 'review and iteration support' on an ad hoc or flexible basis, given the different timeframes of delivering projects. This may lose some of the positive benefits of working with a cohort.
2   Enhance the visibility of implementation. Once there are 'alumni' there could be an element where people learn from their experiences, including implementation. There may be an opportunity to share case studies of how successful iterative implementation has happened in other organisations.

Conclusion

We opened this chapter by positioning the Innovation Lab as an act of hope. Jessica Riddle (2020) contrasts 'critical hope' with 'toxic positivity': the promise that everything will be fine, we should look for silver linings, and we will soon be able to return to business as usual. Critical hope, by contrast, asks us to "open ourselves up to imagine a new model of education that moves us into a future that is better than our present and more humane than our past" (Riddle, 2020). The Innovation Lab confirmed to us the value of service design as a productive approach for this challenging and necessary work. Our participants reported transformative experiences at every level: how they thought about themselves and their agency as well as how they thought about the university. In line with Riddle's characterisation, their feedback stressed the joy and the exciting potential of community and collaboration. As the designers and facilitators of this programme we experienced this joy and excitement too. It was wonderful to work with the participants, each other, and the coaches. Service design offers a way of working which meaningfully forefronts empathy and lived experience. But none of this is easy. We also shared participants' exhaustion, frustration and sadness. The crisis of the pandemic, as we experienced it through the Innovation Lab, has passed. However, the work of imagining and enacting a new model of HE is still very much to be done. We would encourage you to have a go with service design and to find sustenance from the communities already experimenting and working in this way.

Summary of key learning points

1 A structured service design programmes has huge potential in supporting education innovation in universities. We have shared our model and made suggestions for improvement.
2 Social learning in a cohort of educators and students is transformative for individuals and a powerful mechanism for building positive change in universities.
3 Educators and students appreciate coaching from designers.

Acknowledgements

A huge thank you to all the people who made the Innovation Lab possible. The participants and coaches brought such energy, expertise and willingness to have a go. Thank you too to other members of the University of Exeter who were involved, not least Innovation Lab Champions who were informants, gate keepers and enablers to the project teams. Radka and Jean brought such calm and humour. They got involved at a point where it was hard to imagine the Lab becoming a reality and without their service design superpowers it might not have. Tom Ritchie was our administrator for the programme and did amazing work navigating finance systems, organising meetings and solving problems.

References

Aricò, M. (2018) *Service design as a transformative force: Introduction and adoption in an organizational context.* Frederiksberg: Copenhagen Business School.

Boehnert, J., Sinclair, M. & Dewberry, E. (2022) Sustainable and Responsible Design Education: Tensions in Transitions. *Sustainability*, 14(11), 6397.

Design Council. (2023) Framework for innovation. Available at: www.designcouncil.org.uk/our-resources/framework-for-innovation (Accessed: 14 April 2023).

Dyer, S. (2021a) How might we...?. *Exeter Education Incubator blog*, Available at: *#1 Lab blog – How might we...? – The Education Incubator Blog (uoeeduinc.blog)* (Accessed: 12 April 2023).

Dyer, S. (2021b) Where to start? *Exeter Education Incubator blog.* Available at: https://uoeeduinc.blog/2021/05/17/3-lab-blog-where-to-start (Accessed: 12 April 2023).

Dyer, S. (2021c) How can we support innovation in teaching practice? *Times Higher Campus*, Available at: www.timeshighereducation.com/campus/how-can-we-support-innovation-teaching-practices-within-universities (Accessed: 12 April 2023).

Dyer, S. & Deacon, K. (forthcoming) Discovery grants for education innovation- supporting the adoption of people-centred design in HE one step at a time. *International Journal of Management and Applied Research*.

Exeter Education Incubator. (2021) The Innovation Lab. *Exeter Education Incubator blog*, Available at: www.exeter.ac.uk/about/educationincubator/previous_projects/innovationlab.

Exeter Education Incubator. (2022) Discovery Grant. *Exeter Education Incubator blog*, Available at: www.exeter.ac.uk/about/educationincubator/discovery_grants (Accessed: 12 April 2023).

Grabill, J., Gretter, S. & Skogsberg, E. (2022) *Design for change in higher education*. Baltimore, MD: John Hopkins University Press.

Junginger, S. (2015) Organizational design legacies and service design. *The Design Journal*, 18(2), 209–226.

Kurtmollaiev, S., Fjuk, A., Pedersen, P. E., Clatworthy, S. & Kvale, K. (2018) Organizational transformation through service design: The institutional logics perspective. *Journal of Service Research*, 21(1), 59–74.

Kuzmina, K. (2014) *Investigating opportunities for service design in education for sustainable development* (Doctoral dissertation, Loughborough University).

Kuzmina, K., Parker, C., Jun, G., Maguire, M., Mitchell, V., Moreno, M. & Porter, S. (2016) *An exploration of Service Design Jam and its ability to foster Social Enterprise*. In P. Lloyd & E. Bohemia (Eds), Future Focused Thinking – DRS International Conference 2016, 27–30 June, Brighton, UK. Available at: https://doi.org/10.21606/drs.2016.460 (Accessed: 14 April 2023).

Kuzmina, K., Trimingham, R. & Bhamra, T. (2020) Organisational strategies for implementing education for sustainable development in the UK primary schools: a service innovation perspective. *Sustainability*, 12(22), 9549.

Loughborough University London. (2022) Towards a Caring Community at Loughborough University London. *Exeter Education Incubator blog*, Available at: https://blog.lboro.ac.uk/london/community/towards-a-caring-community-at-loughborough-university-london (Accessed: 14 April 2023).

McKercher, K. (2020) *Beyond sticky notes. Co-design for real: mindsets, methods and movements*. Sydney: Beyond Sticky Notes.

Riddle, J. (2020) Combatting toxic positivity with critical hope. *University Affairs*. Available at: www.universityaffairs.ca/opinion/adventures-in-academe/combatting-toxic-positivity-with-critical-hope (Accessed: 14 April 2023).

Santamaria, L. & Kuzmina, K. (2020) Service Design meets strategic action: exploring new tools for activating change. Available at: https://ep.liu.se/ecp/173/082/ecp20173082.pdf (Accessed: 14 April 2023).

Steen, M., Manschot, M. & De Koning, N. (2011) Benefits of co-design in service design projects. *International Journal of Design*, 5(2), 53–60.

Stickdorn, M., Hormess, M. E., Lawrence, A. & Schneider, J. (2018) *This is service design doing: applying service design thinking in the real world*. Sebastopol, CA: O'Reilly.

Wenger, E., Trayner, B. & de Laat, M. (2011) Promoting and assessing value creation in communities and networks: a conceptual framework. Rapport 18, Ruud de Moor Centrum, Open University of the Netherlands. Available at: https://wenger-trayner.com/resources/publications/evaluation-framework (Accessed: 14 April 2023).

Wenger-Trayner, B. & Wenger-Trayner, E. (2019) *Designing for change. Using social learning to understand organisational transformation*. Learning 4 a Small Planet.

Section 3

Institutional Change

Foreword

Sheila MacNeill and Andy Youell

Technology is often hailed as the cornerstone for transformation. Indeed, technology can all too often be seen as the only way to bring about transformation. This techno-centric perspective all too often fails to acknowledge the key to any kind of organisational or societal transformation – people. If you don't fully understand the actual needs and context of your people then you will never be able to enable any kind of transformation.

Service Design provides truly flexible and adaptable keys to understand the context of our students and staff and indeed all users of Higher Education (HE). It is all too easy to assume that we know what our 'users' need and that the curriculum, courses and systems we develop work for them. All too often they don't – or more accurately they don't work as well as they could. Every time I take part in a Service Design workshop, I get a true sense of delight as I see participants so readily engage with persona development, work through scenarios and share their lived experiences to inform meaningful and sustainable change. This book provides a rich picture of the positive impact that a Service Design approach brings to all aspects of the contemporary university experience. I would recommend it to anyone working in HE today who really wants to work meaningfully and collaboratively with students and staff to improve the university experience.

Sheila MacNeill, independent consultant specialising in all
aspects of supporting digital learning and teaching

The power of information technology has increased exponentially for over half a century and with this has come an increase in our expectations of what data and systems can achieve. But meeting these expectations requires transformational change and too many digital transformation projects have stumbled. Technology investments need to be undertaken as part of a broader approach to managing change across the human aspects of organisations. We need to shift our focus from the technology to the people.

This book sets out a manifesto for human-centred design in HE. It brings together coherent, workable theory and lived examples of successes that have been achieved by wrapping services around the people. They say that the only constant is change, so whatever your role in HE, there is something here to help you navigate change and meet the ever-increasing expectations of those around us.

Andy Youell, HE data and systems expert

DOI: 10.4324/9781003383161-16

Chapter 8

An exploration of the relationship between Lean and Service Design for Service Improvement

Mila Bombardieri and Nichole Dunne-Watts

Introduction

This chapter outlines how we integrated Service Design and Lean methodology to promote a different way of looking at problems and designing solutions to enhance ways of working. The aims of this chapter are to share our journey from establishment (promoting a mind-set of continuous improvement using Lean tools) to incorporating service design tools into our ways of working. We share our realisations, a-ha moments and lessons learnt to guide readers in how the two methodologies no longer have to work in isolation but can complement each other.

To note, throughout this chapter, the terms *users* and *customers* are used interchangeably. Users and customers are stakeholders who interact with a service within our institution, for example, students or academic and professional colleagues in departments.

The start of the journey: Continuous Improvement at Middlesex University

A progressively competitive landscape, significant change to the cost of Higher Education (HE) degrees (with fees tripling from £3,000 to around £9,000 per academic year), shrinking resources and the recognition that the students' evaluation of services is central to defining a university's success, saw several institutions invest in the creation of process improvement teams with the aim of increasing 'value for money'. In consideration of this changing and challenging landscape, Middlesex University's 2012–17 strategic priorities looked to enhance student achievement and satisfaction, and to strengthen leadership and staff performance. To take a first step towards facilitating a culture of continuous improvement and enhanced ways of working, the Business Enhancement Team (BET) was created in 2014. The team of five was constructed as a standalone unit to provide neutrality in process improvement across services, ensuring independence from departmental agendas.

DOI: 10.4324/9781003383161-17

The work of the team was underpinned by three core performance indicators to measure success:

- Capacity creation.
- Service quality (now referred to as student and stakeholder / user benefits).
- Leadership and engagement (now referred to as staff benefits).

These performance indicators also internally referred to as our *balanced scorecard*, allow us to demonstrate positive changes to our students' and staff's experience, and to make efficiencies wherever appropriate. In future years these would fall under the term *Value for Money*.

To create a culture focussed on continually working to improve the way we do things and have *the student at the heart* of everything we do we chose to adopt *Lean* as the problem-solving methodology driving our approach. As a brief overview, the Lean Competency System (LCS) organisation defines Lean thinking as 'delivering appropriate customer and stakeholder value with the minimum of resources' (Lean Competency System, n.d.).

The first teams (Financial Services and HR Payroll) we worked with were chosen, owing to the opportunities for process improvements. As we began working with these teams to redesign processes and identify opportunities for capacity creation, we developed an approach that ensured the transfer of all skills and core tools (with a foundation in Lean) to support both continuous improvement and the development and engagement of staff. Services and teams involved in projects were introduced to seven key tools and techniques – namely *communication cells, visual management, performance indicators, process redesign, standard work, creative problem-solving* and *workplace review* – all linked to develop and maintain a continuous improvement culture. While the tools derived from Lean, the language we used was softened as it was recognised that Lean jargon – acquiring from the manufacturing industry – did not fit our HE setting. Therefore, we made several changes to promote easier embedding. In our team's own words from Chapter 21: Developing a Culture – The Essentials for Continuous Improvement in 'Global Lean for Higher Education', 'whilst true to the core values and tools of Lean working, we have taken a pragmatic approach, adopting the language and crafting the message for Middlesex University' (Bennett & Perkins, 2020, p. 346).

Our project work followed five phases, and this structure still broadly guides our work today:

1 Start-up – scoping the project, including identifying benefits.
2 Diagnostic – understanding the current state.
3 Design – create future processes and test and refine new ways of working.
4 Implementation – implementing new processes and ways of working.
5 Embed and sustain – teams take ownership and work to continuously improve.

Working in this way, with solid foundations in the Lean methodology, helped us manage problem-solving work in a way that both helped the organisation achieve strategic goals and promoted the development of our staff. Some early efficiency improvements achieved:

- The Assessment Team reduced the student deferral process time by a third, facilitating capacity to deal with an increase in demand.
- 100 per cent Initial Teacher Training students had placements organised prior to the start of term for the first time.
- The overall reduction of late payment charges to students reduced by 19.5% from 2013–14 to 2015–16.
- The successful upskilling and resource flexing within Student Fees and Finance resulted in a more responsive service delivery and contributed to an 82 per cent staff engagement score.

Early learnings and the shift toward a human-centred approach

Our early lessons learnt through 2018/19 suggested Lean could be challenging on the people side of change: apprehension about job security, feedback on the rigidity of the approach and a focus on efficiencies hampered engagement and did not always sustain a clear sense of purpose in our stakeholders. To address this, we considered other approaches which would better account for the human aspects of service improvement. Developing a learning culture formed a core value in the Middlesex 2017–23 strategy, which provided endorsement and weight behind approaches for improvement, innovation and the associated capabilities necessary to create a culture of high performance. It was through one of our external networks, namely *Lean Higher Education* (LeanHE), that we were first exposed to the mindset and tools behind Service Design.

Radka Newton and Jean Mutton, editors of this book, were presenters at the Tromsø 2018 Global LeanHE conference. In their talk, they advocated using Service Design to define student needs by firstly understanding and empathising with their experiences of engaging with our services over time. We knew that we collected data on number of errors, delayed request fulfilment and process timings, however, were we certain we understood the broader impact of these on the student experience and how it affected their choices and study? The approach was immediately fascinating to us; however, we were yet to make sense of how this would integrate – and indeed whether it *could* integrate – with our existing Lean way of working. At that point, our approach to problem-solving was fundamentally process-driven and rooted in the collection of quantitative data (process timings, error counts, incurred costs), the identification of waste, and the creation of solutions based on the elimination of that waste. We promoted respectful enquiry when investigating processes and celebrated people being at the heart of Lean. We were however becoming increasingly aware of how that could often be lost in the measurables. Service Design seemed to have a lot to offer, however the leap from where we were still felt too great: how might we broker the idea that we would no longer work with set deadlines but iteratively, and in an Agile fashion? How might we help colleagues feel able and empowered to embrace creative ideas harnessing a Human-Centred approach?

First steps into Service Design

To answer these questions, our first step was to gain more knowledge about Service Design. We decided to review the administration process of a problem-solving training our team regularly deliver to staff. Jean facilitated this for us and suggested the use of *emotional journey mapping* (Stickdorn et al., 2018). This was important to us as we wanted to have the experience of being in the participant seat before using this practice as facilitators with colleagues. Before starting, we thought our training administration process was working rather well and were shocked to find it was the opposite: one person was shouldering most of the responsibilities for communicating to trainees, revising training material and organising the training sessions. This took approximately 150 hours across six months. Some colleagues were unaware of how involved this side of the process was. This meant that they unconsciously understated and devalued some of this work by brushing it off as something really easy and quick to do. Talking it out in the safe, contained space of the emotional journey mapping exercise exposed a level of inequity in the distribution of work and allowed the entire team to empathise and appreciate how much work, previously taken for granted, was going into this process. This led to the re-distribution of work, creating more equity and parity across the team. Overall, it was a very productive session where everyone's contribution was appreciated and everyone felt heard and, put simply, happier.

A further step was the opportunity to join the Service Design in Education network, a supportive learning community embodying and promoting the values of Design Thinking in HE. This gave us the space to be able to discuss and trial new things in a safe way.

Thirdly, we immersed ourselves in the three-day Global Service Jam. Much like a group of musicians might get together to be creative to produce sounds and music, a 'service jam' is a global gathering of people interested in a design-based approach to creativity and problem-solving. The GSJ was an important part of our journey as it gave us the opportunity to experience what thinking and doing Service Design actually meant in practice. We were challenged with stepping out onto the streets of King's Cross, London, to talk to people and observe their behaviours to understand their habits when it came to the topic of the problem we were trying to solve. How often were we approaching our students in this way, on a level playing field and in the environment where they experienced our services? It was an inspiring experience which left us wondering how we might weave this research method into our way of working. The '*ideation*' stage positively challenged us to bring a balance to the ideas and to not reject the outlandish or farfetched *a priori* but to build on them. Building prototypes taught us how to tell a story using 'walk-through' LEGO models and role plays to test with the general public. The GSJ was a formative and enriching experience which pushed us out of our comfort zones and challenged our own tolerance for ambiguity and need for answers with a resolution. Reminding ourselves that it is ok to not have all the answers – and that indeed finding them is a co-creative effort – helped us develop greater tolerance for ambiguity and instigated a creative spark that would later become our Innovation Lab.

Reflections on Service Design and its application

As we reflected on what we learned from the exposure to Service Design approach, gaps became apparent:

- *User centredness* – how much – or little – users were involved in understanding the services affecting them *and* creating solutions (Penin, 2018);
- *Radical creativity* – the extent to which staff were empowered to be radically creative; and
- *Managing ambiguity* – pressure to implement new processes scarcely accounted for the ambiguity and uncertainty that comes with designing user-centred solutions.

User centredness

We were clear that our goal was to create an excellent student *experience* and Lean was not doing enough to inject the human element into our way of working. We recognised we needed to place greater focus on the lived experiences of our staff and students, understanding what interacting with our services was like, as well as the ripple effect of those interactions. While we always looked to gather and analyse both the student and staff voices in process reviews – through surveys, focus groups or through representative bodies such as the Student Unions – we recognised that our approach may not have been consistent or inclusive of those students that were hard-to-reach or hard-to-engage. In time, while the naming conventions of our project phases remained unchanged, our practice evolved to align much more with the Double Diamond approach (Design Council, 2004). We started spending more time and effort understanding user journeys, user insights through interviews and observations leading to developing personas. This helped us and the project team to empathise with our diverse community of users, making a difference when designing and developing *how might we* questions and solutions that may achieve 'a perfect balance of desirability, feasibility, and viability' (Brown & Katz, 2009, p. 21) and are fit for purpose.

A breakthrough moment came when we piloted emotional journey mapping with colleagues in the Finance department. While previous attempts to identify and manage process issues felt transactional and duty-driven, adding the emotional portion of the mapping surprised everyone when (a generally very buttoned-up) manager asserted: '*Wao... this really is a cr@p experience!*'. That marked a clear shift in our work together. The team no longer felt defensive as they could appreciate that the aim of reviews was not to attack or undermine their ability to deliver processes, but to tune into what it *felt* like to flow through them as a student. As the pace of change continued slow and steady, we no longer had to expend so much energy in corralling buy-in, the team were now invested in building a better service.

Radical creativity

At the time of writing, '*Radically Creative*' and '*Radically Simple*' are two of the six community principles at the heart of Middlesex University's 2031 Strategy: Knowledge into Action. This is a huge achievement in that it signals the organisation's commitment to a mindset of experimentation and creativity, a mindset we feel proud to have contributed to creating through our learning journey.

Our original approach, characterised by small incremental changes achieved over time, did not account for the larger, more radical shifts needed to transform our services. While actively promoting a mindset of continuous improvement, it seemed to neither engender nor sustain the behaviours needed for true innovation.

Our approach was to foster a growth/designer mindset by creating a safe environment to fail fast and learn quickly. By incorporating the fundamentals of Change Management into our approach, we were also able to assess where there was sponsorship and buy-in for change, both organisationally and at an individual level (Hiatt, 2006). This allowed us to see where we might meet resistance to change, which can derail the best laid processes and plans. When facilitating project work, we changed our vocabulary and rid ourselves of any jargon, which we were aware could be a barrier, often alienating colleagues and hindering appetite for trying something new or giving something a go regardless of the outcome. Moreover, we changed the way we articulated the key tenets of problem-solving, at all levels of the organisation. We were conscious that the common misunderstandings connected to the *Right First Time* slogan and outdated Lean narratives had likely compounded risk-averseness and fear of failure. To counter that, we directed our efforts towards a more coaching-based approach, less dogmatic and constrained by templates but more human-centred and user-led. Our aim was supporting colleagues to build tolerance for ambiguity and harness failure as a learning opportunity instead of perceiving it as something to apprehensively avoid.

Staff and project sponsors gave us confidence that we were moving in the right direction through greater engagement and commitment during improvement work. Through relentless stakeholder management, we built levels of trust and influence at the most senior levels of the University, which allowed us to have an influence on strategic decision-making. It has also allowed us to introduce the language of Change Management and Service Design into the organisation. We are striving to be a truly learning organisation, and we are now giving people permission to fail fast, learn and move on.

Managing ambiguity

Successful change is often associated with transformational leadership styles and may not be consistently found across large, traditional academic institutions. Empowerment, trust, creativity, experimentation and ambiguity can present a challenge for more traditional, risk-averse and transactional approaches to problem-solving. As many other institutions, we also encountered some of these limiting factors, which challenged people's ability to bring about innovative ways of working. As Brown and Katz (2009, p. 11) put it, 'Relaxing the rules is not about letting people be silly so much as letting them be whole people—a step many companies seem reluctant to take'. Traditional approaches to managing people and services may also often favour growth of resources to fulfil tasks on a spectrum of complexity as opposed to trialling creative solutions that may harness technology to address what is simple, standard and repeatable leaving what requires human intervention to people. This was a challenge we encountered when seeking to harness technology to improve both the student and staff experience, which the next section articulates in more detail.

Figure 8.1 Emerging from the tunnel of conventional thinking: expanding problem-solving horizons

How we put our learning into practice: Case Studies

The following case studies illustrate our application of Service Design alongside Lean in improvement activities, and our continued learning while doing so.

Innovation Lab and Harnessing Technology

An opportunity presented itself when the then Chief Financial Officer and Chief Operating Officer approached our team to investigate '*how might we harness technology to improve the staff and student experience?*'. To achieve this, we identified a group of willing colleagues (professional services and faculties) and organised an all-day workshop called the *Innovation Lab* as a pilot for the application of Human-centred Design. We spent weeks preparing and started by following our own advice: talk to people! We were fortunate to find willing mentors in many colleagues we called upon for advice in other British universities and an enthusiastic on-line community with amazing resources. We researched existing data articulating student needs and feedback, and explored how other global institutions were applying Service Design in their work. We were excited and inspired by the work achieved by many, such as Monash University in Melbourne, Australia and Glasgow University in the UK.

On the day, we covered the walls with research findings and facilitated activities aimed at harnessing creativity (brainstorming, 10+10, quick voting, drawing), being open to the wildest of ideas and reminding participants the aim was to experiment and not be crippled by self-consciousness or fear of failure. Harnessing every aspect of the Double Diamond (Design Council, 2004) – existing data, interviews, personas, ideation and prototyping – the approach was geared towards challenging the status quo, refine project ideas to be stress-tested and develop solutions in an agile and iterative way with our staff and students. Three core ideas emerged which the group refined over the coming months. Despite the significant negative impact of the pandemic, we still had successes. Leading and delivering the workshop was a formative experience that crystallised our team's theoretical understanding of Service Design. Through it, we gained new advocates, who maintained their engagement well beyond the workshop.

Student projects

As a spin-off from the Innovation Lab, we collaborated with academic colleagues in our Arts and Creative Industries and Science and Technology Faculties to explore the opportunity to make 'real-life problems' available for Undergraduate and Postgraduate students to solve as part of their dissertation. Initial feedback from interviews highlighted a need for students to be engaged in work that would provide the practical experience they could bring to the world of work. Equally, the institution had more problems to solve than resources available to solve them. To explore this, we agreed on a How Might We question and worked with both students and academic groups to explore requirements and map what the ideal journey would look like for both parties. The work led to the co-creation of a pool of project briefs with potential 'clients' (sponsors) to be offered to students to undertake, with academic supervision, in liaison with the client. From a student perspective, it helped engage students by issuing them with a purposeful problem to solve versus a fictional one and provided them with the experience of working with real stakeholders on real, live issues.

Managing Booking Event Spaces

We (BET) were approached by the Estates Management Head to support on reviewing service delivery within his area. This included how to create a better user experience for university staff to book events space, while ensuring efficiency in delivering the processes for the service staff responsible.

While scoping the project it became apparent that we could make use of our Service Design learnings to achieve these aims, owing to the human-centred, collaborative, iterative, creative and visual approach that Service Design offers (Stickdorn et al., 2018). By integrating this approach with Lean we were hopeful we could redesign processes with the users in mind and improve both customer satisfaction and business. In this case, these pertained to:

- Improved user experience (reduction in paperwork to complete)
- Fewer enquiries: better at providing information before enquiries are raised
- Improved compliance (Risk assessment, Health & Safety and Freedom of Speech)
- Improved collaboration, communication and working relationships across the team
- Clarity of roles and responsibilities
- Capacity creation to do more value-added tasks
- Eliminating waste and reducing variation

To achieve the aims of this project we first had to understand the current state of booking events spaces and the challenges created. In design thinking, this is commonly referred to as the discovery/research phase. We used a data collection plan to identify the data we needed and how we were going to collect it. This included end-to-end processing time, waiting times, the challenges users face and the issues employees came up against when delivering the service. We arranged interviews with new and frequent users and observed them through the process. The observing method – also known as *Go See* in Lean – aided us in gaining key insights, which were further developed through interviews.

We mapped the data we obtained into a service blueprint in the define phase of the project. Using a service blueprint helped the employees become aware of not only how their process affected the experience of their user, but it also provided a view of how process interdependencies affected the overall customer journey. For example, in this project, the process owners learnt how their users interacted with steps that the team complete in the background which aren't visible to the end user. They gained a deeper understanding of the effects of the process on customers which, in turn, helped them identify waste and non-value add activities.

During the design phase, we invited key stakeholders, including customers, into the room to co-design webpages and forms. Focusing on new possibilities, rather than the problem, created a buzz in the room that we had not experienced before. People, especially users, were appreciative about being asked to design something that would work for them. In this case, prototyping helped the team who owned the process produce work which was not based on their own ideas, thought processes, opinions and assumptions. They were able to understand the needs of their users better and avoid making mistakes when designing a new webpage and form. Although, in service design, it is understood you might not get things right first time, co-designing with users allowed for a more desirable, feasible, viable and, ultimately, fit-for-purpose product. We also noticed, working in this way enabled us to achieve stakeholder and sponsor buy-in more quickly and effectively.

Through this project we learnt that data alone is not enough to overcome resistance to change. Providing a space for employees to learn about their customers' needs is paramount to encouraging empathy and implementing and sustaining change. Without the empathy phase in service design it is unlikely this would have been achieved. Another learning from this work is that providing staff with the opportunity to be creative and collaborative without a fear of judgement is essential to generating ideas that may not have developed by only removing waste and non-value-added activities.

Conclusion – Where we are and next steps

In conclusion, in this chapter we have provided an overview of our team's learning journey using Lean and Service Design to enhance our support for the University and our students when designing better services. We have shown through case examples how the different approaches to process improvement can be integrated to help service providers connect with the experiences of their users at a deeper human level. We discussed how this generates the desire and willingness to step into uncertainty when seeking to be 'radically creative' and trialling approaches that are not conventional, or that do not follow a repeatable, standard formula.

Along the journey, through relentless evidence gathering with a particular focus on the user and staff experience, we were able to build a mass of stakeholders who joined us in advocating for and promoting ways of working that are based on radical creativity and user-centredness. The role our communities of practice and networks have played has been pivotal: the privilege of having access to the expertise and insights of colleagues across the globe and their willingness to help us piece together the many pieces of the puzzle has been invaluable. The many learning conversations we had across so many disparate projects – learning how others harness technology, sharing knowledge on Academic Workload Planning, experiences of engaging large groups of people in ideation activities – have enabled us to have the confidence and the ability to be, in 2024, at the helm of the University's Digital Transformation.

As a team, we continue to learn how and where to best integrate appropriate elements of the Double Diamond approach (Design Council, 2004) on a case-by-case basis, without forcing conscious compliance to what could be perceived as yet another problem-solving methodology. We continue to blend Lean, Service Design and Change Management practices to create service experiences that meet the needs of both internal and external service users, students, and to deliver on the financial sustainability and vitality of our organisation. We will be putting this blended approach at the heart of the changes coming and there is an acknowledgement within our Executive Team that this approach will be core to everything we do in the future.

Key learning points

Integrating Lean with Service Design has taught us and our colleagues at Middlesex University about:

1   Empathising with and seeing things from the perspective of the end users.
2   Encouraging colleagues to try new things and establishing an environment where failure is not avoided but learned from.
3   Dealing with the fact that we will not always have all the answers from the start and must manage the feelings of uncertainty which come with that.

References

Bennett, N. & Perkins, J. (2020) Developing a Culture – The Essentials for Continuous Improvement. In S. Yorkstone (Ed.), *Global Lean for Higher Education: A Themed Anthology of Case Studies, Approaches, and Tools*. Oxford: Routledge.

Brown, T. & Katz, B. (2009) *Change by Design*. USA: Harper Business.

Design Council. (2004) The Framework for Innovation, Double Diamond. Available at: www.designcouncil.org.uk/our-resources/framework-for-innovation (Accessed: 5 June 2023).

Design Council. (2023) The Double Diamond. Available at: www.designcouncil.org.uk/our-resources/the-double-diamond (Accessed: 18 February 2023).

Hiatt, J. (2006) *ADKAR: A Model for Change in Business Government and our Community*. USA: Prosci.

Lean Competency System. (n.d.) Lean Thinking. Available at: www.leancompetency.org/about-the-lcs/lean-thinking (Accessed: 20 January 2023).

Lean Higher Education. (n.d.) Lean Higher Education. Available at: www.leanhe.org (Accessed: 17 March 2023).

Penin, L. (2018) *An Introduction to Service Design: Designing the Invisible*. USA: Bloomsbury.

Stickdorn, M., Lawrence, A., Hormess, M. & Schenider, J. (2018) *This is Service Design Doing: Applying Service Design Thinking in the Real World A Practitioners' Handbook*. Sebastopol, CA: O'Reilly.

Chapter 9

Moving from silos to integrated services – a case study of three live experiments

Svein Are Tjeldnes and Karin Eilertsen

Introduction

On a particularly beautiful winter day in Tromsø in December 2020, a teacher from the Faculty of Law enters the University Library at UiT the Arctic University of Norway (UiT), to get help for a problem she had encountered as she was grading exams. In the grading-process she needed access to a specific digital knowledge bank, to which the University had a subscription. She had already been in touch with the IT department, receiving this answer:

> "[Name of the teacher] is only registered as a "specialist" in FS. Specialists can only be affiliated members in relation to FEIDE. It is one of the loosest affiliations there is. If she needs «student» or «employee», she will have to be saved as a student in FS or employee in PAGA. If she receives salary from UiT, it means she is saved in PAGA in such a way that she is not sent to BAS, which is needed before we can upgrade the affiliation. I cannot fix this for you. She must either contact someone at FUF or GENØK [Sic] to change the affiliation to UiT".

To the average reader, this would make little or no sense at all, but does this story ring any bells? If so, it could be the alarm bells you're hearing. The answer given from the IT department bears no meaning to anyone who is not an insider to these specific systems and offers absolutely no help at all to remedy the situation. For the sake of the reader, we should clarify that FS, FEIDE, PAGA and BAS are names for internal IT systems, while FUF[1] and GENØK[2] are abbreviations commonly used for two departments within the professional services.

At the University Library, our teacher found support and help. Unfortunately, the response from the IT department was just as incomprehensible for the librarian. By a stroke of luck, the librarian had knowledge of another colleague at the HR department, who might be able to help. At this stage, and with joint forces from our librarian and the HR colleague, enough was understood from the IT response to fix the problem – still with the need of involving yet another colleague at the Faculty of Law.

DOI: 10.4324/9781003383161-18

In the end, the teacher was able to get hold of the resources needed to do her job, with the help and support from several colleagues, including organisational units like the Faulty of Law, the University Library and two departments.

The story above can easily serve as one of many examples of poor service, despite the best efforts from several employees, through administrative structures that were not designed to make things as easy as possible, use of 'internal language' with customers, silos and compartmentalisation and more. Above all, it serves as an example on how we give good service at specific points in a process, but at the same time display poor understanding of what good, interconnected service looks like for our customers.

At UiT, people working in the professional services are committed to helping students and staff each day, supporting them in their missions, whether it is achieving academic degrees, delivering excellent teaching or doing groundbreaking research. There would be very few, if any, who while travelling to work would think "Today, I am going to do a terrible job. I'll make life miserable for anyone who contacts me". Even with this probably true assumption we see many examples of not-so-great service. How can this be? Would we fix the problems and increase the service-level, thus increasing the number of great user experiences, by simply training our staff members or restructuring our organisation? Or could it be that the basis for our problems (when it comes to service) is more structural and culturally rooted? What if we have an organisation that is not set up for success?

In this chapter we seek to inspire people in Higher Education to go forward with their own service design projects, even though service design might not be the preferred or standard go-to method. We will describe how we got started, what we have done and what we have learned. Please be aware that the narrative is from a practitioner's perspective. This means that the main output will be drawn from concrete experience working with a large-scale service design project and not a theoretically founded framework for a project set-up.

Why approach the problem with service design methodology?

Service design is human-centric and places the customer at the centre of both problem-solving processes and designing new or better services. With a service design approach and mindset, we could aim for solutions and processes that were more tailored to the needs of our customers.

Service design encourages collaboration and co-creation, involving people across the organisation. Our project is at large a cultural re-orientation, as opposed to a formal re-organisation, and we needed to have a holistic approach considering all aspects of the service/user-experience. This 'mission' was initiated by the University Board in 2018, stating the need to create a professional service culture.

A common approach in universities (at least in UiT) is to make hardcoded and elaborate step-by-step plans for what will happen and when, and then stick to the plan no matter what. In addition, public institutions often turn to formal restructuring/re-organisation when facing the need for change. In this project we needed to do something that was not done before at our university, and we needed to make sure that learning was considered when designing the project. To allow learning to impact the process and outcome, means adding more flexibility. By using service design as the main project framework/methodology, we could ensure an iterative process allowing customer and employee feedback to influence and set the direction for our next steps. At the outset of our project, we were unaware of the problems and solutions we would encounter. However, by incorporating service design principles, we were able to better equip ourselves for new ways of working.

How we got started

Providing some contextual remarks about the University's situation at the time is necessary to accurately describe how we began our service design project. Following years of systematic improvement work through Lean thinking and the use of Lean methodology, we became aware of some structural barriers upon implementing new and improved processes. One example is linked to the services regarding staff mobility, which we improved and re-designed in 2013. Part of the solution was to move some of our resources (people and funds) between departments in our organisation. As this was suggested to the process stakeholders, the improvement process came to a full stop. It seemed impossible to relocate resources, as it became a case of arguments over resource ownership, (in the end, the process moved forward as there was an agreement to create a new position, thus hiring new personnel – increase of resources). From one perspective, the proposed changes were considered beneficial for the University, but from the perspective of individual departments, it was seen as "stealing" resources. This situation revealed the siloed nature of our organisation in practice, not just on paper.

This discovery played a part in an emerging realisation of a need to change how the University was operated, and in 2015 this was described in a large project named Adm2020. Adm2020 was described as a transformative re-organisation project with broad goals of changing both the way we were organised and the way we worked. The project was most of all aimed at transforming the administrative organisation and administrative tasks/processes.

Owing to the work with Adm2020 and the knowledge of how near to impossible it was to move resources internally, the university management frequently participated at seminars and conferences where topics like collaboration, work organisation, service and management were discussed. Because of this, it was not a coincidence that central UiT managers, in the fall of 2019, attended a presentation on how Finnish universities had attacked similar challenges. The examples from the Finnish universities became the inspiring input our project needed and made it easier to realise that we needed to think completely differently. Instead of a new round of restructuring the organisation, as we had just undergone, we aimed to reorganise the way we worked. We teamed up with Niclas Lindgren[3], who had been working with several of the Finnish universities, and in December 2019 we invited our university leaders to join a workshop with the following theme: 'To move from control to service – transformation of the administration'. As it turned out, there was a huge interest to participate in the workshop, and with over 80 attendees we had to hold the workshop twice in two days to accommodate actual participation and co-creation.

This workshop became instrumental for the overall service design project we are showcasing in this chapter. The output and action canvas that were produced in this workshop became a guide for the work we have undertaken since. This output also resulted in the model/framework for our service design project, which is now known as "Interconnected Services"[4], consisting of six areas of focus. Those are:

- Identity
- Service culture
- Service leadership
- Internal communication
- Service offering
- Workflows

It is a major point for us to acknowledge that the framework for our service design project was co-created among these eighty leaders. This means that ownership is embedded within large parts of the university management. Another interesting output was that service design came up as a suggestion for how we could proceed with the project, even though it was mentioned only in a couple of the worksheets that were produced.

A more important result was that the participants agreed quite firmly upon which of the six areas of focus we needed to start working on first: To figure out what the total scope of our service offering was. If the workshop was the birth of our service design project, the decision to start mapping our services would be the lift-off.

Hearts and minds – engagement from the wider university community

Even if service design is human centred at its core, it does not in itself create the engagement needed to succeed. There is still a need to engage people widely throughout the organisation, and to do so we wanted to speak both to their hearts and minds – a holistic approach.

Developing the organisation and developing the people within it are two interdependent goals that are essential for long-term success. To engage the employees in our service design project, it became important to create a feeling of trust and a sense of belonging. This would be crucial to gain the necessary level of commitment and motivation, as we knew that changing the way we worked would take some time.

Furthermore, developing people's skills and minds not only benefits UiT as an organisation but also enhances the individual's personal and professional growth. By providing opportunities for learning and development, we can help employees build their skills, increase their confidence and expand their knowledge.

It was important for us to adopt a mindset to test and improve ideas continuously throughout the different phases of the service design project. Such a mindset emphasises the importance of experimentation and learning both from failures and successes as a means of continuous improvement. Instead of waiting for a perfect solution, we could take an iterative approach, testing and refining ideas and experiments based on feedback and data. This approach enabled us to identify and fix problems quickly and make data-driven decisions. To some extent, this was new to our organisation – well used to having elaborate and fixed step-by-step plans.

With a mindset like this, it became easier to encourage employees to take risks (to a certain extent), try new things and think outside the box. These are all qualities that we wanted to lift forward by building safe spaces to experiment and learn. In some ways we were building several small learning labs, fostering curiosity, problem-solving abilities and increased cross-sectional collaboration.

Experiment 1: Developing a cross-organisational service-map

The story from the beginning of this chapter, where our teacher had difficulties getting support from the administrative services, highlights the professional service silos that result in customers being bounced from department to department. The teacher obviously needed something more than each department could deliver by itself, and there seemed to be a mismatch between the service offering and the customers' requirements. In the first experiment we wanted to explore the service offering within the professional services.

What did we do?

A survey was sent to all administrative departments at UiT, to gather information of the service offering. The feedback counted 3,307 services provided to 52 customer groups. When analysing the responses, we realised that the 3,307 services in fact represented a combination of job tasks, processes and a few services.

Separate cards describing each of the 3,307 job tasks were produced, and in a full-day workshop with help from 40 employees, all cards were sorted and collated into 78 services for five customer groups – we had created the first service-map (Figure 9.1). In the following months, through several iterations, the service-map was developed furthermore. We organised several user-test workshops, where students and staff were invited to give feedback on to which extent they found their required services, understood the service names and liked the idea of a visual service-map. Almost 300 students and staff participated during the user-testing, and approximately 700 quotes were processed and embedded in the further development of the service-map.

Key learning points

The service design approach led to a prototype of a cross-organisational service-map, which gave an overview of the service offering from the professional services, regardless of the units involved. The map effectively visualises our services and can facilitate discussions with leaders about the concept and next steps. The main learning points from this experiment are:

- **It is important to define and explain the terms "job-task", "process" and "service".** We realised that we don't have the same definition of these

Figure 9.1 Cross-organisational service-map

terms at a university level. Many departments had already defined their own services and it became confusing when the service-map merged services from the departments into interconnected services on the service-map.

- **All the services need a description.** Even though the service-map represents all the work that is already performed by the administrative staff, some employees found it difficult to recognise their own job tasks on the service-map. We are used to identifying what we do from our organisational structure, while the service-map contains no departments.
- **Administrative staff are not customers of each other within a service.** We learned that we have a strong culture of thinking of each other as customers within the professional services. The service-map is helping us change that perspective and reminds us of who the real customers are.

Experiment 2: Designing and running five pilots

As a next step, the service-map was presented to leaders around the university. The leaders were positive, inspired and curious about the practical impact and requested real life examples of how administrative staff could collaborate across departments to deliver interconnected services. To explore this, we designed an experiment to learn how to build virtual, but functional, service teams across organisational units.

What did we do?

Based on strategic choices and recommendations from the faculties the UiT Rector decided on five services to be run as pilots:

- Exams (for students)
- Student exchange (for students)
- Procurement (for all employees)
- Employment (for leaders)
- Digital study environment (for teachers)

Each pilot involved employees working with job tasks connected to the specific service. To secure daily operations and reduce the risk of overwork, each faculty could decide which of the pilots they wanted to take part in and with how many employees. Consequently, the size of the pilots varied from 11 to 64 participants.

We wanted to explore how employees could work in a matrix-based organisation across units, without getting lost in management discussions. To do this, we created a co-ordinator team for each service pilot, consisting of one participant from each faculty/department that participated in the pilot. The team-members had shared responsibility to facilitate the work in the pilots, secure the progress and to report back to their "home units".

User expectations were explored early, and students and academic staff were invited to share their stories and experiences with each service. In addition, the participants in the service pilots interviewed customers to gain better understanding of the user expectations. The findings allowed for a description of the services, clarifying the content of each service and identifying the contributors responsible for delivering them. Once the service was described, the next step was to explore how to collaborate on a daily basis within each service.

The service pilots were intended to last for three months, after which the participants were expected to communicate, collaborate and deliver excellent service. Following the service pilot period, the teams were to implement the work and expand by involving all staff responsible for delivering job tasks related to each service.

Key learning points

The pilot services faced different problems during the test period, and we gained valuable new insights from each pilot. Working in (virtual) networks was reported as challenging, as was working in a service design mode where the path is created through experimentation and learning. This way of working is after all a huge contrast to what we are used to. Even so, in the evaluation of the service pilots, the majority of the participants stated that it is important for UiT to work with service design (Figure 9.2).

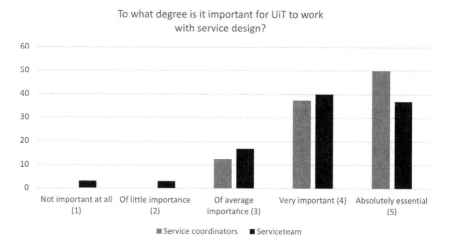

Figure 9.2 After the experiment, the participants in the service pilots were asked how important it is for UiT to work with service design. The answers are given in percent and N=48. Mean value for service co-ordinators = 4.4 and service team members = 4.0

Key learning points from this experiment are:

- **Service leadership.** The experiment gave us insight into the complexity of setting up self-governing cross-organisational teams. Although we succeeded to some degree, we saw the need to understand service leadership. This was our biggest learning point and will be further explored in Experiment 3.
- **Talking to the customer is a good thing.** Many of the participants in the service pilots were not used to speaking directly with academic staff and students. They appreciated the customer feedback and learned that it might be helpful focusing on the customers' needs when building services, instead of how the professional services should organise their work.
- **It is possible to create a network to share best practice.** Although we experienced that it is challenging to work this way, the service pilot "Exams" can illustrate how a network with 160 participants from more than 20 administrative units can communicate, collaborate and learn together. They created a shared Microsoft Teams area, where they actively use the chat function to easily reach all employees involved in exam work.

Experiment 3: Developing a functional model for service leadership

One of the key findings from the second experiment, was that we had unclear descriptions of the role of leadership. In multiple scenarios it became clear that we as an organisation, are quite used to doing regular leader check-ins. Some of the teams had difficulties moving on with the pilot as were supposed to be a self-governing team, hence feeling a lack of leader input. The question of leadership in a customer and service-oriented model also arose in discussions among key stakeholders – and often among senior management. They wondered if and how leading a service differs from leading a department or unit. At this time, there was an urgent need to understand what service leadership is and without this knowledge we couldn't continue building virtual networks around the mapped services.

What did we do?

In this experiment we wanted to understand what service leadership is. In addition, it seemed necessary to break service leadership into specific elements that could enhance the practical understanding of tasks needed to be done.

Initially, a small group of leaders were invited to a quick brainstorming session with the theme "What is service leadership?". This session resulted in five broad topics including a few ideas of content for each topic. Based on this material and further discussions with the leaders, an early model was developed visualising the proposed key elements of service leadership in a simple cake-diagram. The five key elements were:

- User centricity
- Service culture
- Service delivery
- Service competency
- Goals and resource allocation

This prototype model was user-tested in a full day workshop, with 40 leaders across all levels and departments invited by the University Director. The prototype for the service leadership model was presented, and then the participants were given the opportunity to study, reflect and discuss the different aspects of it on large working canvases with questions like:

- Are these five elements the most central components of our future service leadership?
- Seen from your perspective as a leader:

  a   Which two elements (in the model) should we develop first, and why?
  b   Within the two elements you have chosen, what are the key questions to answer, and why?

The output created in this workshop became the core material to develop the next version of the service leadership model (Figure 9.3). This edition was presented at the Rector's leader summit, where all senior leaders at UiT were invited to reflect upon the following question:

'How can we jointly create room to explore what it means to work and lead in a matrix organisation to operationalise customer-centric service?'

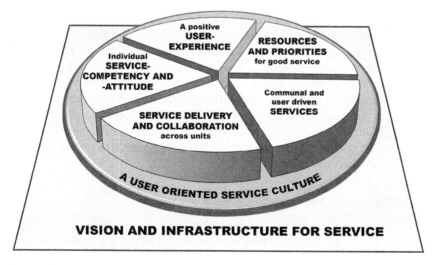

Figure 9.3 The service leadership model with the five key elements with two underlying conditions

After the Rector leader summit, the University Director appointed a small group (model task force) to develop a functional model for service leadership – or how to lead services – and also to suggest how to implement it.

The task force organised the work in the form of a facilitated sprint-week, with three workshops each day for the full week. In the first workshop of each day, the task force looked at one of the items in the model, discussing key questions like: What would it take to operationalise this, and what do leaders need to do? In the second workshop, the task force facilitators designed models based on the ideas, discussions and reflections from the task force members. In the third workshop, the task force reviewed, improved and finalised the models and drawings. After five intensive days, the task force delivered a visual conceptualisation of the service leadership model to the University Director.

Key learning points

During the work with the service leadership model, we found it challenging that the university did not really have a leadership model per se (other than the generic model for all government funded organisations). Leaders quite often ended up discussing infrastructure, finances and resources instead of specific service leadership themes.

As a result of this experiment, we have functional illustrations of a service leadership model. Practical support material for the leaders, in the shape of a guide/booklet/folder etc., still needs to be delivered as well as embedding it into our leader program. Even though we are not finished with leadership discussions, there are two key learning points we would like to emphasise:

- **The work has led to a matured understanding of service leadership.** However, the operationalisation of the leadership model met opposition when presented. The model requires changes to the way we lead and to the role of leaders (as well as changes in budgeting). It also conceptualises service ownership – a discussion yet to be had at the university.
- **Don't underestimate the value of the work done in between activities.** Work done in the in-between-phase can make the difference for the next stage. Preparations can be done to set up tests. Try to provoke reactions. Sometimes it seems to be better to have people react to something rather than just silently consent.

Conclusion and key learning points

In this chapter we have described a large-scale service design project, the creation of a service-map and how we have started to build a professional service culture. Any curious reader would probably wonder how this work will affect the customers of the UiT professional services. Let's revisit the teacher from the Faculty of Law. In a dream scenario the teacher would experience excellent service every time when in contact with the professional services. In the actual example mentioned, the representative from the IT department would not give an answer full of internal language, impossible to understand – but rather take responsibility to remedy the situation, without making it the teacher's problem to seek help elsewhere. In fact, the first point of contact would ensure that the problem would be sorted, handled internally and then happily inform the teacher when problem was solved.

Even though we have worked with the service design project for some years it still feels like we are on the beginning of the journey. There are many more experiments to conduct and challenges to overcome.

Looking back on our service design journey we acknowledge that it has taken longer time than expected. A main reason is probably that it takes time to build a common service culture. There are different levels of service-maturity within the professional services and the work will continue, probably for many years.

During the project we have encountered several challenges, one being nurturing engagement from leaders and employees. The top-level management at UiT have owned the service design project from the start, but there has been some uncertainty among employees and leaders as to how strong this ownership is. When setting out on a project like this, it is vital to have a concrete plan on how the top-level management can support sustainable engagement to change the way of working rather than reorganising.

Employees have participated in the service design project and at the same time taking care of day-to-day operations. It has been challenging and painful "taking the time away from their ordinary tasks". If staff members don't have the time and capacity to join in, the project will suffer. A project like this is a major undertaking with the need for massive involvement, and it must be a leader-responsibility to find the time and resources necessary. Changing the way we work needs to become part of the job, not something that comes on top of it.

When describing the three live experiments, we summarised key learning points tied to each of them. In addition, we would like to highlight three key learning points regarding the overall service design project:

1   Just do it! A well-known slogan, but also instrumental for where we are now in our service design project. As explained in this chapter, it is partly unusual for the professional services at our university to start working on a project that is not carefully planned to the last detail. We would not be able to implement a concrete service-map if we had not dared to take the first step into a service design mindset.

2 In a project like this, it is vital to bring large parts of the organisation along. Likewise, it is just as important to not wait until everyone is ready. It is likely that it will never happen, thus the project never starts.

3 Even though service design came up as a possible way of working at the first exploratory workshop, we have not advertised the label. This has allowed us to work with a service design mindset and service design methods, without having to navigate through debates and resistance on the method itself.

Notes

1 FUF is the department for research and student affairs.
2 GENØK is presumably meant to be ORGØK, which is the HR and Economics department. There is no department or unit called GENØK at UiT.
3 Niclas Lindgren is the CEO and founder of Renesans Consulting Oy.
4 In Norwegian it is called "Sammenhengende tjenester".

Chapter 10

Futurelib

Prototyping library services at the University of Cambridge

Jenny Egan and David Marshall

Introduction

The Futurelib innovation programme, commissioned by Cambridge University Libraries in 2014 and supported by design and innovation consultancy Modern Human, employed user-centred design methods to inform the conception and design of new and reimagined library services at the University of Cambridge. The programme was initiated in response to a rapidly changing landscape for library users, owing partly to an accelerating shift towards digital resources, services and interactions. Futurelib examined the role libraries play for users in the context of learning, teaching and research, with the aim of creating user-centred services which optimise and integrate digital and physical touchpoints.

A phase of exploratory user research (diary studies, contextual inquiry, observations and expert interviews) generated an initial set of 12 concepts for potential new – or reimagined – library services at Cambridge. Some of the concepts made it through to our prototyping and testing phase. We will discuss two of our core concepts – Spacefinder – a service to help Cambridge students find appropriate places to work and Protolib – design of user-centred workspaces to optimise productivity and wellbeing in libraries – throughout this chapter.

The authors, Jenny and David, currently work within the Product and Service Design Division at the University of Cambridge, as Service Design Team Lead and User Research and Data Science Team Lead respectively. However, while working as part of the core Futurelib team, David's role was part of the Reader Services Division at Cambridge University Library, and Jenny was a Design Researcher and Experience Designer at Modern Human.

Two Service Design case studies

Spacefinder: helping Cambridge students find appropriate places to work

Problem to be solved

The University of Cambridge estate has over 100 libraries and has grown and changed organically over hundreds of years. The University's many buildings and

DOI: 10.4324/9781003383161-19

facilities are also spread across an area of more than 40 square kilometres. A recurring theme from Futurelib's research was that it was difficult for Cambridge students to find convenient places to work, especially when they were between lectures or away from their college or department buildings. Since the University is not short of places to work, we described this as 'a problem of hidden abundance' (Priestner, Marshall & Modern Human, 2016a). Observations saw study activity happening in sub-optimal places, for example students doing group work in noisy social spaces or rooms in their college without suitable chairs, tables and other equipment. Students often couldn't find appropriate places to work between lectures, so ended up wasting what could have been valuable study time.

Proposed service

Spacefinder aimed to help students and academic staff to find suitable places to work within Cambridge's complex network of libraries and workspaces, so that they could make the most effective use of the time and resources available to them. It was conceived of as a searchable web-based application (Cambridge University Library, 2023) that sought to catalogue and promote the many and varied spaces across the University. This would enable members of the University to search for workspaces according to their location and/or specific requirements.

Approach

The Spacefinder concept was based on strong evidence, however, we continually tested the concept using rapid prototyping to reach a truly user-centred solution. We ran guerilla usability tests (intercepting users – students and staff – in public spaces rather than recruiting them in advance) as this was less admin-heavy and allowed us to intercept users at moments when Spacefinder was most likely to be of use to them (for example when leaving a lecture). We showed them digitised versions of paper prototypes, using technology which enabled us to quickly iterate and re-test designs while out in the field. This process enabled us to quickly optimise and refine the initial beta release of Spacefinder in response to user feedback.

Protolib: user-centred workspaces to optimise productivity and wellbeing in libraries

Problem to be solved

All students have needs and preferences which inform their choice of workspace. Many students will go to the library when they have a piece of work to complete and see this as akin to going into an office every day. However, we found that the typical library environment doesn't work well for everyone. Some students find formal, traditional libraries too intense and stressful and choose instead to study in their rooms, where they value the familiarity, quiet, convenience and flexibility of making a hot drink or snack. These students only visit libraries to get books or for short periods of time between lectures.

Proposed service

Our aim for this service was to provide students and academics with library spaces which meet their needs and help optimise their productivity and well-being. The final output for the Protolib ('Prototyping libraries') project was a set of principles and patterns that could be used in the design of a cohesive, user-centred, inter-dependent set of working environments that supported students and staff carrying out a wide range of study and work activities.

Approach

We used a range of user-centred methods during the Protolib project. We initially ran a co-design workshop with students using the LEGO® Serious Play® method, 'an experiential process designed to prompt dialogue and encourage reflection, as well as develop problem-solving skills and use of imagination' (LEGO®, 2023). Steps were taken in recruitment to ensure a diverse range of undergraduate and postgraduate students, in terms of their subject or academic discipline and stage of study. The insights from this workshop were used to inform initial designs for our prototype library spaces. A series of observation studies in the prototype spaces enabled us to identify common behaviours and usage patterns. We also conducted guerrilla interviews with people leaving the prototype spaces to gain further insights on our observations. Feedback boards installed in the prototype spaces enabled users to leave comments in their own time. This range of methods enabled us to gather both attitudinal (what people say) and behavioural (what people do) data, which was invaluable in generating the insights we used to inform our final design concepts and layout patterns.

Designing new services within Higher Education: Key learnings from the Futurelib programme

How we solved the right problems with user-centred designs

Watch what they do, don't just listen to what they say

Our concepts were not arrived at through gathering information on professed user need, but by observing and building an understanding of user behaviour using a variety of user-centred methodologies. Our iterative design process, whereby we tested prototypes at varying levels of fidelity, was also essential to ensure we were meeting real user needs and solving the right problem. Our strongest example of this came from our work on the Protolib project. Our initial co-design workshops asked participants to design their ideal study spaces using Lego® blocks. A key theme which emerged was that users wanted spaces designed for specific activities, such as reading, writing, group work and analysis. This informed initial designs for our prototype spaces. A prototype reading space was kitted out with soft furnishings, reading lamps and coffee tables, while a prototype writing space was furnished with generously sized tables for spreading out books and papers alongside laptops.

We conducted an intensive period of testing, during which we installed feedback boards in the spaces, observed people using the spaces and conducted interviews with people leaving the spaces. Aspects of the prototypes (furniture layouts, lamps, plants, plug sockets and other accessories) were iterated in response to patterns of user behaviour and feedback to test the relative utility of different options. We conducted 317 observations, 127 exit interviews and received 664 pieces of written feedback on sticky notes or comment cards.

Analysis of our observation and interview data revealed that, contrary to what our users had requested, they did not in fact use task-specific spaces for reading, writing and analysis. Instead, a myriad of different activities was being conducted in our prototype 'reading' and 'writing' spaces. Over time, we translated these insights into a 'triangle of motivating factors' and an 'intensity gradient' (Priestner, Marshall & Modern Human, 2016b), with these models heavily influencing our future work. The triangle of motivating factors summarised the key factors which informed users' choice of workspace: the task they intended to complete, their intended length of stay and how they felt at the time. The intensity gradient designed and defined individual environments as being either low, medium or high in intensity.

These models worked in tandem as spaces with higher or lower intensity levels were chosen based on the triangle of motivating factors. For example, library users who were tired or stressed were more likely to choose a low-intensity space, as a result of wanting to be comfortable, both ergonomically and mentally. This demonstrates the importance of using multiple complementary methods and continuously observing and gathering feedback from users in context to ensure you are solving the right problem. We would never have arrived at these key insights and uncovered these true user needs had we not followed this process.

Keep an open mind and challenge assumptions

The temptation for (well-meaning) teams can be to create high-fidelity prototypes based on untested hypotheses or anecdotally formed assumptions, which means they end up testing relatively fixed core propositions with users. From our experience it is crucial to start with user research using a variety of triangulated methods, to ensure you are surfacing real needs and behaviours and solving the right problem, rather than the assumed problem. It is important to follow the direction the research is taking you rather than letting your own biases or preconceptions get in the way, as this is how you obtain the most valuable insights.

Our first example of this is when some of our colleagues assumed the soft furnishings in our prototype 'low-intensity space' would detract from 'serious study', encourage more talking/relaxed behaviour and disrupt the serious, more formal working atmosphere in the library. Our observations, interviews and user feedback showed this was far from the truth and led to the concept of the 'relaxed but serious' workspace (Priestner, Marshall & Modern Human, 2016b), which was proven to support students' overall stamina, wellbeing and productivity, rather than detract from it. Feedback from our library users included:

- "I have written my entire introduction in the low-intensity space, which is real academic work, because it's such a relaxed and comfortable environment. I found it much easier to do than if I was sitting at a desk with a neon light, focused intently on the work".
- "It's important to have a room to 'switch gears'. If the body is comfortable it allows the mind to work".
- "This [low-intensity] space supports my needs because I find Cambridge too intense and stressful".
- "I used to have a mental block in more traditional and serious spaces. I can start work instantly in here".

Another assumption made by our colleagues was that removing chairs from workspaces would impact their efficiency, as a result of providing fewer individual places to work. Our iterative prototyping showed that removing more than a third of the chairs from our prototype 'medium-intensity' space actually doubled the average occupancy of the space (Table 10.1). Our user research

Table 10.1 Number of chairs, mean and maximum observed occupancy, in prototype iterations of a space

Prototype iteration	Layout description	Number of available chairs	Maximum observed occupancy	Mean observed occupancy
Original (base-line) layout	A mixture of café-style circular tables and rectangular tables	31	11	7
Prototype 1	Large rectangular tables with four chairs per table and individual task lights	24	15	11
Prototype 2	Same as Prototype 1 but with the addition of plants blocking sightlines	20	18	14
Prototype 3	Same as Prototype 2 but with tables reorientated and placed next to windows	20	20	15

revealed that perceived occupancy and territory had a strong effect on whether people would use a workstation. By removing chairs and adding humanising features such as plants and task lamps, we increased space provision for each user and made the space a more attractive place to work.

Without iterative prototyping, observation and exit interviews it would not have been possible to arrive at these insights. It is important to remember that even if you work with users every day, it does not mean you understand their true needs, behaviours and motivations. If we had just responded to our own or our colleagues' 'expert' opinions and assumptions, we might never have tested some of these concepts. The key learning here is that you need to open your mind, employ user-centred methods, ensure your research is well-designed and trust the process.

Immerse yourselves in your users' context

While the importance of immersion is often acknowledged from a methodological perspective (we need to inhabit the spaces our users inhabit to properly understand and empathise with their experience) this can sometimes be undersold in terms of its importance or represented in quite a mechanical way. We were privileged during the Futurelib work in that we were continually working in and among our users, even when our formal researcher hats were off. Continuously walking through our prototype environments meant we were able to observe and photograph some valuable nuggets of user behaviour and overhear library users when we were not directly interviewing them. All of this helped us to develop a richer understanding of the subject matter we were working with, moving towards the ethnographic ideal of feeling less like we were 'outsiders' (Naaeke et al., 2010).

Live and breathe your data

During one of our longer projects, we had a dedicated project room, which we dubbed 'The Protolib Bunker'. A key benefit of having this room was that no one disturbed us or moved our sticky notes. Being surrounded by our data and being able to map it into themes was the most valuable part of having this space, as it enabled evolving patterns in our understanding. We still reminisce about this time, particularly since the post-Covid world seems to favour online whiteboard tools over old-school war rooms. The limitations (square meterage) of physical spaces can be constraining in a positive sense, while the limitless margins of online tools make it difficult to force a process of convergence.

Start small and follow an iterative design process

Even though service design is broad in scope you can still start small. It's not always possible to work on the big, impactful projects right away, so it's important to prioritise the best places to start to gain traction. This has numerous benefits: small projects and problems are easier and less daunting to tackle; failure (which is part of any good iterative design process) often has lower stakes attached; and, best of all, multiple small improvements to the experience of students and other users can collectively make a significant positive change to people's lives. If you have a low budget or don't yet have buy-in from senior stakeholders, start small and use what you learn to get other people on board with what you are doing.

We adopted an iterative design process on all our projects. During some of our live prototyping phases we updated designs multiple times per day, which meant we could continuously iterate and optimise designs in response to actual user needs and behaviour. Obtaining user feedback early in the design process also meant that any issues with our proposed solutions could be flagged up before any significant expense was incurred.

We would strongly advocate for this 'lo-fi first' approach, regardless of context. Our first step on the Protolib project was not to immediately refurnish two entire library spaces. Our starting point was to put a feedback board in each of the original spaces, observe people using the spaces and interview people leaving the spaces about what they were using them for. We also ran a workshop with students to better understand their library space needs. This low-cost, upfront work helped to inform our next steps and show a need for what we were doing, before we spent big bucks on furniture!

Don't be afraid to 'fail'

Failure is part of any good iterative design process, as something can be learned from everything you do and used to inform your next steps. The three services discussed in this chapter were not our first or only ideas. Following an initial period of research and analysis, a concept ideation workshop generated around 300 opportunities and ideas, which were then whittled down to a final set of 12 concepts over a period of four weeks.

One of these 12 concepts, 'WhoHas?', responded to research that revealed a significant amount of inter-lending of library books between students, outside of the official library systems. We set up a low-fidelity, pilot service in a Facebook group which enabled students to pass books to one another 'in the open', so that librarians could monitor these transactions and update the official lender in the library's system. Despite 174 students participating in the pilot over 6 weeks, only one book exchange was logged. Interestingly, diary studies conducted with some of these participants in parallel revealed that many exchanges occurred outside of the pilot service. This showed us that we were trying to solve a problem which existed for librarians, rather than students. There was no real value for students in legitimising this activity, as it was working well for them already. While this service concept could have been considered a failure, having not passed the pilot stage, we learned a lot from it and were reminded that for services to be used, they need to provide real value for end users as well as for the business.

How we overcame challenges by engaging stakeholders

Community, buy-in and advocacy

People are central to effective service design and delivery; they can either represent barriers to progress or powerful agents for change. We were aware from the outset that building a community of awareness, interest, trust, support and excitement around the work we were doing was critical to its success.

We knew that our stakeholders (senior leaders, managers and librarians) would not buy into or feel ownership of our work if we didn't bring them on the journey with us. We took steps to mitigate this through routinely updating our working groups and maintaining a continually active presence through social media, blogs and other channels. Most of our work took place in library spaces, which give us the opportunity to get to know our service leads on a day-to-day basis.

We put out a request for library staff to help conduct observations in library spaces for the Protolib project and ended up with a relative army of around 50 volunteers. This involved up-front effort from us in terms of training and shadowing them, but it paid dividends in the long run as it meant they trusted in the work, advocated for the approach and believed in the insights it uncovered. It even empowered some of them to start facilitating research in their own libraries and contribute their findings to our central pool of data. Importantly, people became advocates for us when we weren't there, which helped to snowball some of the positive reception we managed to grow.

Working in the open

In response to Protolib's 'relaxed but serious' low-intensity prototype space, which was not as traditional in character as the rest of the library, one of our library users left feedback that "This room hurts me like the world hurts God". While such strongly worded negative comments were in the minority, they may have had more of an impact had we been working behind closed doors. Working in the open increased the visibility of our work and helped to put such comments in context of the sea of positive feedback from other library users. Such comments also tended to get bombarded with sticky notes which leapt to the defence of our less conventional prototype space. This helped to publicly showcase the value of our interventions and made it more difficult for people to argue against what we were doing.

Organisational culture and ingrained mindset

Some of the key challenges we encountered during our work were related to organisational culture. The University of Cambridge is about 800 years old and has a politically dynamic history. Its current devolved structures on one hand allow for flexibility in cutting-edge research and teaching, but simultaneously create administrative minefields and sub-optimal user experiences.

We were fortunate to have backing, sponsorship and representation from a member of the Senior Leadership Team at Cambridge's University Libraries, who had been convinced of the importance of user-centred design, partly through relationships and conversations with States-side peers. We were able to demonstrate value by starting small, gathering evidence and validating service concepts with users, before securing budgets for larger-scale projects and interventions.

On many occasions we encountered either significant resistance or inertia towards change. We helped to mitigate this by working in the open, bringing people on the journey with us and enabling people to witness the impact of our evidence-based designs for themselves. This helped us to build a community of strong advocates within the immediate circles we were operating in. This community was a tiny percentage of the more than 12,000 people employed by the university, but we had to start somewhere.

Longer-term implementation

Our work had impact at a grass-roots level (someone would watch a presentation or read a report and change their service in response) and within a wider context (other universities would express an interest in replicating our solutions). However, it was often more difficult to achieve impact at a business-as-usual, operational level. For example, there was a point at which Spacefinder was handed over to a new technical team and they were considering getting rid of it, as they weren't aware of its context or the value it was providing to users. If we were to do a similar project again in future, we would consider the following as ways of mitigating this:

1 Ensuring provisions are made for managing and maintaining the new service longer term. One way of doing this would be to involve in-house technical teams in the process earlier, so that they would be more aware of the context of the service and involved in decisions about its longer-term implementation.
2 Advocating for dedicated resource in the libraries' staffing to co-ordinate the roll out of offline services.
3 Putting frameworks in place to ensure our work was incorporated into leadership team planning and ongoing service maintenance.
4 Raising awareness of our work with senior stakeholders, committees and groups across the University to help encourage more widespread adoption and implementation. While our work took place within specific library environments and communities, many of its outputs were relevant to other University initiatives, such as student wellbeing support.

The impact of our work

Spacefinder

At the time of writing, Spacefinder is still a heavily used and valued service at Cambridge, around eight years, following its creation. In terms of business benefits, has helped to optimise space usage by promoting library and University spaces which were previously underutilised, thereby increasing the efficiency of University resources. Spacefinder also brings value to individual libraries, whose staff can direct students to other spaces at peak periods such as exam time.

In terms of benefits for users, Spacefinder has facilitated productivity by connecting library users to the right spaces for them, whether those are in or outside of libraries. Users have been better able to find spaces that meet their needs, for example by finding a convenient and suitably equipped space to do some essay-writing between lectures. People are better able to vary the spaces they use when this helps them to maintain productivity and wellbeing. Cambridge students have told us:

- "This is exactly what Cambridge has been crying out for".
- "I've been looking for a service like this for three years!"
- "This is perfect for me. I mix it up all the time and spend an hour in a library then move to another one".

The Cambridge University Students Union's Welfare and Rights Officer at the time also contacted Futurelib to express gratitude for the service, saying:

> "I wanted to write personally, to thank you for Spacefinder and tell you how useful students are already finding it. This is an achievement that shouldn't be underestimated. I thought you might be amused to know that the general response has been one of sheer astonishment that the University have helped produce something so up-to-date and relevant to student life". (Priestner, Marshall & Modern Human, 2016).

Widespread impact has also been achieved by making the Spacefinder codebase open source. It has since been adapted for use as Harvard Library's 'FIND a Space' (Harvard Library, 2023) and several other universities in the UK and internationally.

Protolib

The phased, iterative approach we took to the collaborative design, prototyping and testing of solutions meant that a robust evidence base was established at relatively low cost. The immediate outcomes of the work provided both business benefits (higher occupancy of spaces, improved customer satisfaction) and improvements to users' experiences (increased choice based on preferences, well-designed spaces that met user needs).

Our inexpensive prototyping has also ensured that higher-spend implementation has been based on evidence and an understanding of contextual user needs. Our workspace design principles and patterns for low, medium and high-intensity spaces were used by the architects of Cambridge University's new West Hub, a 4,767-square-metre shared facilities hub which opened to staff, students and the public in April 2022. It has been described as providing 'a huge range of different touchdown spots across the building's large open plan layout, allowing people to choose the kind of mood, light and noise level that suits the work they are trying to do' (University of Cambridge, 2022).

The importance of service design in supporting student wellbeing

We were struck by the fact that, almost regardless of the problem space we were investigating at the time, wellbeing was mentioned again and again by our student participants. Our 'relaxed but serious' space design concepts responded to the needs of a large proportion of the student population. While formality and tradition are partly to be expected in Higher Education (HE) establishments, our work has shown that providing students with opportunities to choose the level of intensity (and formality) which best fits their current task, timeframe and state of mind can help to optimise wellbeing, productivity and engagement. We strongly believe that this concept can be generalised beyond library spaces and services to education and student services more holistically.

Conclusion

We have outlined our approach to designing new and reimagined library services at the University of Cambridge, with the aim of encouraging those working in HE to embark on service design projects within their own establishments.

Solving the right problem with user-centred solutions means abandoning your preconceptions and assumptions and immersing yourselves in your users' context with fresh eyes. This is what will enable you to develop service concepts which are evidence-based and derived from real-life user behaviour. Had we relied solely on the needs users professed to have – or worse still our instincts – we are sure that we would not have gathered as rich and reliable a picture of user needs within libraries.

Change can be hard to effect in older, more entrenched sectors such as HE. It can be difficult to gain traction with service design when people within the organisation see no reason to deviate from the status quo. In HE there is also the lack of a profit-based trigger to pull. This is why the design and delivery of new services is inherently dependent on stakeholder buy-in and positive working relationships. We have seen tangible impact from our work and are convinced this was made possible by engaging others in our journey and being continuously up-front, visible and transparent in what we were doing. We approached everything we did in a highly evidence-based way and made sure we took the time to really get to know and understand our stakeholders.

We want to encourage readers to get started in using service design approaches in their work, no matter how small that starting point may be. The best way to learn is by doing! Your learning journey can be as iterative as the processes we have just described, as you will need to adapt these methods to your own specific context. It's also useful to remember that service design can be applied to anything that helps a user to achieve a goal, whether that is a small, transactional process used by only a handful of users or a larger-scale end-to-end service used by thousands of people. The sooner you get started the better; our work has shown that small changes can have a significant cumulative impact on efficiency, productivity, satisfaction and wellbeing within HE.

Key learning points

1   Abandon your preconceptions and employ a range of complementary, user-centred methodologies to ensure you are solving the right problem.
2   Start small, follow an iterative design process and don't be afraid to fail, as failing comes with valuable learnings!
3   Encourage stakeholder buy-in by engaging others in your process and being continuously up-front, visible and transparent in what you are doing.

References

Cambridge University Library. (2023) Spacefinder. Available at: https://spacefinder. lib.cam.ac.uk (Accessed: 14 April 2023).

Harvard Library. (2023) *FIND a Space*. Available at: https://library.harvard.edu/spa ces (Accessed: 14 April 2023).

LEGO®. (2023) *Serious Play*®. Available at: www.lego.com/en-us/themes/serious-pla y. (Accessed: 13 April 2023).

Naaeke, A., Kurylo, A., Grabowski, M., Linton, D. & Radford, M. L. (2011) Insider and Outsider Perspective in Ethnographic Research. *Proceedings of the New York State Communication Association*, Vol. 2010, Article 9. Available at: http://docs. rwu.edu/nyscaproceedings/vol2010/iss1/9 (Accessed: 14 April 2023).

Priestner, A., Marshall, D. & Modern Human. (2016a) Spacefinder: Illuminating study spaces at the University of Cambridge and matching them to user need and activity. Available at: https://futurelib.files.wordpress.com/2016/06/the-spacefinder-p roject-final.pdf (Accessed: 14 April 2023).

Priestner, A., Marshall, D. & Modern Human. (2016b) The Protolib Project: Researching and reimagining library environments at the University of Cambridge. Available at: https://futurelib.files.wordpress.com/2016/07/the-protolib-project-final-report.pdf (Accessed: 14 April 2023).

University of Cambridge. (2022) West Hub: new, flexible work and study space opens at West Cambridge. Available at: www.staff.admin.cam.ac.uk/general-news/west-hub-new-flexible-work-and-study-space-opens-at-west-cambridge (Accessed: 14 April 2023).

Chapter 11

Designing for a Gender-Inclusive Campus

Bernadette Geuy, Daphne Ogle and Rachel Hollowgrass

Introduction

Universities and colleges are places where academic and personal transformations happen in people's lives, particularly with young adults. It is a time of growth, exploration, and introspection, including with one's gender identity and sexual orientation. A Pew Research Center study (Brown, 2022) found young adults, under 30, are more likely than older adults to be transgender or nonbinary. About 5 percent of young adults in the U.S. say their gender is different from their sex assigned at birth. This is a population whose needs cannot be ignored.

This group is also very vulnerable. The Trevor Project's survey on mental health in 2022 found that 45 percent of LGBTQ youth seriously considered attempting suicide in the past year, including more than half of transgender and nonbinary youth (Trevor Project, 2022). Universities and colleges face mental health crises on their campuses and must find ways to be more welcoming and to help everyone feel like they belong. Having only male/female gender options leaves genderqueer, nonbinary and transgender students feeling not seen and not represented by the institution.

This best practice guide describes how to make structural changes in support of a gender-inclusive campus. The guide centres on enabling *gender identity, lived names,* and *pronoun* options in the institution's Student Information System (SIS), Human Capital Management (HCM) system, and downstream business applications. Researching, designing, and planning for gender data enablement can take years and happen in phases. Many complexities will need to be navigated; for example, revising policies on privacy and data sharing, and leading the campus community through changes that will challenge many peoples' thinking about gender and identity.

Service design tools and methodologies provide a framework for approaching a whole campus project from a human-centred lens, facilitating information gathering and discussions across many university departments and schools. A service design approach differs significantly from traditional technology-driven projects, where human needs and experiences are more often an afterthought and considered late in the process.

DOI: 10.4324/9781003383161-20

Anatomy of a Gender Data Project

> Do you feel reflected on campus? "Oh no, no, no!"
>
> Interview quote from a transgender student

The Impetus for Change

A gender data enablement project is initiated in one of three ways: a compliance mandate; a software update; or an initiative to address the needs of a vulnerable population. An institution working under a mandate is frequently provided with pre-defined design choices by the mandating entity. The focus of these projects is on seeking the best and easiest way to reach compliance. When the release of a software update initiates a project, new gender data functionality in the campus's student and employee systems of record (SIS or HCM) is enabled by the information technology team with limited forethought on the business needs and human impact. Finally, and ideally, an institution can take a pragmatic *outside-in* and human-centred approach. This starts with understanding the needs of impacted community members, ensuring LGBTQ voices are included in design choices, and that they inform how changes are communicated and implemented with care. Regardless of the impetus for change, there is always room for incorporating human-centred design methods, including researching human needs, and developing change communications to improve trust, belonging and outcomes for LGBTQ community members.

Visioning and Organizing for Change

Statements about diversity and inclusion are often central to a university's mission and values. However, enabling a vision of gender inclusivity has broad implications and is only possible with the buy-in of executive leadership, who can prioritize and allocate campus resources toward the effort. While the starting point might be different, the case for change is often advanced by a coalition of motivated LGBTQ staff, students, and allies with the goal of a more inclusive campus. Providing their time and expertise voluntarily, such groups will invariably need dedicated and authoritative resources to make timely progress. The group will need to coalesce into a formally recognized working committee, such as a steering committee, under the auspices of an executive sponsor. An executive sponsor is frequently from the campus' Diversity, Equity, and Inclusion (DEI) organization.

Typically, this sort of committee will be divided into working groups responsible for making informed decisions about what gender data options to offer and how to responsibly manage the privacy and security of the data collected. Expert service design help will be needed in designing the necessary technology changes with change management, helping students understand

and feel comfortable entering their data in the student portal and practical support for faculty adjusting to pronouns on rosters. At the heart of this change is a vulnerable person trying to make sense of the world around them, navigating systems based on pre-set binary gender categories. Focusing on that person and understanding the world through their eyes is an essential first step in this fundamental paradigm change.

Understanding Gender and Gender Data

Gender is a social construct of norms, behaviours, and roles that varies between societies and over time, and often includes categories of man, woman, or nonbinary. Gender is frequently conflated with someone's *sex* (male or female) on a birth certificate or government identification record. *Sex* is associated with one's biology, hormones, and genitalia, while *gender identity* is one's sense of self and is not outwardly visible to others (Wamsley, 2021). Assumptions about gender are made based on a person's name (male or female sounding), appearance (*gender expression*) and presumed *sexual orientation*. However, gender is not binary, and gender does not inform someone's sexual orientation.

To be inclusive of all genders, we need new data elements that:

1   Describe *gender identities* beyond the male/female binary
2   Enable the preferential use of *lived names* in place of legal names
3   Support the sharing of *pronouns* to convey how someone wants to be addressed

With these three data elements in place, community members can feel seen gender-wise, have less fear of being *outed* by a system that displays their 'dead name', and experience less misgendering with incorrect pronouns. People on campus will have varying degrees of familiarity and understanding of gender data and will need to be considered and supported through change communications.

External Factors and Influences

There is growing socio-political discord about gender identity in the United States, including hundreds of legal efforts to dismantle DEI initiatives at educational and public institutions (Kelderman, 2023). There are also growing attacks on the LGBTQ community and laws aimed at restricting health services for transgender youth and adults in some states (Hassan, 2023). These negative forces impact people on a very personal level. Being 'othered' with ongoing fears of verbal or physical harm weighs heavily on someone's mind as they consider the risks and rewards of disclosing their gender identity (Parks, 2023). Additionally, executives at institutions in very conservative states may be reluctant to sponsor a gender enablement project unless mandated.

On a more positive front, Federal and liberal-leaning American states are normalizing and enabling support for a third "X" gender on passports and driver's licenses. However, gender-expansive data options will take years or decades to be generally recognized in private and public institutions. Today, no nationally agreed-upon standards exist for gender identity data options and pronoun sets. This space is evolving, and data elements and options will need to be revised over time.

Recommended Approach

> "I don't know what to do when I get continuously misgendered, and it seems inappropriate to correct a senior manager in a department meeting."
> Interview quote from a staff member who identifies as nonbinary

It is important to understand the context and influencing factors for a gender inclusivity project that are explored in the prior section. Once executive approval has been obtained and funding secured, a project team can be assembled to begin the work. Regardless of the impetus for the change, and based on the authors' experiences and expertise, the best practice for approaching a gender data enablement project is to be human-centred and follow a service design methodology.

Higher Education (HE) institutions generally find it very challenging to plan for and implement complex campus-wide and culture-impacting initiatives, especially those involving significant human, business, and technology considerations. The authors recommend engaging an outside service design firm that has the cultural competence and subject matter expertise to facilitate and navigate the project from problem framing, through research and design, to testing and implementation. A service design approach creates a framework for looking holistically and critically at a complex problem space and then facilitating the work to achieve essential outcomes on many fronts and for many stakeholders.

Frame the Problem Space

It cannot be overstated how important it is to get grounded in the identified needs, motivations, goals, and considerations for the project through interactive planning meetings with sponsors, the committee, and other key stakeholders. Individual committee members, representing many parts of the institution, will have different perspectives and ways of thinking about the problem. Individuals can include people focused on students and student services, on institutional data and reporting, and on LGBTQ issues and needs. Service design consultants are skilled at facilitating discussions and synthesizing inputs to gain alignment from the group on a 'how might we...' statement. For example:

> **How might we** thoughtfully and purposefully enable gender data in our university systems so that campus community members are recognized in campus settings by their appropriate gender in respectful and inclusive ways while also meeting institutional reporting, security, and privacy needs?

Designers, working with the project team, will develop a Design Brief that describes the research hypothesis, high-level questions, the target research subjects, methods and a plan.

Conduct Research

Research must be conducted across human, business and technology domains to understand the key factors that inform the final design and gender options. The design tension is in recognizing that what is *desirable* for community members may not be *viable* from a data governance perspective or *feasible* with the campus technology. For example, students have told us that they would like to specify by class if their pronouns appear on the class roster. This, however is very costly and challenging to design for and implement in today's student information systems.

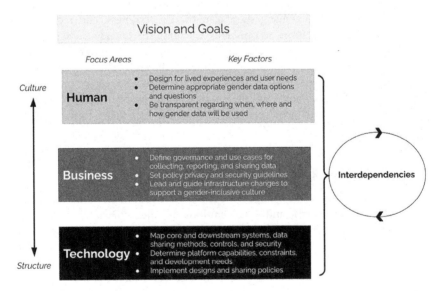

Figure 11.1 Designing for a Gender-Inclusive Campus

Understanding the Human Needs and Experiences

Researching the needs of campus community members is critical. One goal is to gather sentiments (positive, negative, and indifferent), from a broad audience to gauge how the planned changes will be received. This input can be collected effectively through surveys.

The most important goal, however, is to learn from individuals who identify as gender-nonconforming and who will be directly impacted. This research should be conducted through interviews, where researchers can learn about a person's goals, needs and motivations with 'why' and 'tell me more' prompts. As an external design consultancy, we have had success securing interviews by working with the client to send out invitations to students, post-doctoral fellows, faculty, staff, and alums through audience-specific channels. To reach impacted people, it will be important to engage with committee members who have trusted relationships in the LGBTQ community, and who can include personal messages to encourage participation.

The interview protocol must be thoughtfully developed to put the interviewee at ease and set the context by describing the purpose of the research, and the confidentiality of responses. Participants must be informed that they can opt out of any question or terminate the interview at any point. Open-ended questions developed from the design brief will guide the interview flow. Remember that asking vulnerable people to talk about their gender identity is very personal, and sharing stories about lived experiences can be trauma-inducing. It takes a skilled researcher to develop trust, put someone at ease, sense when the participant is stressed, and adjust the questions as needed.

Lastly, learning from faculty who will be asked to use pronouns in the classroom is essential. Anonymous surveys provide a way to get candid feedback on the initiative, and to hear their questions and concerns.

A Findings document should include analysed survey and interview data, anonymous quotes and personas or archetypes from the research as we could read in Chapters 14, 15, 16 and 17.

Determine the Business Needs for Data Governance

Business research must include a review of relevant policies and procedures defining how the new data will be classified from a security and privacy perspective and the institution's reporting and data governance needs. We recommend researching state and federal websites for relevant laws and policies to inform campus requirements. Peer institutions can also be a rich source of information, and good practice can involve reviewing website resources and asking for informational interviews. The project should produce an output from the business research in the form of a Data Definitions and Guidelines document describing and defining data governance of gender data, the classification of data elements, access controls, approved uses, and related policies and procedures.

Discover and Map Technical Considerations

A prerequisite for the project is the readiness of the campus' student and employee systems of record, (SIS and HCM), to support the collection of gender identity, lived names, and pronoun data. While service design focuses on improving human experiences, research must look end-to-end at the technical underpinnings and ask what-if and how questions to determine feasibility and business needs around data sharing. Enabling gender data elements is a whole system problem, and service designers play an essential role in facilitating the discovery of the ecosystem, mapping systems, and visualizing data flow. Universities and departments can have several hundred applications, each with different data sharing modes, unique purposes, and varying needs for gender data access. Assess the catalogue of systems, with the help of technical staff, to determine *where*, *why*, and *how* data flows from the primary systems of record downstream to various business applications. If lived names are being implemented, for example, it is critical that the institution knows which applications are consuming legal names so that an action plan can be made to transition them to lived names. Legal names will still be required for select applications and business processes, for example by payroll, taxes, financial aid, and travel services. Efforts should be made to minimize the sharing of legal names and provide appropriate training to personnel who have access to confidential data.

The recommended output from technical research is a comprehensive Systems Catalogue or assets database. For example, this can be a large spreadsheet, with a row for each system that includes its business function, a description, and users, with current and planned uses of name and gender data. We found it very helpful to create visuals describing how data flows from student admissions to the SIS, then through different data integration methods to downstream systems, like healthcare and housing applications. These visuals helped communicate complexities to technical and non-technical stakeholders and facilitated design decisions.

Design the Experience and Technical Requirements

Design, informed by data-driven research, includes developing gender data questions and selection options. *Wireframe* screen prototypes help visualize the proposed student and employee experiences as someone reviews, enters, and updates their gender data. Prototypes are shared with the committee in design critiques, where questions and input are solicited for future refinements and subsequent approvals of a final design. We recommend sharing the designs with a student advisory group – volunteers who are compensated for meeting periodically to provide input on the project.

An effective design visual for describing the future state is an ecosystem map of people, systems, and support functions. In the example, we depict gender-queer students in the classroom after pronouns have been added to class rosters and the students' expectations of faculty using them. This is made possible by the infrastructure and supportive changes on campus.

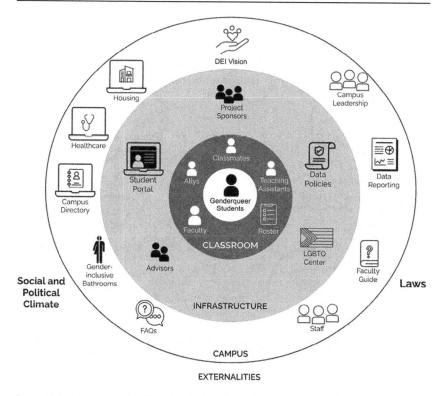

Figure 11.2 Ecosystem map, designing for gender-inclusive learning

The recommended output from this part of the design phase is a Requirements document for technical staff with data definitions, screen designs, and logic.

User Testing

Before implementing, it is essential to review the screens and workflow experience with students who may be impacted by the changes and who are unfamiliar with the planned designs. They will be experiencing the screens, options, and onscreen help for the first time. Setting up a test system with the technology team can be complicated and requires a lot of coordination. It is important to setup a test experience where the user logs on and sees their own information, not a generic test student's data, to avoid confusion, and negatively impact testing outcomes. Testers are instructed to complete a set of tasks, without hints, and to verbalize what they are thinking and doing along the way. Spoken thoughts can be enlightening and informed the development of Figure 11.3, depicting the many considerations going through a student's head as they contemplate selecting and saving their pronouns in the student portal.

Figure 11.3 Entering Gender Data, Risks and Rewards

Likewise, testers help you understand where instructions, options and navigation are challenging. The output of user testing includes a Test Results report and design revisions, as necessary. Without a student portal, and because the user interfaces and page navigation on student information systems (SIS) are often difficult to modify, desirable changes may not be possible, and instead be supplemented with onscreen help and links to reference websites.

Implementation

The project will likely need to be implemented in phases. For example, phase one could include the SIS and changing three priority downstream systems to support 1) sharing pronouns with instructors on rosters in the learning management system; 2) passing gender identity information for gender-informed housing assignments; and 3) sharing gender data with clinicians via the student healthcare portal. The data flows and impacts on each downstream system must be carefully planned for with the business owners and technical teams.

Here, the output will focus on monitoring the change and delivering change management content from the communications plan, including a faculty guide and student FAQs.

Key Findings

> "I still can't figure out what information they have for me and where."
>
> Interview quote from a transgender student

Understanding the Human Experiences

While the research must be extensive and include business and technical considerations, a key finding is understanding the human needs and experiences of gender-nonconforming people on campus. Following is a persona, Vivi, who represents a vulnerable person on any campus. Interview findings provide insights that inform the data Vivi needs, the screen designs for the student portal, and change communications that answer her vital questions and encourage participation.

Meet Vivi

Vivi is gender-nonconforming, identifies as a woman, and uses *she* and *they* pronouns interchangeably. At birth, Vivi's doctor recorded her sex as male on her birth certificate, and her parents gave her the name Victor. At an early age, Vivi understood and identified with a different gender than the one assigned at birth. Her journey as a college student has been fraught with difficulties, including coming out, being accepted by her family, and transitioning to a life lived as a woman. It was challenging for Vivi to find inclusive housing, a roommate, and a community of friends. She fears being outed or misgendered as a man, *dead-named* as Victor and abused by verbal or physical violence on an ongoing basis. Vivi embraces her female self and the community of friends she has met through her journey. However, suicidal thoughts and depression have been a constant for Vivi for many years.

Students like Vivi receive micro-invalidations of their identity daily and encounter cultural biases and structural systems that let them know they do not fit in. Enabling gender data helps make people like Vivi feel seen and that they belong, enabling the context for her to achieve her academic goals and to thrive.

Here, we must consider how to humanize Vivi's experiences with technology (Geuy, 2017). This illustration provides a glimpse into the many thoughts going through a gender-nonconforming student's mind as they contemplate entering their pronouns. This is an example of making the invisible visible that helps people not impacted by the change to empathize with the concerns of a vulnerable community member.

The Work is Complex and Nuanced

Institutions will underestimate the deep and extensive work necessary to implement gender data on rigid campus systems of record. The complexity comes from a lack of national or authoritative gender data standards, while at the same time, gender identity for students on campus is fluid and expansive. A gender data initiative has campus-wide implications, but oversight and execution do not naturally reside in any single division and require the input and expertise of many people. On a human level, gaining the trust of impacted and marginalized community members in interviews and as project advisors is critical. Here, service designers are skilled at navigating bureaucracies and working agnostically across areas to gain alignment in conducting research, synthesizing insights, leading decision-making, and communicating findings with stakeholders. Service designers are adept at bringing together stakeholders' inputs through visualizations and the final deliverables, helping people see the whole project and situate themselves in the solution.

Best Practice Recommendations

This section provides a compilation of best practice recommendations from experiences researching, designing for, and working with universities enabling gender data.

Organizing People for Project Success

A successful project will need many people with diverse perspectives and expertise. Success is contingent on the executive leadership team for funding, for communicating the institution's commitment to the project, and for escalations when roadblocks are encountered. A cross-department, working committee is created and aligned around the problem space and into functional sub-committees. Experienced human-centred design consultants help manage the project, conduct the research, and facilitate trade-off discussions with stakeholders when goals and desires cannot be easily met.

Gender Data Use Cases

Gender-nonconforming people have four primary needs around collecting and sharing their gender data.

1   For self-identification and receiving gender-appropriate services
2   To support personal interactions and campus communications that reduce incidents of misgendering
3   To support the desire for transparency and sovereignty around one's data
4   To gain visibility to the community in aggregate reporting and equity assessments

Data Privacy

Gender data elements have very different privacy and usage characteristics.

The data should be compliant with relevant campus policies and have the support of institutional research and data governance leaders.

Pronoun Options

When someone shares their pronouns, they are specifying how they want to be addressed in the third person and thus avoid being misgendered. Research and testing resulted in the following design that aims for easy-to-interpret and pronounceable pronouns on instructors' class rosters.

Pronoun options are grouped into *three sections* separated by dashed lines for ease of visual scanning. Students and employees can pick one option, i.e. a familiar pronoun set of *she/her*, etc., or a combination pronoun set with an "*or*" to signal either pronoun is acceptable, or a pronoun alternative.

Table 11.1 Gender Data Elements

Data Element	Privacy	Appropriate Uses of the Data
Gender Identity	Private	Gendered services, e.g. Student housing and healthcare
Transgender Status	Confidential	Aggregate reporting only, not shared
Lived Name	Public on campus	Use in all situations except where legal name is required
Pronouns	Public on campus	Class rosters and campus directory

Table 11.2 Pronouns Questions and Options

Question	Pronoun Options
What pronouns would you like to be addressed by? Select one (optional):	*Any* *He/him* *She/her* *They/them*
	He or She *He or They* *She or He* *She or They* *They or He* *They or She*
	Use my name *Please ask me about my pronouns*

Gender Identity in Three Questions

Research with gender nonconforming people asked what gender identity options the institution should collect and report on. 'No one needs to know my transgender status,' was an overwhelming response. However, the same interviewees were very interested in seeing aggregate transgender population data on their institution's demographic dashboards. This was an *ah-ha moment* for the team when we determined that transgender information should be collected separately, not shared with downstream systems, and only used for aggregate reporting.

The best practice is to ask about gender identity in three optional questions: 1) to allow individuals to fully express who they are by selecting multiple options; 2) to accommodate situations where only a single gender identity is supported by a downstream application; and 3) to maintain transgender status as a separate and confidential data element for aggregate reporting.

Institutional transparency on data usage is critical. It is critically important that the user interfaces for pronouns and gender identity data include answers to questions about *how, why,* and *where* the data collected by the institution will be used, given the associated risks to people disclosing personal information.

Design the Experience

Service designers consider the journeys and experiences documented in student personas, created in the research, as they engage with new gender data options

Table 11.3 Gender Identity Questions (3) and Options

Questions (3)	Gender Identity Options
1. Which best describes your gender identity? (select all that apply)	*Agenda* *Genderfluid* *Gender-nonconforming* *Genderqueer* *Man* *Nonbinary* *Questioning* *Two-spirit* *Woman* *Prefer not to say*
2. Selecting a single category to describe your gender identity (select one)	*Man* *Nonbinary* *Questioning* *Woman* *Prefer not to say*
3. Do you identify as transgender or under the trans umbrella?	*Yes* *No* *Unsure* *Prefer not to say*

in the student and employee portals. It is crucial to situate new gender data options (gender identity, lived names, and pronouns) on the same screen and in proximity with the person's demographic data (name, sex, date of birth, race, and ethnicity, etc.). Without customization, the student and employee systems of record (SIS and HCM) typically present gender identity, lived names and pronouns on separate screens. Navigating to these sub-pages is not intuitive, and the experience of entering and checking on options entered will be off-putting. A Profile Page is recommended for this purpose, which is easier to deliver on the student portal.

Outcomes

> "When I hear my pronouns, I feel seen and heard and that I belong."
> Interview quote from a nonbinary student

Outcomes are best examined against the best practice goals below and by looking at the impact on stakeholders.

Data Enablement

Implementing gender data creates the conditions for culture change and is the visible manifestation of an institution's inclusivity values. The project is costly to implement, however, and designs can take years to fully realize. Campus enterprise systems of record for students and employees are generally not designed with the user experience in mind. Delivering easy-to-use navigation with a profile page requires modifications to vendor software pages. IT organizations are reluctant to introduce customizations, like the three-gender questions, that must be maintained and tested with each new software release. For this reason, a phased approach is often necessary. We recommend adding pronouns and lived names first, with gender identity later, to positively impact daily interactions on campus.

Support Respectful Communications

Allowing people to self-identify with a lived name and pronouns, and then including them on class rosters and in the campus directory, creates the conditions for respectful communications on campus. Each incidence of misgendering is felt as a sting and a micro-invalidation by the person impacted. It detracts from their academic or professional experiences.

Research shows some instructors are reluctant, and many more need help to address students with the correct pronoun and to know how to recover from making a mistake. To support this change, offer workshops on creating an inclusive classroom and resources on using pronouns. When change management is designed and delivered well, anticipated pushback from faculty will be negligible, and the adoption of lived names and pronouns by students will be significant.

Data Security, Privacy and Transparency

Gender data elements each have privacy and security needs that must be established as part of the project. Impacted community members need to know why, how, and where their data will be used before they trust, feel comfortable, and participate in sharing their information with campus systems and the institution. Transparency is critical, which can be achieved through on-screen help, web resources listing where pronouns will be shared, and a feedback form. The potential for harm is great, if data is not protected and governed appropriately.

Representative Reporting

Institutions need aggregate data to report on which represents the various gender identities on campus, including the number and percentage of people who identify as transgender. This information supports decisions by campus leadership on allocating resources to support marginalized groups and DEI initiatives. The data may also be required by external grant requestors with diversity and inclusion criteria. Transgender folks on campus want to feel confident that their individual status will not be shared with downstream systems or outside entities. Research showed that while reluctant to add this information to their campus record, transgender community members strongly desire to be represented on campus dashboards.

Serve the Needs of Impacted Community Members

After years of advocacy, the power of seeing concrete institutional investments that allow for greater gender inclusivity cannot be overstated. It signals that everyone belongs. Serving the community means listening to their needs and lifting their voices through project artifacts that raise awareness and facilitate greater allyship. Our experience of undertaking these sorts of projects shows us that the impact on campus culture is difficult to directly measure but can be assessed anecdotally from the overwhelmingly positive feedback received from those involved in the project. Additionally, the small number of help desk tickets and the strong student response to entering their pronouns reflect the successful design. At one institution, 17 percent of students entered their pronouns in the first six months.

Key Learnings

> "It is so clear that your goal is making changes for students. I have never felt so centred in it."
>
> Emailed quote from a member of the Student Advisory Group

I Design for the Few, Impact Us All

HE institutions have a lot of competing demands on resources. It can be argued that a gender data project is costly and only benefits a few. This thinking discounts the overall benefits of well-being and respectful communication on campus. Lived names provide people with a way to designate a Western name when studying abroad, however it is problematic option for people preferring to be known by the name from their own culture (Warwick University, n.d.). Lived names also provide a way to maintain anonymity for someone trafficked or in an abusive relationship and clarify preferences when names or appearances do not signal the person's gender. There is an analogy here with *sidewalk curb cuts*, designed to help wheelchair users; they also benefit people with strollers, luggage, the elderly, delivery drivers and all of us (Sheridan, 2021).

2 Design with the Dimension of Culture

Designers' tools and methods are used to research human needs within a particular context and to design better experiences for these needs. A gender enablement project creates structural changes, without which cultural conflicts are perpetuated, and gender continues to be defined as binary. You cannot escape the fact that you are designing for cultural outcomes and that there is no perfect solution that everyone will embrace. *Systems thinking*, and the framework of an iceberg (Cababa, 2023) is an excellent way to get beyond the visible 'events and patterns' of a problem space and into the invisible 'structures, culture and vision'. It is essential to map stakeholders, look for cause and effect loops, plan for unintended consequences, and include this thinking in your design.

3 Design for Social Impact: it is the Most Important Work You Will Do

Rarely do you get the opportunity to develop and advocate for designs that improve the lives of vulnerable people. Immersing yourself in the research and being curious and empathetic with the people you meet, can and will impact you profoundly. Research reveals the challenges that some must navigate regularly, and the harm done. We recognize that well-designed findings and storytelling can sway hearts and minds, drive change initiatives, and positively impact practices on campus. The power of a gender data enablement project is that it shatters the binary structural construct and starts to normalize the breadth of gender identities present in society. Be an ally. We challenge the reader to push against the forces that want to perpetuate the status quo and do your bit to create a culture of belonging, for everyone (Wise, 2022).

References

Brown, A. (2022) About 5% of young adults in the U.S. say their gender is different from their sex assigned at birth. *Pew Research Center*. Available at www.pewresearch.org/fact-tank/2022/06/07/about-5-of-young-adults-in-the-u-s-say-their-gender-is-different-from-their-sex-assigned-at-birth (Accessed: 7 June 2022).

Cababa, S. (2023) *Closing the loop: Systems thinking for designers.* New York: Rosenfeld.

Geuy, B.*et al.* (2017) '*Humanizing the Organization through Digital Experiences*'. Cincinnati: International Association of Societies of Design Research.

Hassan, A. (2023) States Passed a Record Number of Transgender Laws. Here's What They Say. *The New York Times.* Available at www.nytimes.com/2023/06/27/us/transgender-laws-states.html (Accessed: 18 November 2023).

Kelderman, E. (2023) The Plan to Dismantle DEI. *Chronicle of Higher Education.* Available at www.chronicle.com/article/the-plan-to-dismantle-dei (Accessed: 18 November 2023).

Parks, C.*et al.* (2023) Most trans adults say transitioning made them more satisfied with their lives. *Washington Post.* Available at www.washingtonpost.com/dc-md-va/2023/03/23/transgender-adults-transitioning-poll (Accessed: 23 March 2023).

Sheridan, E. (2021) The curb cut effect: How universal design makes things better for everyone. *Medium.* Available at https://uxdesign.cc/the-curb-cut-effect-universal-design-b4e3d7da73f5 (Accessed: 3 September 2023).

Trevor Project. (2022) The Trevor Project's 2022 National Survey on LGBTQ Youth Mental Health found that 45% of LGBTQ youth seriously considered attempting suicide in the past year. The Trevor Project. Available at www.thetrevorproject.org/resources/article/facts-about-lgbtq-youth-suicide (Accessed: 27 August 2023).

Wamsley, L. (2021) A guide to .gender identity terms. *NPR.* Available at www.npr.org/2021/06/02/996319297/gender-identity-pronouns-expression-guide-lgbtq (Accessed: 18 November 2023).

Warwick University. (n.d.) Say my name. https://warwick.ac.uk/services/dean-of-students-office/community-values-education/saymyname/research (Accessed: 18 November 2023).

Wise, S. (2022) *Design for Belonging.* Ten Speed Press, California.

Chapter 12

Intelligent Automation

Integrating human-centred design thinking into an Automation Service

Jennifer Robertson

Introduction

The art of the possible

What you would think if you were told you could recruit a team who could take away the monotonous, low value but high-volume activities of your service? What would you think if that team could also reduce errors, reduce backlogs and work at times that fit into your service model saving thousands of hours in time per year to reinvest into value-add activities? Let's go on a journey and explore how this might be possible by embracing Intelligent Automation and Artificial Intelligence (AI), specifically Robotic Process Automation (RPA) deployments as a precursor to more transformative AI solutions.

Leading edge early adopters such as retail banks and energy providers are using Intelligent Automation technology at an enterprise level, globally adopted, demonstrating scalability, stability and security. These early adopters have shared lessons learned by trial and error and provide best practice for other sectors considering Intelligent Automation. This provides institutions with a wealth of experiences and examples to demonstrate and de-risk some of the barriers to adopting Intelligent Automation providing a solid foundation to build on.

The University experience

As institutions plan for an improved, responsive University experience of the future, Intelligent Automation has the potential to form part of our standard service offering. Students are able to access resources such as banking, energy and other external support services via highly automated, responsive self-service entry points that are low friction, accessible and available on demand. There is an expectation that a similar experience should also be available across their academic career. The British Government has set out a clear agenda to use technology as, '... an effective tool to help reduce workload, increase efficiencies, engage students and communities, and provide tools to support

DOI: 10.4324/9781003383161-21

excellent teaching and raise student attainment' (Department of Education, 2019, p. 2). How do we as Higher Education practitioners ensure that we retain the core principle that services are human-centred, ensuring we maintain the 'human in the loop'?

This chapter explores the journey that the University of Glasgow has been on. It considers how creating an Automation service enables the University to become more efficient and effective. It considers how approaching this service from a human-centred mindset takes staff and students on the journey using human-centred design principles and methods. A set of guidelines are proposed, based on the lessons learned so far, for other institutions considering embarking on their own RPA journey.

I was part of a small team leading the Automation Proof of Concept, from early 2022, to establish the case for an Automation service. I am now Head of Automation at the University of Glasgow and have been leading the creation and development of the Automation Service since January 2023. I lead a small automation team and am supported by a strategic partner, working with the internal team as they grow and develop their expertise and experience.

What do we mean by Intelligent Automation?

Intelligent Automation has been adopted at scale by a handful of institutions in the UK to date. At time of writing, a simple search to identify which institutions are using automation provides limited results. This is a new area, but there are examples of how automation is benefiting universities across the globe, demonstrating how a slow adoption of automation could 'contribute to higher tuition, frustrated students, educator flight and missed education opportunities' (Walker, 2023).

Intelligent Automation is an umbrella term. There are multiple ways to use the different technologies under this umbrella and the opportunities and benefits are growing and developing at pace:

- Automation covers things like document ingestion through computer vision, natural language processing as well as forecasting models that could be used across multiple activities and processes such as timetabling, examination planning and enquiry management.
- Large language models are a specialism of AI and cover any language model such as Amazon Alexa and Google Translate. They can be used across multiple student touchpoints, available 24/7 and accessible from any location.
- Generative pre-trained models or GPTs cover things like Open AI Chat GPT and Google Bard. At time of writing, this is a very popular technology that can be used in multiple learning and teaching settings, but also carrying multiple challenges from ethics through the way assessments are designed.
- Robotic Process Automation (RPA) is used for work flow automation which covers the bulk of automation opportunities and is able to orchestrate other technologies.

The choice and possibilities Intelligent Automation offers are far reaching. This chapter will focus on RPA across supporting and administrative services. It does not explore the use of automation across learning and teaching or research areas. RPA may also be referred to as a 'virtual worker'.

What do we mean by a virtual worker?

RPA is accessible, has 'relatively low barriers to personal usage and has the potential to be applied across multiple service settings' (D'Souza, 2023). When exploring the opportunity of RPA as a service tool at its most basic level we start by asking the question:

What does a member of staff or team do today that is keeping them away from more focussed, value add activities?

RPA can be brought in as a 'virtual worker' to complete those tasks by using technology to give time back to the staff member or team.

In plain terms, the service asks; *if you could employ someone tomorrow to lift the work that gets in the way, what would you design your virtual worker to do?*

Figure 12.1 Humans at the centre of automation choice and selection

Why RPA?

Higher Education Institutions are large, complex organisations with multiple processes, departments and specialist areas. Making changes and/or organising services across this landscape can be challenging. The University of Glasgow identified Intelligent Automation as an opportunity to address some of the challenges. The service focusses on three main problems to fix:

Problem 1: Resources are stretched

Resources are locked in transactional activity; we need to unlock time to focus on students and research. Staff need to be able to respond to enquiries and other daily demands, but also need the time to review and develop their services. They need more time to focus on the student experience, offering service excellence but don't have the space to do this, often focussing on this activity 'at the side of their desk'.

Problem 2: Need to do more with less

Staff are being asked to do more with the same or less which is creating additional burden, backlogs, burnout and frustration. The student community is constantly evolving, with increased student numbers, changing demographics and expectations and there are multiple changes to the way our staff work and complete tasks.

Problem 3: Difficult process landscape

Sub-optimal processes, customisation and systems do not allow agility to respond to market changes quickly. Data can be inconsistent, processes are not streamlined, there is duplication of effort, multiple hand-offs, backlogs and this all impacts the student and staff experience.

RPA offers a tactical, relatively quick solution that can provide support and help to staff working in high demand, high pressure services. It can help achieve efficiencies and faster turnarounds that can improve student and staff experiences, providing more streamlined access to services, information and decision making.

RPA is not going to fix all the issues, nor is it necessarily going to be the long-term solution, but it is an option to provide the breathing space and support to staff and students at critical points across the academic year. When the right processes are identified and RPA is used as the right solution, there is an opportunity to consider RPA to streamline and improve services.

The University of Glasgow Automation Service

The Automation Service is new and has been operating, post-Proof of Concept, since January 2023. To date, the service has delivered virtual workers across multiple areas including:

- **Learning and Teaching:** Automation of student extension requests
- **Human Resources:** Automation of the staff recruitment process
- **Admissions:** Automation of the student agent process

Feedback on the service so far has been positive and teams are keen to engage with the service:

- "Where we had lots of people doing slightly different things, this has made it much more consistent, and we know the process is now exactly the same for every transaction. Consistency across the whole of process has been improved".
- "We can see the benefits with team members being able to take on other pieces of work and projects that they just would not have had the capacity to do when they were processing this high-volume task manually".
- "The bot not only saves staff time, but it improves student experience and is allowing us to review process data to help offer more proactive support for our students in the future".
- "Due to the automation of this process, the business team was able to define the optimal way this process should be carried out".
- "Fantastic to be able to drive this on behalf of other Colleges, as I think this will help all of the Research Support teams".

What happens on an automation journey?

Each automation experience is unique, but the service is broadly organised across the following framework, inspired by the Double Diamond methodology (Design Council, 2023):

Discover: The service meets with service owners and subject matter experts to understand the current state. We identify any areas that can be improved as part of the automation solution and/or any blockers that may lead to part of the process being automated but not the full end-to-end process.

Design: The service creates the automation solution. This is done in partnership with the subject matter experts, and they are partners across the full automation lifecycle. This includes daily stand-ups and an active role across testing and user acceptance testing.

Deploy: The service delivers the automation. Teams are fully supported across a 'hyper care' stage where we ensure the solution does what we anticipated and make any fixes that may be needed. We then move to an 'adoption support' phase which is a bit like an induction for a new member of staff. We support the subject matter experts to understand what they need to do if things go wrong, how support is organised and how to ensure they are supported to own and realise the benefits of automation.

The importance of human-centred design: design the right thing and design the thing right

Services, at their core, are human-centred. Ideally, they are designed with people, for people, to enable outcomes that enhance and deliver experiences to 'get things done'. A strategic driver for the Automation Service is to understand and be aware that while a key driver for automation is value, the longer-term impact is more human and has the potential to realise much more than time or cost savings.

Approaching automation from a human-centred mindset anchors the benefits of automation to be driven by how they benefit humans. RPA replicates what the human is doing. This approach ensures, from the start, any RPA decision is challenged by asking the question 'are we automating for the sake of automation or because this will make a difference to teams/employees' (Babb, 2023).

To embed this thinking across the automation service the focus is on the what, when and why we use virtual workers:

- **Why are we planning to use RPA?** What benefit will this bring to staff and students? How does this improve/evolve a service and/or process and what positive difference might it make?
- **What will we be automating?** Just because we can automate it, does not mean we should automate it! Consider the process from the end user perspective: how will this solution improve/change the user journey? Will there be a positive impact and where do we need to ensure we design in human interactions? How complex is the process and is RPA the best solution?
- **What is the value of doing this automation?** Ultimately, the automation should enable a change that improves a service/experience and provides a measurable return on investment (ROI). Will there be fewer errors, will time to respond improve, will there be more time given back to staff to focus on more complex tasks, will there be a reduction in cost?
- **The unintended consequences of automation.** We need to think through the impacts that may occur that are unplanned and unintended and be ready to mitigate them. For example, does reducing the lapsed time in a process give the end-user time to fully engage? Does it erode confidence that their application or request has been duly considered?

Rather than looking for opportunities that need 'RPA', it is about looking at service pain points and issues where automation might be an option to consider during the ideate stage of our design process. By embedding the above approach, the service challenges each solution to ensure the right choices are being made and that solutions will provide a positive impact.

To bring the service to life, the next section of this chapter provides a case study of a delivered automation.

The story of an automation: Student extension requests

Students can request extensions to their studies of up to 5 days, based on criteria/rules defined by academic policy. There can be thousands of these requests per year. The criteria are the same, but the way requests are handled differs across Colleges and sometimes at a School level. Requests can be submitted by email, in person, on the phone and through the University helpdesk system. Students may ask for a request from different staff members and the approval of requests is allocated to different staff members, depending on the approach that College/School uses. Owing to the volume of requests, at peak times this can become a full-time activity.

How did automation help?

The Automation service initiated a discovery activity within a University College to understand the problem. By starting in this way, we were not focussed on the solution, but on what the actual pain points and issues were. We ran workshops with the teams who delivered the process, organised one-to-one interviews to gain a deeper dive understanding on the current state and ran some 'service safari' events, where we watched the staff and students who delivered and used this service. We were able to identify:

- There was no central place for students to make their request.
- Staff did not have easy visibility on the requests at an individual student or course level.
- There were long waiting times in some areas.
- Staff working on requests were not able to focus on other activities, leading to additional backlogs or a need to work additional hours.
- No standardised approach existed across the College, and Schools were approaching this activity in different ways.

Moving from current state to solutions

Once we had a better understanding of the current situation, we were able to focus on how and if RPA would be able to help. RPA could help, but for the most effective user experience, we identified that the solution should be embedded in the Virtual Learning Environment. This meant students and staff could access a solution in an environment they were familiar with, located in the same space a submission would be made for the assignment they were requesting the extension for.

The next step was to agree where to start. This was a big change to the way things had been done so it was agreed that we should prototype the solution before we scaled it. This was important because to get the best out from a solution there was a necessity to streamline the process so that all Schools within the College followed the same approach.

We had a wicked problem to overcome:

> Custom and practice over time had led to wide variation in how this process was delivered. A key by-product of automation is that by its definition it drives out standardisation. However, when faced with multiple stakeholders all claiming their process was essential, we needed a creative approach to achieving consensus.

The solution:

> We created a low friction, standardised process as a starting point before designing the RPA solution. As a next step we created a prototype with a single School, tested it, iterated it and then demonstrated it was a success. This was done in partnership with the teams delivering this service so they could see the prototype in action and visualise how their needs would be met. By approaching the solution in this way, we removed the barriers to adoption and the College took ownership of their new virtual worker as a joint endeavour.

Impact: Did it make a difference?

At time of writing the extension request automation has (per year):

- Saved c.1,000 hours and processed over 5,500 student requests in one School, as the solution scales to handle even more requests the projected benefits will be much higher.

The solution provides:

- A reliable and consistent data source that the School is able to use to inform the proactive monitoring of the student experience such as (i) identify students who may be making multiple requests, so that additional support can be provided as soon as possible; and (ii) courses that may be receiving a high proportion of requests indicating that the assessment design may have unexpected issues for students.
- The opportunity for the College to create dashboards that staff can use to better support students and plan assignments and submissions across courses.

The automation is now being scaled across all Schools and Colleges using the same standardised process. At the start of this journey, we were not able to get agreement on one way of doing things. After creating a prototype, developing and enhancing it based on user feedback we were able to create a solution that was adopted by all because we could demonstrate that it worked!

The next section of this chapter will reflect on some of the challenges to date, the conclusions from the journey so far and share key learnings.

Automation Service: Some of the challenges

- **Current state:** before we automate a process, we need to understand how things are currently done. We have experienced some challenges including the same thing being delivered differently by multiple teams & services. For RPA to be most effective we need to streamline and have one shared process to enable scaling. Getting multiple teams and services to agree to one approach can be time consuming and difficult to gain agreement on.
- **Staff time:** to create effective RPA solutions, it is important to take subject matter experts on the journey. Staff are focussed on their day job and asking staff to attend workshops, complete user testing and sign off on solutions can be difficult to organise and prioritise. This is a critical element to get right. RPA will only work if you have access to the subject matter experts who can design and own the virtual worker. We have developed our service communications to provide an estimate of the time and effort needed to take an automation forward and contract with service areas to ensure the time and commitment is ready. If not, we come back later and move to the next automation in the pipeline backlog.
- **Data:** getting access to reliable data to create baselines can be difficult. To understand what benefits we may realise from an RPA, we need to understand the current situation, validated using service data. This includes metrics like workflow, throughput, time to complete tasks and annual variations. We have seen some variation in the benefits we anticipated and the benefits that we realise. We are working together as a team to design methods to enable higher confidence and reliability in the baseline data we have access too.

Impact of RPA

1   The change management aspect of using virtual workers and how this is communicated to staff and teams, must be carefully managed, especially the message that this is not about headcount reduction but freeing up time to focus on more complex and value add activities.

2   With the ownership of the solution and realisation of the benefits by service owners, there is a delicate balance to be struck so that the automation service is not seen as a tool to reduce head count. When automation is used to improve efficiency and effectiveness, business areas need to take ownership on how they will use the time, cost or other benefit savings to improve and maximise their service offerings.

3 We need to be cognisant of the impact on our technology and policy landscapes and how that affects our work with supporting services like IT services, infrastructure, security and data protection. These stakeholders need to be consulted and included as part of the adoption journey. These are new technologies which challenge services to consider new approaches and ways of doing things that may not be as thoroughly tested or as understood as more familiar, established solutions and approaches. Blockers can be experienced, and the adoption of automation can be at risk of being slowed down if engagement and partnership working isn't agreed early on the journey, endorsed and encouraged at a senior level.

Conclusion

RPA provides an exciting opportunity for institutions to identify pain points across multiple services and processes and can provide a quick solution in partnership with service owners and subject matter experts. It is a business-led process and provides a unique opportunity for service teams to be involved from ideation to implementation, across the full automation lifecycle.

The end goal is not to automate as much of a service as possible, but instead create a hybrid service that uses RPA for repeatable, rule-based tasks, freeing up service teams to focus on more value-add activities. The service is driving the adoption of new tools and technologies for the future of work. This helps to develop skills and mindsets across the institution encouraging us to think about what we do and how we deliver our services as part of our day-to-day decision making.

Key learnings

1 **Start with a proof of concept, design in collaboration:** use a PoC to illustrate the benefits of working with subject matter experts across the design journey to create solutions that are embedded and adopted by service teams, rather than them have a feeling of being 'done to' by subject matter experts. Bring the teams, staff and students who deliver and use the services on the journey to ensure that the pain points, issues and challenges are understood and planned for, not worsened, misunderstood or over-looked. Acknowledge that RPA is a business-led initiative not technology-led.

2 **Be transparent and explainable, safe and secure:** the virtual worker's activity, purpose and reason for existing should be clear and easy to explain. This includes ensuring that any data and privacy aspects are clearly communicated and understood. RPA should be designed to be inclusive and ethical. Work with internal specialist teams to ensure that RPA features on your technology roadmap and is integrated into data protection, privacy and academic policy design and requirements.

3 **Design with a clear purpose and benefit(s):** identify early on what the benefits of the automation will be, how they will be measured and realised. Ensure that the service owns the benefits and uses them to enable improved user experiences. Don't lose sight of the longer-term benefits that reach beyond time and cost savings, and continuously ask: *what difference will this make to teams and employees,* don't solely lead with how much money will this save.

References

Babb, B. (2023) What is Human Centred Automation? Available at: www.pipefy.com/blog/future-of-work-human-centric-automation (Accessed: 15 November 2023).

Department of Education. (2019) Realising the potential of technology in education: A strategy for education providers and the technology industry. Available at: https://assets.publishing.service.gov.uk/media/5ca360bee5274a77d479facc/DfE-Education_Technology_Strategy.pdf (Accessed: 15 November 2023).

Design Council. (2023) Framework for Innovation. Available at: www.designcouncil.org.uk/our-resources/framework-for-innovation (Accessed: 19 September 2023).

D'Souza, D. (2023) Why artificial intelligence in OD is the new frontier of change. *People Management*, August-October 2023, 21.

Walker, J. (2023) Higher Education and Automation! Available at: www.linkedin.com/pulse/higher-education-automation-jim-walker (Accessed: 15 November 2023).

Section 4

Student Experience

Foreword

Sue Morrison and Jacqui Jackson

Most students study a degree once, possibly twice, in their lifetime. Students have a range of expectations about their university experience. They may be motivated by passion for a subject, unlocking career opportunities, meeting new people, expanding horizons, making a difference to the world around them or a natural next step after school or college. Whatever their motivation and intentions, going to university is a big step with potentially lifelong consequences. Universities have a responsibility to provide opportunities and experiences that meet – and ideally exceed – expectations. The more we consciously design curriculum, services and opportunities with a student-centred approach, the less is left to chance in the experience and outcomes for students. So, how do we design to meet the needs of students, now and in the future? We live in a complex and changing world, the expectations of students entering university evolve and every student has their own, unique experiences and goals. How do we shift from rhetoric and assumption to adopt an evidence-informed, empathetic approach to design?

Student-centred design requires understanding of the expectations, feelings and motivations of students and the impact of their diverse lived experience on their learning. This book takes the reader though the research underpinning an evidence-based approach to human-centred design and forms an accessible and informative introduction to student-centred and inclusive education design. It is valuable for policy and practice, curriculum and service development.

Sue Morrison, Programme Director for Curriculum Nottingham at the
University of Nottingham

As a business owner and Honorary Teaching Fellow who fully embraces the opportunities Human-Centred Design can bring, for me this book represents an exciting leap in reshaping Higher Education (HE). In the world of academia, where student and staff experiences drive success, this book emerges as a real catalyst for change which can ultimately help drive business forward.

Human-centred design isn't just a methodology; it's a requisite tool in both Business and HE and is the conduit that aligns institutions with the evolving needs, aspirations and challenges faced by learners and educators.

This isn't merely theoretical jargon. This book is a practical handbook, illustrating how human-centred design principles can overhaul services, curriculum

DOI: 10.4324/9781003383161-23

design and the overall educational experience. Its relevance extends beyond educators and managers; it's invaluable for anyone invested in HE – from tutors, advisers and administrators to the very students they serve.

By advocating for a human-centred approach, this book empowers us to create learning environments that nurture creativity, inclusivity and innovation. It's about not just adapting to change but actively driving it.

Jacqui Jackson, Director, Thomas Jardine & Co

Chapter 13

Warwick Secret Challenge

Design thinking for re-imagining student engagement

Bo Kelestyn

Introduction

The dynamic of student engagement with their education and university is transforming; demanding more participatory approaches where all parties can be equal partners in engaged learning (Healey et al., 2014). Students place more value on universities being able to identify and solve problems that are 'felt viscerally' by the student body (Dickinson, 2020). The increased diversification of student cohorts (Mercer-Mapstone & Bovill, 2019) is another driver for change, demanding diversification of institutional approaches to student engagement and student voice. Homogenising data and compounding the student experience, driven by rankings and quantitative measurements of student satisfaction, conceals the true nature of issues such as the black degree awarding gap (Greaves et al., 2022). As such, there is a need to shift away from a focus on capturing retrospective quantitative data to a more proactive and participatory approaches with an emphasis on qualitative data that seeks out heterogeneity of lived experiences.

New tools for decision making, problem-solving and ideation have been created in the business and digital realms to reflect the complexity and uncertainty brought about by the accelerated levels of innovation and change, which old management tools could no longer speak to (Ries, 2011). These tools are also relevant for the Higher Education (HE) context. Applying design thinking, one of these new tools, to student engagement proposes new and exciting areas of innovation and research (Dunne, 2016). Design thinking appears in several papers, including Snelling et al. (2019) and the recent special issue of the International Journal of Management and Applied Research, led by Nerantzi et al. (2023), but the methodology has not fully been operationalised for wide use in the sector.

Used for student engagement, as part of a wider student voice portfolio and traditional data capturing methods (such as student-staff liaison committee, student voice panels and groups, student barometers and surveys), it creates a new space outside of the formal structures of the university and the Students' Union, and the tensions associated with these structures (Kelestyn

DOI: 10.4324/9781003383161-24

and Freeman, 2021). This chapter focuses on the Warwick Secret Challenge (WSC), a model based on design thinking principles and tools, which reimagines student engagement and creates several distinct benefits including increased diversity, active creativity around policy and experience design, community building and skills development. As the creator of the WSC, I will position the Challenge as a novel conceptual model for engaging students as partners in the co-production and co-creation of their experience and their institutions.

What is the Warwick Secret Challenge?

The University of Warwick achieved a Teaching Excellence Framework Gold standard in 2023, with co-creation having a prominent role in the overall success of the institution. In 2017, however, the University was less successful, with a Silver award, and a range of projects were conceived to boost the visibility and consistency of the three (at the time emerging) Education Strategy pillars: Student Research, Internationalisation and Interdisciplinarity.

When it came to the latter, a wide range of definitions, approaches and relationships existed across the institution with its devolved departmental structures. Students' understanding of and relationship to the Interdisciplinarity pillar was not well articulated or understood. It was important to change this to support student engagement in this area, build their sense of community and belonging in relation to the University (and not just their department and discipline) and to boost their overall interdisciplinary learning experience. As part of the project to ensure students have a larger stake *in* and a stronger sense *of* interdisciplinarity at Warwick (led by the Institute for Advanced Teaching and Learning (IATL) and funded by the Warwick International Higher Education Academy (WIHEA), I was selected to lead the project as a student project officer. As a doctoral researcher specialising in teaching and learning design thinking, I pitched a design led co-creation workshop idea to the project steering group. I designed it as a contained experience for the student participants that would boost engagement with the project while giving students an opportunity to learn about design thinking and collaborate with other participants different to them.

It was very important to invite as many different viewpoints and perspective as possible into this process. As a student myself, I envisioned the WSC becoming a way to democratise leadership opportunities. Existing and more traditional student voice opportunities (e.g. Student-Staff Liaison Committee or Sabbatical Officer within the Students' Union) can be quite intimidating and often not equally accessible to all students. This was my own experience, especially as a busy postgraduate international student. Design thinking and the shorter WSC experience seemed a powerful way to democratise access to student leadership, allowing students to engage with university innovation challenges in a way not seen before at Warwick.

The project steering group, comprised of students and Warwick's key Interdisciplinarity experts from IATL and WIHEA, played a pivotal role in shaping up and approving the workshop design. After a few discussions with the project steering group to ensure the workshop was inclusive and met the project aims, the WSC and its key premises outlined in this chapter were born. I defined the WSC as a method for exploring and responding to university innovation challenges with students as equal partners. At its core, I saw it as a problem-solving workshop with elements of design thinking, used as an effective tool for student engagement and learning experience enhancement and as a complementary approach to some of the more traditional methods of capturing student voice. At Warwick, the creation of the WSC in 2018 was the first discipline agnostic, student-centric, student engagement experiment with design thinking.

Mixing design thinking with student engagement

Design thinking, which I learnt about in the context of studying management and digital innovation at Warwick, jumped out at me as having a lot of relevance to student engagement and student voice. The focus on the human, user, student, etc. was at the core, despite being seemingly unrelated domains with significant differences in language. In both innovation and student experience, co-creation generally leads to better solutions and more diversity in thinking about the problem. It is more likely that the intended audiences will embrace solutions because they have co-created them, rather than simply validated an idea at the final stages of its development.

In the application of design thinking within the WSC, design thinking is considered as both a mindset and a process. This was a key part of my pedagogy when teaching and learning design thinking because it allowed me to create temporary spaces for creative thinking, to help think differently and reconsider the problem in a different way. The WSC from the beginning has been about creating temporary spaces where experimentation, and therefore tolerance to failure, ambiguity, willingness to be more creative, are invited and celebrated even if only for a few hours. Challenging entrenched ways of doing things in HE requires thinking differently, calling all involved to become authors of the change (Grabill et al., 2022). Design thinking allowed students and staff involved to be more courageous, to look at the ordinary to see the extraordinary.

Another aspect of my pedagogy that influenced the WSC, was viewing design thinking as a social technology (Liedtka, 2018), defined as a blend of tools and insights applied to a work process. This elegant conceptualisation allows us to rethink and democratise the use of design thinking. It somewhat lowers the barriers and removes the need to arrive at 'the perfect outcome', to practice design thinking 'perfectly' and to be part of the selected few with the expertise to be able to do it.

Adding a touch of secrecy

This distinctiveness also needed to be reflected in the identity of the workshop. In the early stages of the WSC, it was an experiment, a one-off, making both the designing and the naming less risky and easier to buy into. The student members of the project steering group led on the selection of the challenges for the initial three workshops. Broadly speaking, these were focused on: Coventry City of Culture, sustainability and entrepreneurship, employability education. These challenges helped to align the design thinking workshops with the Interdisciplinarity focus of the project but risked attracting a student persona interested in the specific challenge. It was decided to keep the challenge a secret until the very last minute to prioritise attracting diverse students. The name *Warwick Secret Challenge* was born:

- 'Warwick' was important, as it allowed for the experience to be connected to the wider university identity and be rooted in the needs of the community, but at the same time without foregrounding words like 'education', 'policy' or 'student experience', keeping it open and unbiased towards a specific topic or agenda.
- 'Secret' became something that made a difference to the overall experience and the impact of WSC. The challenge itself was intentionally kept a secret so that participants attracted to the workshop could make a more objective decision when deciding to join a problem-solving activity. This way the Challenge appealed to a more diverse student population, as opposed to appealing to business, economics or engineering students when advertising, for example, a sustainability and entrepreneurship challenge. Those kinds of topics, if advertised upfront, could be connected to disciplines, particularly where students derive their identity from their departments.
- The 'Challenge' was something intended to be exciting to the students, who are often focused on and motivated by creating impact and being problem-solving-oriented. In the description of the experience, 'Challenge' was where the emphasis was placed. Something that was the easiest for students to understand and be drawn to, considering the secrecy of the rest of the workshop experience.

So, students would be signing up to a problem-solving experience without really knowing anything about the challenge they would be working on.

Proof of concept and first lessons

After the initial three workshops as part of the Interdisciplinarity project, student feedback was very positive. As part of the experience, students were more forthcoming with their feedback, views and ideas, their very authentic visceral experiences on the topic. This was partly the effect of me, a student facilitator, leading the workshops at the time. And by doing so, equalising some of the dynamics that can exist in more traditional feedback mechanisms such as focus groups. The Interdisciplinarity project WSC insights exceeded expectations and were not seen before in any other source of student voice and student engagement. Students saw the WSC as an opportunity to learn new skills, experience an exciting problem-solving activity, meet other people, contributing to the feeling as part of a community. The students felt they could do something different, felt their voice was important and felt as if they were a part of the broader innovation culture within the University. Those early experiments with the WSC demonstrated clear wins for both the staff and student communities within the University. The next step was obvious: test the methodology on an institutional challenge.

The first institutional innovation challenge

The first institutional WSC explored the digital student experience, commissioned by the newly appointed Director of Innovation. The open-ended nature of the WSC presented the Challenge to the participants very broadly ('Digital student experience @ Warwick'). This openness was a source of some frustration with students often accustomed to and wanting more clarity in their learning experience. The ambiguity was intentionally baked into the experience to allow participants to construct and build the definition of digital experience bottom up, to uncover themes and pain points. The methodology of the WSC applied to the institutional challenges had two intended outcomes:

1 Uncovering student creativity, ideas and suggestions as *outcomes* of design thinking
2 Capturing student insights from discussions and reflections in the design thinking *process*

For example, mapping out the digital student experience led to several distinct student-led problem reframings, challenging the assumptions of staff commissioning the Challenge. One candid student quote highlighted the need for more constructive student engagement in university's digital transformation, which often takes place behind the curtain:

> "Students understand the internet and digital media better than people developing it."

The institutional Challenge was presented to the participants with the rationale, and some context of the strategic push and pull forces influencing the University (e.g. change of leadership and strategy with the arrival of the Director of Innovation). This openness had a positive impact on the candour of student feedback. When asked whether participants had a positive digital experience at Warwick, no

Figure 13.1 Student Challenge roadmap

student participant said 'yes'. Not only did the WSC surface this trend, but it also presented insight into the reasons for negative student experience and ideas about how to tackle those. Several students stayed behind to ask questions about the University and enquire about further opportunities to feed into innovation efforts. This was based on their positive WSC experience and the introduction of the reason and rationale for exploring the digital student experience.

- 78 per cent said that the workshop met their expectations,
- 100 per cent would like to see more similar workshops,
- 93 per cent would recommend the workshop to their friends.

This was a powerful finding that led to a hypothesis that:

- Students that take part in a WSC get exposed to the backstage activities (Stickdorn *et al.*, 2018), insights and university decision making in a very unique way.
- The design thinking experience engages them with their university in a way that generates curiosity for further opportunities, shifting student openness to participate in co-production (Penin, 2018) from passive to a more active engagement.

In turn, these insights and facilitated design experience give students a more pragmatic and holistic understanding of what goes into creating the experience they are on the receiving end of, creating longer-term ripples in their learning, including about design. On the staff side, especially those in non-student facing roles, engaging with students through design is a powerful and tangible reminder of the messiness but also excitement of innovation in HE.

In total, in this first instance of tackling an institutional challenge, 45 student participants took part across two workshops of three hours each, generating eight student presentations and ideas. These were presented to various stakeholders and led to the commission of another Challenge which resulted in the redesign of the University's module and course catalogue (Kelestyn & Freeman, 2021). Students taking part in the initial institutional Challenge were invited to take part in the module catalogue Challenge and were informed about their impact via email and university newsletters.

Towards a replicable methodology

Since then, and especially during the pandemic, the WSC continued to iterate beyond its initial design. Although scalability was not something I thought too much about in the early days, the purpose and DNA of the Challenge was carefully thought out. When zoomed out, the distinctiveness of the WSC is based on these key premises:

1 Adopting an open-ended problem statement, presented as the focus of the Challenge, prevented participants from converging on a solution too fast and created more authentic engagement with the brainstorming activities. Students were encouraged to bring their discipline, expertise and skills to the Challenge. This process helps to develop a shared and comprehensive understanding of the Challenge rooted in each student's experiences.

2 Keeping the Challenge a secret allowed us to advertise to and attract students from all disciplines, study levels and background and helped to maximise cognitive diversity.

3 Connecting with the Warwick Award (formerly known as the Warwick Skills Portfolio Award) gave students an additional incentive to attend and to develop their skills. The WSC has been designed to first and foremost deliver value to students.

4 Maintaining transparency in introducing the Challenge as an ongoing institutional innovation project was important for clarity. The facilitator remains clear and upfront about the challenge, as well as the use and value of student input.

5 Working with University 'client' teams helped us to define the challenge and frame it in a way students can easily relate to. This also required the facilitator to have some background knowledge of the Challenge.

Zooming in on the design of the workshop, I designed it with the experience of the student participant at the centre, which can be broken down into three key parts:

a   Introduction to WSC and design thinking – which includes an overview of the workshop, house rules and some guidance on giving and receiving feedback such as I like/I wish (Kelley, 2018a). This is followed by the introduction to the concept of creativity, a creative exercise, usually the 30 Circles Challenge (Kelley, 2018b), and an activity to help students develop team coherence fast using tools such as the team CV, an A3 handout with headings that students might typically see in a CV (e.g., skills, experience, interests, education). While mapping out experiences relevant to problem-solving, students get to know each other.

b   Introduction to the Challenge – design challenges for the WSC are intentionally open-ended. Although it is, at times, frustrating for the students to work on a very broad problem (as shown by patterns in student feedback), this helps get a richer student viewpoint on the challenge and allows students to define and frame the challenge in relation to their experiences. In a single workshop, a group of 30 students can generate around six problem framings (about six teams of five students) and more than six ideas to tackle the problems in the experiences identified. The process of framing and reframing the problem (IDEO.org, 2015), especially where discussions are captured, allows participants to deep dive into the positive and negative elements of the student experience that are invisible to the existing student voice mechanisms such as surveys or focus groups.

c   Design thinking mini-sprint – which can be customised based on the logistical constraints such as time, space and mode of delivery. It usually consists of activities that can be easily explained and used by beginners such as mind maps to map out the challenge by each team; storytelling to generate patterns across diverse student experiences; abovementioned re(framing) of the challenge; empathising and digging deeper into student experiences; and ideating. Student teams then present ideas and solutions and vote on the best solutions and presentations. The WSC is concluded with a small prize-giving.

All of these key steps are led by one or two (where possible) student facilitators, trained in design thinking and the basics of facilitation, as well as briefed on the details and context of the Challenge by a relevant University team. As the methodology evolved beyond just my involvement, student facilitators are presently selected out of Warwick Innovation Fellows. This role has been inspired by the University Innovation Fellows programme of Stanford University's Hasso Plattner Institute of Design (d.school), which seeks to empower students to be agents of change in their departments and faculties (Hasso Platner Institute of Design at Stanford, 2023b). At Warwick, they are embedded within the Warwick Enterprise team, which is a central team that supports student innovation and entrepreneurial activities.

The process of commissioning and running a WSC can further be broken down into several stages, nested within the Stanford d.School or the Hasso Plattner Institute of Design (2023a) five-stage design thinking process of Empathise, Define, Ideate, Prototype, Test, which the WSC is built on:

1 Recruiting and training student facilitators (Empathise, Define)
2 Commissioning of the Challenge (Empathise, Define)
3 Stakeholder engagement I: data analysis, challenge framing, recruitment (Empathise, Define)
4 Logistics and preparation (Define, Prototype)
5 Stakeholder engagement II: recruitment, engaging departments (Empathise, Define, Ideate, Prototype)
6 Delivery of the Challenge (Empathise, Define, Ideate, Prototype, Test)
7 Data analysis and collation (Define, Prototype)
8 Stakeholder engagement III: reporting, disseminating, implementing (Define, Prototype, Test, Empathise)
9 Stakeholder engagement IV: Student facilitator reflection and participant data collection and follow up, if needed (Prototype, Test, Empathise)

The scaling of the WSC

The first replication of the institutional challenge became 'wellbeing in relation to the teaching and learning environment'. Still new and not well understood at the time, the WSC was getting interest predominantly from staff and teams close to the initial Interdisciplinarity project. In the case of the wellbeing WSC, it was commissioned by IATL, where the WSC was incubated, looking to push the boundaries of student engagement with one of their projects. Due to the complex and sensitive nature of wellbeing, traditional approaches could miss crucial parts of student wellbeing stories. Staff members did not lead the workshops due to the potential for bias or influencing students. Students leading and facilitating these workshops were more likely to help student participants feel relaxed, understood and heard, generating authentic and candid insights that were both quantitative and qualitative in nature. In the instance of the wellbeing WSC, design thinking was used alongside focus group interviews as part of a University-wide research and student experience project. This iteration for the first time included both staff and students in the same workshops. This risk paid off and allowed staff to experience the WSC, creating some positive buzz around the methodology. The success of the wellbeing WSC then led to further iterations that touched on different parts of the University's strategic priorities such as internationalisation and the creation of a global and connected campus.

At this stage, the impact of the student facilitators became better understood. Leading the process across its all stages, the student facilitators' unique position allowed them to 'translate' the institutional challenge into student facing language or contextualised in a way that student participants could better connect with. This also includes facilitating the workshop to support student participants through making the most of the design thinking activities. In turn, student facilitators would then share insights from the WSC with the University team or individual who commissioned the challenge. The student facilitators leading the WSC were also tasked with condensing and crafting WSC insights, presenting them to staff in an easy to understand, actionable, professional, but also visceral way. As a result, this double 'translation' became a key part of why the WSC has re-imagined student engagement at scale across Warwick.

What worked well?

First, co-creation and student centredness was already at the core of how many Warwick educators think, helping to make the case for design thinking when adopting the methodology. Getting that initial buy in from colleagues can be a challenge because design thinking can look and feel so different and unfamiliar to something like a SSLC or a focus group. Empathy and human centredness, starting points of design thinking, are fundamental touchpoints between design thinking and HE (Dunne, 2016). This message was and continues to be a key part of the WSC identity, as well as a helpful guiding principle on the use of design thinking for re-imagining student engagement at Warwick.

Design thinking is about designing *with*, not just *for*, making it a bottom-up approach to innovation. It is very much about the students and the intended audience. The 'nothing for/about us without us' continues to be a message in student engagement with their institutions across campuses all around the world. And that really is meaningful because with design thinking, students are given that voice and are at the centre in terms of co-creating in the process, but also deeply rooting any solutions and decisions in their needs and evidence that is often hidden with other sources of data. "There's no such thing as a 'normal' user" (Downe, 2020, p. 162), or in this case student, and the WSC allowed us to explore heterogenous ideas and experiences, instead of collapsing them and generalising using more traditional quantitative sources of innovation insights in HE.

Design thinking has also been shown to have tremendous power to contribute to student employability and skills. Engaging in the process does something to participants; the process changes the innovator (Liedtka, 2018). Facilitating a Challenge is about creating a temporary space where students can show up as themselves and become innovators, even if temporarily. Students get to learn about design thinking as a skill, get to practice it and walk away from a co-creation activity having learned something new, not just having shared their feedback.

And finally, there is community. The WSC has had an impact on students as a contained interdisciplinary opportunity where they can meet new people and engage in the wider conversation about their experience. Design thinking has the power to impact on how students (as well as any staff participants) feel as part of the university, their sense of belonging and their ability to see themselves as part of the wider learning community, not just their course, department or faculty (Barile & Kelestyn, 2023). This is also fundamental for capacity building to ensure the longevity of design thinking projects (Stickdorn et al., 2018).

What could be improved?

Within the WSC and its related time constraints, opportunities for prototyping and testing are limited. While small 'stealth' or 'island' projects (Stickdorn et al., 2018, p. 456) are a recommended way to get started with design, in the case of the WSC, the one-off nature created a flaw that did not honour the latter stages as much as it ought to. This had to be rethought in later experiments with different and more extensive formats. These have been successful, engaging more than 70 staff and students over two-week sprints. More work however is needed to understand the right timing, length, incentives and challenges to engage all parts of the University at a scale where prototyping, making and testing are essential. The reality is that the WSC is constantly competing with many other opportunities and priorities in busy student lives.

Diversity, although positively impacted by the secrecy of the WSC and openness of design thinking, can always be enhanced. Making the WSC even more accessible and making sure that all students are aware of the opportunity, find it interesting and engaging is important and continues to be the focus of innovation with design thinking at Warwick.

The WSC could also be better at closing the feedback loop. There are still unanswered questions to ensure consistency of communication within the methodology, especially as it is getting used and iterated on by other teams across the University and around large institutional change projects that take longer than the average student experience/lifecycle. Design thinking helps to close the feedback loop better than some of the more traditional tools, but the methodology should be viewed as part of a portfolio of tools and efforts. Including and formalising guidance on the use of such a tool within the wider University co-creation strategy and toolkits is something that is starting to positively impact consistency over time and across disciplines, while also giving the methodology room to grow and innovate. Using the WSC as a complementary methodology, alongside other data capturing and ideating, can help to close the loop faster and can also help with buy-in and a more sustainable implementation and scaling of the methodology.

Finally, making sure the right tools are being used, taking the best of design thinking, contextualising it for HE and learning from institutions is an ongoing effort at Warwick. This would not only get more colleagues and teams excited, familiar and comfortable with using design thinking, but would also contribute to the overall development of student experience by design across the sector. Be it small or big, every experiment with design thinking for student engagement contributes to the development of the collective toolkit and mindset, and we need to seek out opportunities to share and learn more. After all, design thinking is 'borrowed' from other domains. As it becomes a more widely accepted and used methodology within Warwick, maintaining the humble beginner mindset inherent in design will be the litmus test for authentic uses of design thinking.

Generating buy in for the WSC and getting people engaged in and excited was possible due to the small-scale nature of the initial experiments that ended up growing into a bigger, albeit slow, cultural shift. Design thinking applied to student engagement saw students become more open to joining the dialogue with their University in a different way; in ways that meet them 'where they were at' and that help students express those 'visceral feelings', facilitated by design thinking tools that honour individual storytelling (Kelestyn & Freeman, 2021). With more iterations of the WSC and over time, the perception of design thinking is shifting from being a novelty to a methodology for routine student-staff innovation, becoming less about the particular tools used and more about the mindset that spills over into all parts of how the institutions runs and how people across its complex hierarchy relate to each other.

What's next for the WSC

At Warwick, design thinking has opened a new kind of dialogue, reframing what student and staff expertise mean. The methodology continues to evolve and adapt to the overall institutional, as well as specific departmental, context developing an internal library of experiments while learning from others externally.

Further embedding of such design-led and informed methods demands fresh thinking and candid feedback. The next steps will focus on moving away from just one-off experiences of design thinking, to learning from continuous activities that change the culture, embedding the values and cognitive skills that come with design thinking into everyday practices for all students and staff across the institution. Experiments with the institution-wide two-week long Warwick Employability Challenge (Reid & Kelestyn, 2022) and the Warwick Sustainability Challenge (Barile & Kelestyn, 2023) acted as prototypes and tests for further design thinking experiments.

Key learning points

1   Design the experience *with*, and not just *for*. Design thinking has the power to shift student engagement with their university from bystander to agent of change/activist. Shifting these perceptions is akin to cultural

shifts. It takes time and requires small and frequent experimentation, coupled with an open ongoing dialogue with all stakeholders.

2   Continue to iterate and share. Colleagues looking to implement design thinking into their work should seek to explore a range of tools and methods, not being afraid to pick and choose, as well as pivot away from the aspects that do not work for the individuals and the institution. The methodology should be seen as a guide, not a dogma, at least in the early experiments. Colleagues should seek to be open about the challenges and lack of answers (even about the methodology) with students and staff and invite them to co-create in ways that honour their time and personal growth. This will not only help make any efforts truly aligned with the principles of design thinking but is also a great way to think about scalability from the onset. After all, it is the community that will be implementing and embedding any innovations that may come from the applications of design thinking.

3   The medium is the message. Play with the uses of design thinking and its related experience, including the identity of any activities. Seeking out empathy for the student and staff experiences requires a level of discomfort and ongoing work. Radically caring about the experience in the workshop and during the co-creation activities, regardless of how short that may be is what will either spark or put out the excitement about institutional innovation.

References

Barile, L. & Kelestyn, B. (2023) Using Design Thinking to Create Sustainable Communities. *International Journal of Management and Applied Research*, 10(2).

Dickinson, J. (2020) Wicked Problems: (How) Does Higher Education Solve Problems for Students? *WonkHE*. Available at https://wonkhe.com/blogs/how-does-higher-education-solve-problems-for-students (Accessed: 6 March 2023).

Downe, L. (2020) *Good Services. How to Design Services that Work*. Amsterdam: BIS Publishers.

Dunne, L. (2016) Design Thinking: A framework for student engagement? A personal view. *Journal of Educational Innovation, Partnership and Change*, 2(1).

Grabill, J. T., Gretter, S. & Skogsberg, E. (2022) *Design for change in Higher Education*. Baltimore, MD: Johns Hopkins University Press.

Greaves, R., Kelestyn, B., Blackburn, A. R. & Kitson, R. R. A. (2022) The Black Student Experience: Comparing STEM Undergraduate Student Experiences at Higher Education Institutions of Varying Student Demographic. *Journal of Chemical Education*, 99(1), 56–70.

Hasso Plattner Institute of Design Stanford. (2023a) An introduction to design thinking: process guide. Available at https://web.stanford.edu/~mshanks/MichaelShanks/files/509554.pdf (Accessed: 17 December 2023).

Hasso Platner Institute of Design at Stanford. (2023b) University Innovation Fellows. Available at https://universityinnovationfellows.org (Accessed: 6 March 2023).

Healey, M., Flint, A. & Harrington, K. (2014) Engagement through partnership: students as partners in learning and teaching in higher education. The Higher Education Academy. Available at www.heacademy.ac.uk/system/files/resources/engagem ent_through_partnership.pdf (Accessed: 3 June 2019).

IDEO.org. (2015) Frame Your Design Challenge. Available at www.designkit.org/m ethods/frame-your-design-challenge.html (Accessed: 17 December 2023).

Kelestyn, B. (2021) Get Started Using Design Thinking in Higher Education with These 10 Steps. Available at https://uoeeduinc.blog/2021/10/04/get-started-using-de sign-thinking-in-higher-education-with-these-10-steps (Accessed: 6 March 2023).

Kelestyn, B. & Freeman, R. (2021) How to Design Our Way to a Better Future. *WonkHE*. Available at https://wonkhe.com/blogs/how-to-design-our-way-to-a -better-future (Accessed: 6 March 2023).

Kelley, T. (2018a) Build Your Creative Confidence: I Like, I Wish. Available at www.ideo. com/journal/build-your-creative-confidence-i-like-i-wish (Accessed: 17 December 2023).

Kelley, T. (2018b) Build Your Creative Confidence: 30 Circles Exercise. Available at www.ideo.com/journal/build-your-creative-confidence-30-circles-exercise (Accessed: 17 December 2023).

Liedtka, J. (2018) Why Design Thinking Works. *Harvard Business Review*. September –October. Available at https://hbr.org/2018/09/why-design-thinking-works (Accessed: 6 March 2023).

Mercer-Mapstone, L. & Bovill, C. (2019) Equity and diversity in institutional approaches to student–staff partnership schemes in higher education. *Studies in Higher Education*, 1–17.

Nerantzi C., Hammersley, J. & Lopez, I. (2023) Uncovering people centred design in the context of curriculum and learning design in higher education. *International Journal of Management and Applied Research*, 10(2), 81–91. Available at: https:// doi.org/10.18646/2056.cfp010 (Accessed: 27 July 2023).

Penin, L. (2018) *Designing the Invisible. An Introduction to Service Design*. London: Bloomsbury.

Reid, E. & Kelestyn, B. (2022) Problem Representations of Employability in Higher Education: Using Design Thinking and Critical Analysis as Tools for Social Justice in Careers Education. *British Journal of Guidance and Counselling*, 50(4), 631–646.

Ries, E. (2011) *The Lean Startup*. Portfolio Penguin: London.

Stickdorn, M., Lawrence, A., Hormess, M. & Schneider, J. (2018) *This is Service Design Doing. Applying Service Design Thinking in the Real World. A Practitioners' Handbook*. Sebastopol, CA: O'Reilly.

Snelling, C. A., Loveys, B. E., Karanicolas, S., Schofield N. J., Carlson-Jones, W., Weissgerber, J., Edmonds, R. & Ngu, J. (2019) Partnership through co-creation: Lessons learnt at the University of Adelaide. *International Journal for Students as Partners*, 3(2), 62–77.

Chapter 14

Service Design in Education

A mindset towards Inclusive and Accessible Learning Experiences

Kim Anderson and Christopher Sze Chong Lim

Introduction

Inclusive design is an approach to design that considers the needs of the widest possible audience, exploring and examining similarities – but also differences – to inform design decisions. When we think of inclusive design there are many examples that probably come to mind in physical environment, visual, product or even the service design space. When we do not use an inclusive design approach within these spaces, we can unintentionally exclude people from them. Inclusive design and service design are both human-centred approaches that complement each other and can be brought together to create inclusive experiences. But what about education and learning, how can we use service design to ensure that we are creating truly inclusive and accessible learning experiences for as many people as possible? We have brought our combined knowledge and passion for inclusive design together alongside our experiences as design educators in both Higher and Further education to explore the impact that service design could have on learning experiences. In this chapter we explain what inclusive design is, where accessibility fits within it and why it's important in education, while answering the question "How can service design inform an inclusive design approach to learning and teaching?" through two praxis-based case studies.

Universal Design, Inclusive Design and Accessibility

You might have heard the term Universal Design or Inclusive Design and might have used either word interchangeably in your practice? Universal design is a term coined in the 1900s by Ron Mace, a disabled American architect who because of his own experience of finding it difficult to access buildings and environments using his wheelchair decided to produce a set of principles to support better design for all people not just disabled people (Null, 2013). Universal Design is defined as 'design of products and environments to be usable by all people, to the greatest extent possible, without the need for adaptation or specialised design' (Coleman *et al.*, 2003, p. 13). Essentially,

DOI: 10.4324/9781003383161-25

Universal Design calls for a single solution to reach the broadest range of users possible and is underpinned by the seven design principles (Coleman et al., 2003, p. 13) which are: 1) equitable use; 2) flexibility in use; 3) simple and intuitive use; 4) perceptible information; 5) tolerance for error; 6) low physical effort; and 7) size and space for approach and use. Everyday examples of how Universal Design principles are implemented include single lever faucets, signage that has both graphics and braille included, and curb cuts where wheelchairs users, parents with prams and travellers with luggage benefit from transition between roads and pavements.

Inclusive Design is the UK expression for Universal Design. In Europe, Design for All (as well as Inclusive Design) is also used (Coleman, Bendixen & Tahkokallio, 2003, p. 290). The British Standards Institute defines Inclusive Design as 'The design of mainstream products and/or services that are accessible to – and usable by – as many people as reasonably possible ... without the need for special adaptation or specialised design' (BSI 2005). Inclusive Design is very much about including people with disabilities and the consideration of other aspects of human diversity including language, culture, gender and age that may affect use of a product, service or environment. Inclusive Design is also a design process that involves end-users' participation right from the start of a project; however, this may not involve disability depending on the project and user or stakeholder group.

Accessibility refers to designing and creating environments, products and services (physical or digital) that have no barriers to prevent interaction or access to them. Accessibility is enforced by legislation, for example in the UK, the Equality Act 2010 ensures that people are not discriminated against because of a disability, including access to goods, facilities and services. Beside direct discrimination, failure to make a reasonable adjustment is also a form of discrimination. For example, if you have difficulty reading your bank statements in standard print, you should be able to ask your bank to send the statements in your preferred format. If your bank refuses or continues to send you information in a format you cannot read, they have then failed to meet reasonable adjustments. In relation to the Universal Design principles, the bank has not provided perceptible information to its customer by not providing essential information legibly.

Inclusive Design and accessibility work together, in the Inclusive 101 Guidebook (Microsoft, 2016a) Microsoft describe Inclusive Design as the approach, and accessibility as the attribute. An experience cannot be inclusive if is not accessible and vice versa. For example, you could have a technically accessible form on your website, but it may contain language or terminology that exclude some people. In this chapter, when we refer to inclusive design, we talk about a wide spectrum of human differences/attributes and accessibility (some of which are shown in Figure 14.1).

It is however important to note that accessibility is very important in its own right, and most educational institutes will have their own accessibility standards

Figure 14.1 The approach of inclusive design

or guidelines to help support the creation of accessible learning experiences. These are typically based on existing digital standards which means that they often give guidelines or examples for making digital files and online platforms accessible. This can lead to a learning experience being disjointed when only some aspects of a learner's journey have been built with accessibility/inclusion in mind.

Why is inclusive design important in learning?

According to the World Health Organisation an estimated one in six (or 16 per cent; about 1.3 billion) of the world's population experience significant disability (World Health Organization 2023). This means that the individual will have a severe physical, cognitive or sensory impairment that limits their ability to function independently in the family or community or to obtain, maintain or advance employment.

Of course, not all disabilities are apparent, the Hidden Disabilities Sunflower Scheme estimates that 80 per cent of disabilities are invisible. The UK Parliament POST on invisible disabilities in education and employment highlighted that students with invisible disabilities are less likely to disclose their disability than those with physical disabilities (particularly on admission) or identify as disabled (UK Parliament POST, 2023). The briefing further reports that according to the 2021 National Disability survey, lack of awareness, understanding and stigmatisation is a major issue for people with invisible disabilities as this creates barriers for them in their interactions with others as well as access to services and facilities.

Inclusive design can benefit everyone because we can all experience exclusion at some point. That is because inclusion or exclusion are not fixed states, and the degree to which we each experience barriers can depend on the situation and the context. This can be demonstrated through the spectrum of temporary, situational or permanent barriers (Microsoft, 2016b). For example, captions on video content could benefit learners who might have an ear infection (temporary), be studying in a noisy environment (situational) or have a hearing impairment (permanent).

Points of exclusion or barriers can exist because services were created based on assumptions. Kat Holmes (Lindberg, 2018) said, 'The things we make reflect our own biases'. This can also apply to the learning experiences that we create as we each hold different unconscious biases based on our own individual experiences. These biases can lead us to make assumptions that can get in the way of creating inclusive learning experiences. We can unintentionally exclude people when we make assumptions about abilities, what we know about other types of people, and the thoughts or behaviors of others. Some ways that these assumptions could show up in education are the use of confusing language or terminology, lack of gender inclusive language or limited instructions on how to use a digital platform.

We all experience the world differently and that includes how we experience or interact with products, services and learning. When we acknowledge that we each have our own biases and assumptions we can begin to appreciate different perspectives of the same experiences. Learning about differences is a way that can help us to avoid some of these common biases and prevent us from making assumptions as we create learning and teaching experiences.

Universal Design for Learning

In the 1990s researchers at the Centre for Applied Technologies, in Massachusetts, proposed three principles that make learning more inclusive (Meyer, Rose & Gordon, 2014). The first principle is providing *multiple forms of representation*. This means showing or presenting content flexibly by using several different mediums, for example, text, images, diagrams, videos etc., so that learners can find the content accessible.

The second principle is about providing *multiple forms or means of expressions*. This involves allowing learners to show what they know about what is being taught. Learners for example, who are dyslexic, have cerebral palsy or experience language barriers will approach learning tasks differently with some expressing themselves well in verbal communication or presentation but not in written work or vice versa. Allowing learners to leverage their expressive strengths in demonstrating what they know is thus important in deciding if they have met their learning outcomes.

The third principle involves providing *multiple means of engagement*. Learners can become frustrated or disengaged during their learning journey and start to withdraw from learning. Some might not even initiate a first attempt at engaging if they are not interested or find that the task too challenging. To engage learners, we need to consider their interests, challenge them appropriately and support continuous learning by encouraging sustained persistence and effort. Indeed, service designers are also encouraged to design for engaged behaviours by thinking carefully how to create more motivating services by enabling service users to 'do' or interact (and continue to interact) with the services designed (Bisset & Lockton, 2010). In the context of inclusive learning, there are several factors that influence an individual's motivation and engagement to learn. They include personal relevance, background knowledge, learning and instructional environment, peer learning and ways to actively process what they are learning, for example, reflecting and writing on their learning experience, monitoring their own goals for what it is they have to learn and their progress or achievements. This involves engaging with values, benefits and knowledge structure of the service experience.

UDL thus allows students (and educators) to assess how they are engaged in their learning process, allows them multiple ways to access information and new and innovative ways to express their learning. UDL is more than accessibility, it is about enhancing learning and expanding the learning opportunities of a wide diversity of learners which includes not just the students but staff as well. It is important to plan for and address learner diversity and being responsive to the needs of all learners. This means that the institution of learning is responsive too, ensuring that academic support services (e.g. Disability services) can help students and staff to embed UDL into their learning and teaching.

These principles are a good place to start when thinking about how to make your learning and teaching experiences more accessible and inclusive and have been shown to improve the learning process of all students (Capp, 2017).

Case studies

UDL and Service Design are two concepts that share a common goal of improving user experiences and inclusivity. By integrating UDL principles into the process of Service Design, we can create services that are universally accessible and responsive to diverse user needs. For example, when designing a service, UDL principles can inform the consideration of multiple means of communication, providing alternative formats or channels for information delivery and accommodating various modes of interaction to ensure accessibility and engagement for all users. In the following two case studies, we will share how UDL in the context of Inclusive Design and the mindset of service design was used to design and deliver learning and teaching experiences.

Case Study 1: Applying Service Design Mindset and UDL in the teaching of a Design module

'Changing Populations' is a four-week design module taken by students from the Product Design, Design for Business and Design for Healthcare Masters programme and led by one of the authors. The module is about students rethinking the role of design and designers in contemporary society through the lens of Inclusive Design which emphasises the inclusion of broader social groups in the design of products, services and environment. The context of this module revolves round the phenomena of societies throughout the world that are ageing rapidly and will do so for the next 40 years. This brings a big societal impact that is unprecedented in human history and in response, design can contribute to the wellbeing and quality of life of older people and people with disabilities. Central to the module's learning outcomes is the introduction and application of a user or people-led approach rather than a designer-led approach in design. As an educator, adopting a service design mindset is helpful in considering how best to improve the student learning experience and achieve the intended learning outcomes.

Challenge of directing and supporting individual's motivation and engagement to learn

In Stickdorn and Schneider (2010) *This is Service Design Thinking*, Bisset (p. 302) posed the question whether we need to more clearly conceptualise, visualise and question our motives behind the service we provide and the motives of the stakeholders or users who use the service we design to understand and 'energise and direct' people's behaviour. As an educator (and wearing the hat of a service designer) delivering a module (as a service) for the learner (who is a stakeholder of the experience and user of the service), motivation plays an important role as it is required to understand, regulate and support human behaviour when designing and experiencing the service. 'A good service clearly explains its purpose' and '... users with no prior knowledge must understand what a service will do for them and how it will work' (Downe 2020). Bringing this into what and how we teach, the intended learning outcomes, is the purpose of the service (i.e. module) and to motivate and support students in achieving their learning outcomes, we need to consider appropriate learning and teaching methods or strategies that encourages a deep approach to learning. Factors that encourage a deep approach to learning (Entwistle, 1981, 1988, 2000; Ramsden, 1987; Biggs, 1999) that also align with the UDL principle of engagement are: 1) linking course content to real life; 2) relating new and previous knowledge, ideas and knowledge; 3) focusing on knowledge and ideas needed to solve a problem in familiar or unfamiliar contexts; 4) organising and structuring content into a coherent whole; 5) allowing students time to reflect, room for making mistakes without penalisation and rewarding effort made in learning; and 6) planning and using activities and task that requires students' active participation.

What did we do?

To move students into the 'intrinsically motivated' space (see Figure 14.2.), it is important to give students briefs that relate to real world / life challenges. For example, project briefs were formulated in collaboration with charities such as Versus Arthritis or a condition like Multiple Sclerosis. To encourage "engaged behaviour", people with lived experience are invited to give students an insight into their lives. Students would work closely with volunteers to understand their needs and wants, generating ideas and developing prototypes with and for the volunteers to respond to and give feedback on. By going through this process, the student learning experience is then 'empathetic' and 'authentic'.

To support students in their learning experience, students with disabilities are encouraged to register with Disability Services to ensure individual support from disability support officers and educators. Universities under the Equality Act 2010 are required to make reasonable adjustments in anticipation of – and in response to – disabled students' needs and must ensure that disabled students are not

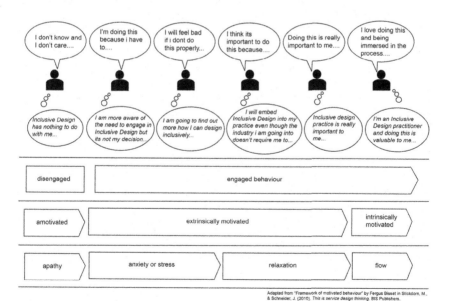

Figure 14.2 Framework of motivated behaviour for learning

treated less favourably than other students for reasons relating to their disability. Information around what support is needed can be accessed by lecturers and reasonable adjustments are usually around teaching and assessments, for example students needing to record lectures, have presentations available before the lecture starts or been given extra time during written examinations.

To ensure that UDL principles are considered when planning and delivering the module, personas of disabled students are created as an aide memoire to avoid making assumptions on the needs of students. Disability support information for each disabled student is mapped onto the UDL principles of representation, engagement and expressions. This process aids the educator in visualising how the adjustments are related to the UDL principles and helps seed any further ideas or actions that are required by the tutors to ensure that the needs of students and the intended learning outcomes are met (see Figure 14.3).

Where did we get to?

Engaging with the persona and reflecting on the journey this student might experience led to an iteration of the module's learning plan to support the adjustments and learning outcomes. Learning activities or 'touchpoints' such as lectures, workshops, practical work sessions, tutorials and independent work were re-adjusted and woven into the learning journey so that new knowledge and skills learned from the module (and combined with what was learned from other modules and from their disciplinary background) can be used to respond to the brief. These *multiple means of engagement* supporting a deep learning approach and providing multiple options for engagement are important as there is not one optimal means of engagement that will suit a diversity of learners.

Part of *engagement* is about providing *multiple forms of expressions*, allowing learners to show what they know about what is being taught. To this end, students are given two deliverables to assess whether they have met their intended learning outcomes. One involves an individual design response work assignment and the other a reflective report which covers a set of tasks with learning reflections that informs both the students/assessor if they have fulfilled the learning outcomes. As students who undertake this module are from Product Design, Design for Business and Design for Healthcare Masters programmes, the different disciplinary backgrounds of the students need to be considered. The individual design response work assignment allows for *multiple forms of expressions* through a combination of portfolio and presentation to show critical thinking, creative process and development. This further helps support the idea that learning is a journey. In addition, portfolio allows learners to document their expressive strengths in a tangible way, leveraging their interdisciplinary knowledge and skills in response to the brief.

The potential drawback of using the persona to iterate the curriculum is that any considerations are only as good as the quality of information you have received. In one case, it was not made clear in the disability support information

ASHLEY (pronouns: she/her)

22 year old, female illustration graduate

Ashley graduated with a first class honours in illustration from University School of Art. She is studying in the Design for Business programme because she is interested in business models, strategies and marketing and wants to explore new opportunities where she could apply both combine business and illustration skills. She enjoys business challenges and being part of a team.

(taken from personal statement and expectations of the course)

Multiple forms of representation

Ashley would benefit from having her module timetables in advance of the module commencing, or as soon as possible and it would be beneficial for her to have this as a list or PDF as due to her difficulties with visual processing, she struggles to follow this on My University.

Ashley will benefit from the use of clear and concise language. This should be undertaken discretely and without drawing attention to Ashley in front of others.

Audio recording of lectures should be permitted in line with University recording policy. Lecture material/alternative adjustment should be provided in teaching situations when audio recording is not permitted e.g. when other students have not given their consent to be recorded in classes that involve substantive student participation.

Tutor's Actions

- Timetable as a list and in PDF. To be given in advance at least a week before the start of the module

- The written language used in module guide, lecture slides or notes given must be clear and concise

- Audio recording for lecture to be expected

- For group discussion ask consent for audio recording

- Online lectures or video recording of lectures to have subtitles

Multiple forms of engagement

Ashley should be provided lecture material in advance if not on My University. Ashley may be unable to attend her classes at times due to her disability and should be provided with any missed material.

Questions should be presented in a clear manner and the meaning explained if necessary. This should be undertaken discretely and without drawing attention to Ashley front of others.

Verbal instructions to be confirmed in writing. Ashley should not be asked 'on-the-spot' questions in classes without preparation time.

Presentations and Group work to be discussed with Ashley in advance to determine any support needed.

Ashley is taking medication which impacts on their ability to wake in the morning and as such, may miss morning sessions at university. Therefore she would benefit from afternoon crit appointments.

Ashley requires to leave classes without giving notice and will return if her symptoms subside.

Ashley may be unable to meet deadlines at times and some flexibility is recommended.

Ashley may require reassurance and clarification of information and tasks. This should be undertaken discretely and without drawing attention to Ashley in front of others.

Any questions and answers in teaching situations should be repeated to Ashley to ensure they have understood what has been said.

Tutors Actions

- Lecture materials (slides and presenter notes) to be given in advance

- Questions should be directed at all students in general and presented in a clear manner with the meaning explained if necessary. Responses are voluntary.

- Tutorials or crits to be scheduled in the afternoon. During tutorials or teaching sessions questions and answers should be repeated to ensure that its been comprehended. Verbal instructions to be confirmed in writing.

Multiple forms of expressions

- NA -

Tutors Actions

- As Ashley's background is in illustration, ensure that outcome(s) of design project are not 3D object orientated. Ensure that students can identify different opportunities in the design project that will leverage their strengths.

Figure 14.3 An example of a persona created from mapping disability support information to UDL

that the student is neurodivergent and is sensitive to noise and certain physical sensations. This only became apparent during part of their learning experience – a half-day workshop organised to enable students (with and without prior experience) to engage in the process of making a walking stick using a pre-prepared shaft and handle. This revealed the need for better communication between disability support, student and educator. The neurodivergent student tried engaging with the workshop activity but in the end the noise from machinery in the workshop and the sensation of working with tools was too overwhelming and the student had to abandon the process. Flexibility was needed thereafter to adjust the learning experience and learning outcome to ensure an equitable experience for the student. The student experience and learning journey does not start when the module starts but extends back to when they plan to come into university and how they interact with other services within the university. Moving forward, better collaboration with disability services and getting in touch with disabled students to understand them better and co-design the persona with them before the module starts would help to make the curriculum more inclusive.

Case Study 2: The Professional Development Award in Service Design

The Professional Development Award in Service Design is a Scottish Qualification Authority qualification that develops learners' skills in service design. The six-month course is delivered by one of the co-authors, Anderson and the team at Dundee and Angus College of further education in Scotland.

As a result of this being a professional development qualification, learners of this course are typically adults who are currently employed. There is also a wide mixture of learner backgrounds, nationalities and other attributes. The motivations for learners studying the course and the individual initial knowledge about the subject matter of service design are varied.

The qualification consists of four units, each unit is assessed in the form of a summative assessment. Each assessment is based on a workplace or community project which is undertaken by the learner. Following the Universal Design for Learning (UDL) principles, the course provides learners with:

- *Multiple means of representation* with various ways to access knowledge and course materials, for example, live classes and online course content that has a variety of different media and formats.
- *Multiple means of expression* through a portfolio assessment that demonstrates what they know and have learnt through practical application of the subject matter.
- *Multiple means of engagement* with self-chosen workplace challenges that motivate and ensure learning through meaningful projects.

In mid-2020 the course was redeveloped in response to the Covid-19 pandemic moving from in-person to online live classes. A service design process, involving mindset as well as tools and methods, was utilised for this project involving interviewing learners, journey mapping current and new learner journeys, prototyping and then testing with learners.

Every learner is different so we aim to discuss accessibility needs individually and early so that we can understand how to best support each person throughout the course. When learners require support in relation to accessibility, they are first discussed with the student support team. Previously we have encountered issues where neither team had enough understanding about what the other does, and where there were assumptions made on both parts. We have since collaborated to ensure that the student services process and learner journey were better understood by everyone involved.

We recognise that adult learners can experience different types of challenges and barriers in their learning experience. These can be related to lack of time for course work or assessment, owing to caring, work or other responsibilities. Alongside the clear benefits of the workplace project, it can also bring its own challenges, for example, if learners are not well supported in the workplace in relation to the course, if job security is an issue, and if priorities change in their roles. These specific factors mean that we consider learner well-being at all stages of the learning experience. We design to support learners who might be experiencing anxiety or stress whether this is permanent (a recognised anxiety disorder), situational (submitting an assessment) or temporary (a short-term issue with assignment planning). We have also aimed to remove barriers for learners at moments when stress may be naturally higher, for example, by drafting clear and easy to understand submission instructions. We also provide examples of issues and how appropriate help can be accessed and created a space where questions can be asked openly so that other learners can view the answers if they have a similar question. These interventions have meant that learners can get help more quickly and don't become as stressed or anxious while they wait, as there are clear expectations about what happens next in the process.

Challenge of removing barriers to the learning experience created by a visual subject matter

Recently we have been working with a learner with low vision. We began by thinking of the whole learning experience as a journey made up of multiple parts. This meant looking at every aspect of the learning experience from the induction email, online learning content, online classes, as well as the assessment process. By mapping out the end-to-end journey we could start to identify where, what and why barriers might exist for this learner.

Alongside the practical aspects of the learning experience, we had to consider the subject matter itself. Service design is a 'visual' practice, and because of this a lot of the theory, tools and methods are visual in nature.

What did we do?

We have asked ourselves how we can create a course that can support a learner for whom 'visual' has a different meaning. We considered this in three contexts and aligned these with the UDL principles:

- **Participation in learning** (classes and content) – *multiple forms of representation*
- **The submission projects** (completing workplace projects) – *multiple forms or means of expressions*
- **Practicing service design** (as part of the course and beyond) – *multiple means of engagement*

Once we had taken some time to do general research on the topic of best practice for designing for low vision and screen reader assistive technology, we were able to highlight areas that needed the most attention and begin to create a plan of priorities. As well as the desktop research on low vision, the learner has been involved in user research to inform the learning experience. This has prevented us from making assumptions. For example, initially we had assumed that they might not be comfortable with creating visuals within exercises in the classes, however after involving them in those conversations we found out that they actually enjoyed making visuals and that it was something they did a lot in their workplace. This co-design approach has also meant that we could test solutions making sure that we have solved the right problems before going too far with development.

Where did we get to?

As this work has progressed, we have been continually sharing the challenges, changes and learnings within our wider team. This was to make sure that everyone not only knows what changes have been made but why they have been made and the impact that they could have for learners if not implemented. We have also shared what hasn't gone so well and solutions that didn't work, for example file formats that we were not able to make accessible. Our thinking on the three contexts that we had defined and how we can further embed the UDL principles into the learning experience has developed as we have progressed with the project.

Multiple forms of representation: We have learnt new technical skills, programmes and teaching techniques. This has meant we have grown the inclusiveness of the **participation in learning** (classes and content) for all our learners.

Multiple forms or means of expressions: A more inclusive **participation in learning** experience better supports learners with their **submission projects** (completing workplace projects). This work has also pushed us to expand our thinking and approach in this area specifically related to the visual aspect and evidencing the practical application of the subject matter for assessment purposes.

Multiple means of engagement: As with any learner **practicing service design** (as part of the course and beyond) this isn't something that we can fully teach. Every learner develops their own ways of practicing service design through **participation in learning**, their **submission projects** and beyond. What we can do is develop classes and content that support each learner alongside engaging assessment opportunities to grow their confidence and their own individual way of working.

Although this is an example of one specific learner and how we have looked to remove barriers for one aspect of accessibility we have made improvements that will support many different learners. To continually improve the learner's experience, feedback is regularly gathered from each class. The team investigate any issues or potential barriers to ensure that issues are highlighted early and can be solved quickly with and for future learners. Inclusive Design in any context is an evolving journey and we understand that it's something that we will continually need to revisit as learners and as technology changes over time.

Conclusion

Inclusive Design is important for everyone in all aspects of our lives, including education where it can be used to ensure that barriers within learning experiences are removed. As well as the positive impacts on the learning experience for students, Inclusive Design can provide a positive challenge for educators to produce innovative and creative ways to enhance the learning experience. Removing barriers in education can create a sense of belonging for learners which could then support positive wellbeing and academic success. Service design can inform an Inclusive design approach to learning and teaching, and there are many ways that you can build service design into the creation and experiences of learning and teaching.

To begin thinking about how we can use service design to inform an inclusive design approach in learning and teaching, first we need to shift our perspective on education - by seeing it as a service where we (the people who work in education) are the service providers or designers. No matter what your role is in education you create and/or provide part of the learning and teaching service.

Our case studies highlighted how UDL principles with service design thinking are used to develop and continuously improve inclusive teaching and learning experiences. We shared and reflected on teaching and learning challenges faced as educators to encourage discussion on how praxis could be improved for those who experience unintentional exclusion in education and particularly to support students with invisible disabilities.

Key learning points

1 **Be aware of your own biases and assumptions:** Consider how these might impact the learning experiences that you create. Learn about different types of people, technology and disability.

2 **Collaborating and sharing with learners as well as colleagues:** Involve others in the creation of learning experiences. Share stories about when things go well and when they don't go so well.

3 **Always improving:** Developing a feedback process to enable you to make informed decisions. Continually improve learning experiences based on learner's feedback.

References

Biggs, J. (1999) What the student does: teaching for enhanced learning. *Higher Education Research & Development*, 18(1), 57–75.

Bisset, F. & Lockton, D. (2010) Designing motivation or motivating design? Exploring Service Design, motivation and behavioural change. *Touchpoint: The Journal of Service Design*, 2(1) 15–21.

British Standards Institution. (2005) *Design Management Systems – Part 6: Managing Inclusive Design Guide (BS 700006:2005)*. London: BSI Group.

Capp, M. J. (2017) The effectiveness of universal design for learning: a meta-analysis of literature between 2013 and 2016. *International Journal of Inclusive Education*, 21 (8), 791–807.

Coleman, R., Lebbon, C., Clarkson, J. & Keates, S. (2003). From margins to mainstream. In J. Clarkson, R. Coleman, S. Keates & C. Lebbon (Eds). *Inclusive Design: Design for the whole population*. London: Springer.

Coleman, R., Bendixen, K. & Tahkokallio, P. (2003) A European Perspective. In J. Clarkson, R. Coleman, S. Keates & C. Lebbon (Eds). *Inclusive Design: Design for the whole population*. London: Springer.

Downe, L. (2020) *Good Services*. Amsterdam: BIS Publishers.

Entwistle, N. (1981) *Styles of Learning and Teaching: an integrated outline of educational psychology for students, teachers and lecturers*. Chichester: John Wiley.

Entwistle, N. (1988) Motivational factors in students' approaches to learning. In Schmeck, R. R. (Ed.). *Learning Strategies and Learning Styles. Perspectives on Individual Differences*. Boston, MA: Springer.

Entwistle, N. (2000) *Promoting deep learning through teaching and assessment: conceptual frameworks and educational contexts*. Paper presented at the ESRC Teaching and Learning Research Programme Conference. Available at: www.leeds.ac.uk/educol/documents/00003220.htm (Accessed: 20 November 2023).

Hidden Disabilities Sunflower Scheme. (2022) What is a hidden disability? Available at: https://hiddendisabilitiesstore.com/uk/what-is-a-hidden-disability (Accessed: 20 November 2023).

Lindberg, O. (2018) How Kat Holmes Transforms Businesses with Inclusive Design. Available at: https://staging1.xdideas.site-review.net/ideas/perspectives/interviews/user-experiences-kat-holmes-transforms-businesses-inclusive-design (Accessed: 20 November 2023).

Meyer, A., Rose, D. H. & Gordon, D. (2014) *Universal design for learning: Theory and Practice*. Wakefield, MA: CAST Professional Publishing.

Microsoft. (2016a) Inclusive 101 Guidebook. Available at: https://inclusive.microsoft. design/tools-and-activities/Inclusive101Guidebook.pdf (Accessed: 20 November 2023).

Microsoft. (2016b) Support Card | The Persona Spectrum. Available at: https://inclu sive.microsoft.design/tools-and-activities/InclusiveActivityCards.pdf (Accessed: 20 November 2023).

Null, R. (2013) *Universal Design: Principles and Models*. Boca Raton, FL: CRC Press.

Ramsden, P. (1987) Improving teaching and learning in higher education: the case for a relational perspective. *Studies in Higher Education*, 12, 274–286.

Stickdorn, M. & Schneider, J. (2010) *This is service design thinking*. Amsterdam: BIS Publishers.

UK Parliament POST. (2023) Invisible Disabilities in Education and Employment. Available at: https://researchbriefings.files.parliament.uk/documents/POST-PN-0689/ POST-PN-0689.pdf (Accessed: 20 November 2023).

World Health Organization. (2023) Disability. Available at: www.who.int/newsroom/fact-sheets/detail/disability-and-health#:~:text=Key%20facts,earlier%20than% 20those%20without%20disabilities (Accessed: 20 November 2023).

Chapter 15

Reflection by Design

Embedding Reflective Practice into the Student Learning Journey

Ksenija Kuzmina and James Moran

Introduction

This chapter focuses on learners and seeks to add to debates around how and when reflective practice itself may be embedded within Higher Education (HE) provision. We hope this is useful for educators and learners who are interested in understanding and engaging with reflective practice throughout the student learning journey. The chapter may provide inspiration to adopt some of the approaches to explore how service design can support the development and implementation of reflection that is student-centred and holistic.

Discussions around the complexity and diversity of approaches to embedding reflective practice within education are not a new phenomenon (Clift et al., 1990). Nor are epistemological questions which explore how reflective practice fits within pedagogical practices (van Manen, 1995). However, despite the length of time these ideas have been debated, there remains a high level of superficial engagement with reflective practice when utilised in teaching and learning in HE, and although established practical guides to support implementation of reflective and experiential learning have long been available (Moon 2000, 2013), few methods have been definitively adopted by institutions. Within the literature there is some recognition that reflective practice should be 'taught', rather than presuming students inherently understand the difference between personal and more critical reflection (Russell, 2006). But equally others argue that rather than focusing on 'teaching' reflective practice, the emphasis should instead be values-focused and consider which practices we should introduce to those in education (Edwards and Thomas, 2010). Debates on how and when to engage learners in reflective practice also persist; positive results have been seen from engaging students with reflective practice at the start of an academic journey (Pretorius and Ford, 2016) and there remains a need to 'implement ... longitudinal curricula in reflective practice' (Butani et al., 2017, p. 1) while also recognising the importance of reflection and experiential learning to affect transformative learning (Moon, 2013). This chapter adds to these discussions by exploring service design approaches to inform student engagement with reflective practice and the implications for teaching it in HE institutions.

DOI: 10.4324/9781003383161-26

Student Learning Journey

Service design in HE has been associated with a market-driven logic for service innovation and management (Wolfe, 2020), utilising the concept of student as a consumer to measure the quality of education and develop opportunities for market differentiation (Cassidy et al., 2021). Such commodification of education has been widely problematised, among other things for its power to suppress and devalue HE as a developmental place for finding self, connecting with others and discovering new ideas (Schwartzman, 2013).

In this chapter, we reconceptualise the student as a learner aligning with the notion of education being transformative, rather than transactional, and learning as embodied and experiential (Dewey, 1910). We draw on Dewey to understand the transformative learning journey as a process of emotional, cognitive and moral growth through reflective inquiry and ask how such reflective inquiry can be enhanced while undertaking study in HE. Reflection can be understood as a practical engagement with one's situated experience of the environment through which one can discover, know and act differently (Dicker, 1972). 'Reflective practice can enable professionals to learn from experience about: themselves; their work; the way in which they relate to home and work, significant others and wider society and culture' (Bolton, 2014, p. 2). Yet, we argue, as a result of our learning from this project, current pedagogical frameworks for intentionally educating for reflection in HE settings are too generic and are introduced to the students in transactional and analytical ways, rather than attending to one's learning that is embodied and experiential. As will be seen in the development across the interventions, practice in this area can be advanced by building upon concepts and theories of reflection (e.g. Kolb, Gibbs, etc.) We will highlight interventions that draw on the student learning journeys shaped by contextual factors including structural and institutional conditions (Holdo, 2023) and individual experiences.

Service Design and Reflective Practice

We propose to use service design methods and tools to facilitate students' reflection on their situated experience in HE. As such we do not use service design as the means to suggest new value propositions for the student as a customer, but to utilise the ethnographic nature of these methods, building a rich picture of students' learning journeys and as interventions that promote learner's situated reflective practices.

Service design tools and methods have the capacity to facilitate reflection through narratives and visual representations of a particular service experience and as such enhance contextual understanding (Yeo & Lee, 2018; Blomkvist & Segelström, 2014) that can be reflected upon. Neubauer (2022) highlights how visual representations order the relations of artefacts, processes and resources. As a result, service design tools and methods bound and frame the object of reflection from a service design perspective. For example, tools such as user journey maps and personas (see Chapters 11, 14, 16 and 17), place people and their experience at the centre, emphasising that services are human-centred, relational and co-produced through interactions between various actors. Furthermore, user journey mapping captures the temporality of the service, representing interactions with the service as a linear and consecutive process, while visualising complexity through a series of overlaying pathways that link visible and invisible activities and resources. Less material methods such as contextual interviews evoke personal narratives which draw on individual experiences, bringing to the fore the personal and the contextual, describing how things are from the participant's perspective and imagining alternative ways of being and doing. The participatory nature of these methods further promotes an understanding of services as collaborative and co-created. As such, it opens up opportunities for exploring curriculum design approaches that are student-centred, systemic and link action and reflection.

Designing Interventions

Over the course of two years, the authors undertook action research (Swann, 2002), exploring, designing and evaluating new service design interventions for reflective practice with students from Loughborough University London and engaged with multiple cohorts of students who undertook a one-year full time MSc course. Four methods from service design were adapted as interventions into the student learning journey: user research, student journey mapping, personas and contextual interviews to frame, describe and in some instances visualise students' reflective learning journeys. Each method was introduced to the students at different times of their studies. The learning experience of the MSc student in the British institution tends to be bounded by time. Thus, the structure of pre-, during and post educational learning experience was utilised while understanding that it simplifies and reduces comprehension of the experience and the complexity of service provision.

Interventions

Forming part of a wider project on reflection, the chapter presents four examples on how service design was used to enhance student engagement with reflective practice and discuss how it can inform curriculum design and its evaluation.

Intervention 1: Onboarding – User Research

Feedback suggested students were unprepared for reflective assignments. There seemed to be an expectation from staff that students would be able to apply reflective practice within their studies without it forming an intrinsic part of the taught curriculum. While acknowledging that 'reflective practice is a state of mind, an ongoing attitude to work and life' and being aware of the 'danger of it being a separate curriculum element within a set of exercises' (Bolton, 2014, p. 1), students still need to be introduced to the concept and practice of reflection long before it is used as an assessment method.

As such we sought to find a way to introduce the concept of reflective practice earlier in the student journey and explore its context as a tool for academic and professional development. Upon approaching the institution, we were allocated time within the 'welcome' week for all new students arriving at the campus. The intake was just over 1,000 postgraduate students of whom more than 75 per cent were international students. Within the timetable of activities, the overall cohort were broken down into three groups and we were allocated approximately one hour with each group. So, the challenge was to try and introduce reflective practice to a group of 350 predominantly international students within one hour.

Given the diverse experiences and educational backgrounds of participants we had to assume a relatively low level of knowledge of reflective practices (which was confirmed by student feedback following the event). Thus, the session was required to introduce students to the concepts of reflective practice but also to give them a chance to engage with the basic tenets of how they might make use of it in their assignments and to support their academic development.

As an icebreaker we got participants to spend two minutes drawing the person sitting next to them with their non-dominant hand. Next, they had to talk to the person they had just drawn about how they felt about the experience. This exercise was chosen as it can be done with hundreds of students at a time, it is relatively equitable as most people have little experience drawing with their non-dominant hand, and it was also mildly uncomfortable without being acutely stressful. The latter point was intended to foster a sense of honesty within a safe environment; there are no 'right' answers in reflective practice and it may occasionally feel slightly uncomfortable and out of synch with other academic practices.

While recognising that 'reflection and reflexivity is grounded in and springs from individual practice...rather than theory' (Bolton, 2014, p. 45), we found that students still benefited from a tangible structure to support engagement with the reflective process. As such we introduced some of the more common reflective practice models such as Kolb (1984) and Gibbs (1988). The focus here was not simply on conveying the informational aspects of reflective practice models but to begin to think about how they could be used by students to engage in aspects of their own development on the course. A short reflective writing exercise was undertaken to facilitate application of a reflective model in practice and then students were asked to critique their writing and consider how they would transition from descriptive to more critically reflective writing. Finally, students were introduced to a follow-up assignment, a short piece of reflective writing of around 500 words, which would be undertaken within the first few weeks of the term and could be reviewed by their personal academic tutor.

Overall, feedback suggested that most students had found the sessions useful "I love reflection which makes me rethink and grow up; looking back is help [ing] me move forward" and "I liked learning about experiential cycle models – I think these will come in useful for me to refer to in my studies". However, the limitations of the event were also clear given the limited time and large numbers of students "Actually I'm a bit confused about today's lecture" and "I'd just start a bit slower, so we could all catch up". Overall, we would recommend building in space to welcome activities for an active workshop as it can be a useful introduction and initial engagement with reflective practice. However, to develop reflective practitioners, a more substantive engagement with the concepts and tools of reflective practice are required across the student journey to avoid the sessions simply being a superficial "separate curriculum element" (Bolton, 2014, p. 1).

Intervention 2: Student Journey Mapping

In this intervention we facilitated a substantive journey mapping (Kimbell & Blomberg, 2017) to inform the mapping of reflection opportunities within the student journey and to correlate this with the formal provision within the published curriculum. The mapping was co-created with one MSc student and tested with four MSc students, who had previously undertaken service design modules and had knowledge of the mapping tool. As a result, there was no need to introduce the concept nor the process to the students.

The journey mapping aimed to visually capture students' experiences of engaging with reflective practice as they went through their learning journey, identifying points of interaction between the students and the university as a service provider. The mapping captured a broad set of touchpoints that crossed formal and informal curriculum, including modules and assignments in class, formal and informal feedback, employability workshops, hackathons and other activities. In addition, it identified areas of 'in between' reflections, such as holidays, waiting for assessment feedback, discussions with classmates or just entering the class for the first time. The mapping provided an insight on how various components in education link together to facilitate the learning journey for the student and how the experience of the learning journey is entangled with self-reflection. In their summary of the activity, our participants noted the emergence of three ongoing self-reflections that they experienced before they entered the studies, during and after:

1   Reflection and assessment on personal attributes. These are questions on the background of the student that keep coming up in terms of self-worth, capabilities, personal strengths and weaknesses.

2   Questions about alignment between what is provided by university and the vision/reasons the student had for continuing their studies, whether it matches or exceeds their expectations or falls short of their expectations.

3   Reflection on past experiences, for example, how different induction at Loughborough University London is compared to what the student had before, the formation of friendships, the delivery of content and similarities and differences to their previous studies.

The mapping prompted consideration on how and where within the studies some of these reflections can be facilitated. There was a sense that learning experience can be enhanced if some of the reflections are guided through a scaffolded and supportive route rather than leaving students to interpret expectations on their own. This lent itself to a development of a journey map for students and staff that defined more relational touchpoints for reflection, such as with the Personal Tutor, with guiding questions.

Intervention 3: Reflective Student Persona Tool

This section presents the service design intervention that was introduced to the cohort of 50 MSc design students at the Institute for Design Innovation in the six-week module, Design Research. The aim was to facilitate reflection on students' design practice as it is developing through their MSc studies and as it is practiced in the field of design. The purpose was to build capacity for reflexivity in the context of 'designing one's own Dissertation project', a major assignment that students undertake at Loughborough University London. To develop an intervention a commonly used Persona tool (Trischler & Scott, 2016) was integrated with theories of strength and deficit-based approaches to reflection (Ghaye, 2010), to develop an innovative Reflective Persona Tool for the students to facilitate individual and collective reflection for meaningful action.

In design, the persona tool aims to 'narrate different types of users, based on clusters of behaviours and needs' (servicedesigntools.org, n.d.; and see Chapter 17) and is used in projects to understand and design for a particular archetypal user. Personas are typically created by designers and in the process promote discussions and collective sensemaking. However, they represent the 'user' rather than 'designer' and this 'otherness' has been critiqued for leading to overly simplified and false representations. The *Reflective Student Persona* tool has been developed in the context of supporting students to design a Dissertation project that is meaningful for them. To do so, students were tasked to individually develop and reflect on two 'personas' that represented them as project users. The first persona was based on a set of questions linked to deficit-based theory (Dixon et al., 2016). This takes a reductionist view of the world that emphasises the existence of problems, failures and weaknesses. It asked students to develop a sense of 'self' based on the needs, goals and values rooted in one's problems or frustrations. The second persona asked students to explore strength-based values and goals that linked to one's flourishing. The experience of creating such personas as well as the output of the two personas promoted not only deep self-reflection but the imagination of multiple paths into the Dissertation projects that one can undertake. Personas utilised the strengths of the original tool by enabling students to externalise their self in multiple forms and engage with the notion of multiplicity by promoting several representations of self. When presented and discussed in the group, these personas promoted important discussions about motivations for studying, underpinned by various worldviews, interests and future directions.

Yet, this process was not straightforward. Many students struggled in the classroom to develop a persona that would represent them from a 'human flourishing' perspective. This stumble, in itself, led to a whole-class reflection and critique of the design practice and the need for more content in the lectures and workshops that supported work based on strength-based rather than deficit-based design. Further, this intervention explored how to further facilitate students' agency and participation in their studies, it opened up space for reflection on students' own design practice in relation to the Dissertation. For many participants this exercise shifted a view on the Dissertations from a box ticking exercise to an assignment that can be leverage for one's future activities.

Intervention 4: Testing, implementation and evaluating the impact and through interviews

In the final intervention, a set of contextual interviews was undertaken with nine design students, who were at the end of their studies between 2018 and 2020. The aim was to undertake a critical evaluation (Trichler et al., 2019) with students on reflective practice and the designed interventions, to promote what Schön calls reflection-on-action (Visser, 2010) and to consider future iterations of the interventions themselves.

All participants agreed on the importance of reflective practice for their work and described it as the active process of 'self-questioning, self-exploring and self-learning'. Many associated it with the independent study that they experienced during their MSc, particularly during their Dissertation. For others, it was linked to their evaluation of their future direction and a general life skill. To this end, there was a desire to gain capacity to learn and practice reflection to enhance one's learning, professional and life experiences.

Having space throughout their learning journey to explore reflection in its many different forms, seemed to be valued and desired by the students. There was a general agreement that theories and concepts introduced in Intervention 1, raised basic awareness on the topic, yet were difficult to put into practice. Through Interventions 2 and 3, students explored their own learning process and for some this "triggered a new mindset" and helped them to develop their own reflective practice that some continue to undertake after their studies. For example, students reported on developing "a habit of writing diaries when new ideas are presented to them", "creating a list in [the] computer ...[adding] skills I would like to develop or things I am interested in" and using a well-being app that activates daily reflection. Only one student mentioned the use of a theoretical model of reflection based on flourishing (Ghaye, 2010) whereas others drew on generic processes and experiences of reflection throughout the year to underpin their activities.

As such, reflective interventions that linked directly to the decision making about their studies (i.e. Dissertation) were received well by the students. These interventions were able to support students in navigating from theory to direct action. In addition, the proposed interventions may be seen as the springboard for the students to develop their own reflective practice, rather than a blueprint that dictates a course of action. This poses a question of how to consider designing curriculum that considers student reflective capabilities *after* they finish their studies, rather than *to* finish their studies.

Discussion

Within the UK most curricula are founded on the concept of constructive alignment and are designed to meet the needs of an outcomes-based system (Biggs & Tang, 2007). Students should thus be able to demonstrate the intended learning outcomes of a programme via assessments at the modular level. Successful completion of all module assessments results in the demonstration of all the programme level outcomes and thus graduation from the programme. To this end, methods for summative assessment of reflective practice 'which focus on the outcome of reflection by creating a product (e.g. portfolio)' (Norrie et al., 2012, p. 570), are favoured in curriculum design. Yet, in line with this research and Dewey's notion of the 'transformative learner', these methods need integrating more closely with formative assessment methods where learning and self-development is the focus and promoted in classroom activities' (Norrie et al., 2012, p. 570). Intervention 3 exemplifies how this can be achieved and Intervention 4 evidences the longer-term impact of such work on students' personal development of the individual reflective practice.

As a curriculum is linear by design it requires an entry point for students to join a course and an exit point to leave with qualifications. This is counter-intuitive to most reflective processes which, by necessity, are cyclical to enable a revisitation of an experience to enable the application of learning derived from the reflective process. The weakness of this transactional approach can be seen within the modular structure in universities where a single reflection-based assessment is often used. Though a student may reflect on their experience and identify changes to practice, unless explicitly designed into the course structure, it is unlikely that the student will actually have the opportunity to apply learning derived from their reflections as they will move on to a new module with a new learning context. Thus, following on from the on-boarding stage in Intervention 1, this project looked at how to break the model of isolated pockets of reflective practice and link targeted reflective engagements to enable learning from reflection to be implemented and subsequent reflective cycles to be undertaken. The journey mapping in Intervention 2 visualised, framed and revealed these opportunities integrating cycles of reflection on the formal curriculum with reflection on self, one's capabilities and self-worth.

Reflective practice has, at varying points, found itself to be included within the formal curriculum as an assessment but also in the domain of the 'informal curriculum' as there can be an implicit expectation that students will simply know 'how' to reflect or be able to do so effectively with little support. Similarly, while experiences taken outside of the formal curriculum may be identified to address issues such as employability, few linkages are made to reflective practice activities that may appear within the formal curriculum itself. This research emphasises making reflective practice visible and explicit throughout the student learning journey and suggests that narration and visual representation that is inherent in the service design tools, as well as the concepts that service design operates, including experience, journey, touchpoints, etc. can support such a process.

Interventions prompted students to structure their experience in a particular way that led to questioning of one's actions and thoughts, rather than simply accepting them. Dewey sets out that it is purposefully seeking the foundation of a belief and evaluating its effectiveness and capability to substantiate this position which is the basis of reflective thought (Dewey, 1910). It is only a 'person who understands what the better ways of thinking are, and why they are better, [who] can...change his own personal ways until they become more effective' (Dewey, 1933, p. 3). Thus, seeking to embed this core principle of questioning thoughts, a core tenet of this project was to provide time and space for students to both engage with differing conceptions of reflective practice as a subject, but also to ensure that there was time to apply these at different points across their student journey.

Though steering clear of prescribing a specific model that students should favour, there were none the less some overarching principles which informed the design of this approach. It was felt important that students were able to take ownership of both their understanding of and engagement with reflective practice but that they may still need some support in this process. Thus, adopting principles from Dewey, design interventions were guided by an ontological position of social constructivism. This positioning frames learning as constructed through building on personal and shared experiences to form understanding, thus students would develop learning through engaging in the reflective process in both individual and collective activities. Service design tasks to support engagement with reflective practice were designed around the principles of experiential learning, reflection and use of visual and narrative representation and structuring. This was required to be undertaken by students across the academic year rather than simply providing them with information on reflective practice as a subject.

Echoing the core tenets of Dewey's philosophy, but also recognising the traditionally disjointed approach to the teaching of reflective practice, this project also adopted a broad interpretation of the pedagogic approach of a 'gradual release of responsibility' (Pearson & Gallagher, 1983). Seeking to initially instruct students on ways to reflect there was a transfer of responsibility to the students for engaging with and undertaking reflection. This was aimed to develop their individual agency in this field beyond the bounded elements of the curriculum and was felt key to transfer ownership of the reflective practice process from those who may be teaching it to the students themselves.

In conclusion, we found a service design approach to developing reflective learning can strengthen the human-centred and transformational aspects of reflection. It helped provide a holistic approach to developing reflective skills throughout a student's learning journey while service design methods offered new ways of engaging with reflective practice. Our hope is that the reflective skills and experiences our students have acquired through this process will go on to inform their personal development and professional practice far beyond their time studying with us.

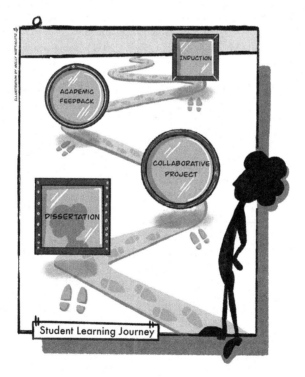

Figure 15.1 Opportunities for Reflective Touch Points in the Student Journey

Key learning points

1   Reflection is a lifelong capacity that is valued by students, yet educational approaches that link theory and practice are missing.
2   Student journey mapping is a valuable tool to understand where and how reflection is taught across formal and informal curriculum within a HE institution from the student's perspective.
3   Service design tools can be adapted to design coherent interventions across the curriculum that support reflective practice in students, underpinned by Dewey's transformative learning approaches.

References

Biggs, J. & Tang, C. (2007) *Using Constructive Alignment in Outcomes-Based Teaching and Learning Teaching for Quality Learning at University* (3rd ed.). Maidenhead: Open University Press.

Blomkvist, J. & Segelström, F. (2014) Benefits of external representations in service design: a distributed cognition perspective. *The Design Journal*, 17(3), 331–346.

Bolton, G. E. J. (2014) *Reflective practice* (4th ed.). London: Sage Publications.

Butani L., Bannister, S. L., Rubin, A. & Forbes, K. L. (2017) How Educators Conceptualize and Teach Reflective Practice: A Survey of North American Pediatric Medical Educators. *Academic Pediatrics*, 17(3) 303–309.

Cassidy, K. J., Sullivan, M. N. & Radnor, Z. J. (2021) Using insights from (public) services management to improve student engagement in higher education. *Studies in Higher Education*, 46(6), 1190–1206.

Clift, R. T., Houston, W. R. & Pugach, M. C. (Eds) (1990) *Encouraging reflective practice in education: An analysis of issues and programs*. New York: Teachers College Press.

Dewey, J. (1910) *How we think*. Lexington, MA: D.C. Heath.

Dewey, J. (1933) *How We Think: A Restatement of the Relation of Reflective Thinking to the Educative Process*. Lexington, MA: D.C. Heath.

Dicker, G. (1972) John Dewey on the Object of Knowledge', *Transactions of the Charles S. Peirce Society*, 8(3), 152–166.

Dixon, M., Lee, S. & Ghaye, T. (2016) Strengths-Based Reflective Practices for the Management of Change: Applications from Sport and Positive Psychology. *Journal of Change Management*, 16(2), 142–157.

Edwards, G. & Thomas, G. (2010) Can reflective practice be taught? *Educational Studies*, 36(4), 403–414.

Ghaye, T. (2010) In what ways can reflective practices enhance human flourishing? *Reflective Practice*, 11(1), 1–7.

Holdo, M. (2023) Critical reflection: John Dewey's relational view of transformative learning. *Journal of Transformative Education*, 21(1), 9–25.

Gibbs, G. (1988) *Learning by Doing: A Guide to a Teaching and Learning Methods*. Oxford: Oxford Polytechnic Further Educational Unit.

Kimbell, L. & Blomberg, J. (2017) The object of service design. *Designing for service: Key issues and new directions*, 27, 20–34.

Kolb, D. (1984) *Experiential learning*. Englewood Cliffs, NJ: Prentice-Hall.

Moon, J. A. (2006). *Learning Journals: A handbook for reflective practice and professional development* (2nd ed.). London: Routledge.

Moon, J. A. (2013) *A handbook of reflective and experiential learning: Theory and practice*. London: Routledge.

Neubauer, R. (2022) Materializing the Agency of Design in Innovation Practices. *Design Issues*, 38(1), 81–91.

Norrie, C., Hammond, J., D'Avray, L., Collington, V. & Fook, J. (2012) Doing it differently? A review of literature on teaching reflective practice across health and social care professions. *Reflective Practice*, 13(4), 565–578.

Pearson, P. & Gallagher, M. (1983) The instruction of reading comprehension. *Contemporary Educational Psychology*, 8(3), 317–344.

Pretorius, L. & Ford, A. (2016) Reflection for Learning: Teaching Reflective Practice at the Beginning of University Study. *International Journal of Teaching and Learning in Higher Education*, 28(2), 241–253.

Russell, T. (2005) Can reflective practice be taught? *Reflective Practice*, 6(2), 199–204.

Schwartzman, R. (2013) Consequences of commodifying education. *Academic Exchange Quarterly*, 17(3), 41–46.

Service Design Tools (n.d.) Personas. Available at: https://servicedesigntools.org/tools/personas (Accessed: 30 April 2024).

Swann, C. (2002) Action Research and the Practice of Design. *Design Issues*, 18(1), 49–61.

Trischler, J., Dietrich, T. & Rundle-Thiele, S. (2019) Co-design: from expert-to user-driven ideas in public service design. *Public Management Review*, 21(11), 1595–1619.

Trischler, J. & Scott, D. R. (2016) Designing Public Services: The usefulness of three service design methods for identifying user experiences. *Public Management Review*, 18(5), 718–739.

Van Manen M. (1995) On the Epistemology of Reflective Practice. *Teachers and Teaching*, 1, 33–50.

Visser, W. (2010) Schön: Design as a reflective practice. *Collection*, 2, 21–25.

Wolfe, K. (2020) Service design in higher education: a literature review. *Perspectives: Policy and Practice in Higher Education*, 24(4), 121–125.

Yeo, Y. & Lee, J. J. (2018) *Mapping design capability of public service organisations: A tool for collaborative reflection*. ServDes2018. Service Design Proof of Concept, Proceedings of the ServDes. 2018 Conference, 18–20 June, Milan, Italy (No. 150, pp. 534–549). Linköping: Linköping University Electronic Press.

Chapter 16

Discovering the untold story

Emotional journey mapping of learners' educational experience

Radka Newton

Introduction

Journey mapping is a frequently used method in service design, and you can find many templates (Ivey-Williams, 2016a) and even software applications, such as Smaply, that provide guidance on how to map user experience. In an education context there are lots of opportunities to understand our interaction with the university world through the lens of a member of staff or a student, a frequent traveller or a temporary visitor navigating a complex journey without a map or a compass.

A service design approach to journey mapping helps us turn the intangible and invisible into a visualised and tangible account of steps that help us reflect on our learning, communicate our experience and identify opportunities for improvements. The sequencing and evidencing nature of service design turns attention to the service user who we follow through the service as if we were watching a film assembled from a series of scenes in which we look for evidence of their experience, their emotions and actions (Stickdorn et al., 2018).

Developing journey maps as a method of mapping user experience falls under the umbrella of ethnographic research (Segelström et al., 2009) that is adopted in service design, allowing us to develop an understanding and appreciation of our users' lived experience. Ethnography also enables us to consider the context of the user holistically rather than looking at the service in isolation. Therefore, the journey maps often include seemingly unrelated activities to the service that is delivered. For example, mapping student experience of a particular course may include moments of homesickness, a birthday celebration or a sleepless night. And it is these human moments that can lead us to the root of any problem and help us demystify assumptions.

In this chapter we will discuss various applications of journey mapping with cases from education practice that will focus on mapping the emotional journey. The education context offers an opportunity to explore the different purposes of journey maps including personal reflection and communication across boundaries. A distinctive feature of these case studies is that they all demonstrate journey mapping *owned and created by the users themselves* and will

DOI: 10.4324/9781003383161-27

hopefully inspire other possible applications contributing to making our education journeys better, more enjoyable and memorable for the right reasons.

Mapping the invisible

Education is not only about the excellence of the content. It is also about understanding how to deliver and reach diverse audiences with different needs and learning backgrounds. Our learning experiences shape our attitude to acquiring new knowledge, our relationship to risk when it comes to gaining new skills and our personal connection to people, places and spaces that we associate with learning. The steps we take during the learning process remain invisible to us and too often we are focused on the end result. The education environment encourages us to learn for assessment, get good grades, perform well and yet the journey we take towards the outcome remains unnoticed.

Universities are complex systems with multiple interdependent actors who impact on our learning experience and our ability to learn. It is not all about our lecturers who deliver the content of our curriculum. Our learning journeys are impacted by factors such as the accessibility of learning resources, the living environment in our student accommodation or the expectations imposed on us by our families and friends. Our learning is also influenced by our previous learning experiences, habits and routines developed before we came to the University. Journey maps allow for us to see what may otherwise remain invisible and unattended for. They provide tangible clarity to student and staff experience with the acknowledgment of feelings and emotions, not only processes and tasks.

Putting journey maps into action

The concept of customer journey mapping was introduced in marketing in the 1960s to encourage a better understanding of customers (Whittle & Foster, 1991) and to respond to the commercialisation and growth of consumerism (Crosier & Handford, 2012). It then became well adopted in exploring customer experience from the customer perspective, rather than from the point of view of the service provider. In service design projects, journey mapping became one of the key parts of the research and insights stage, mapping the current state of user experience, as well as being used as a prototyping tool envisioning the improved state of the service (Følstad et al., 2014). More recently we have seen powerful applications in public services and in the endeavour of the UK Government to understand citizens' experiences outlining the two dimensions of journey mapping – the time and emotional response (Cabinet Office, 2007).

Journey maps have been widely applied to map out patients' experiences in hospitals, and in education we have seen some sporadic examples documented in literature mainly related to user experience in libraries. As we have seen in our persona profiling chapter, university libraries have been one of the first adopters of service design principles incorporating Customer Service Excellence Accreditation, a government standard awarded by the Cabinet Office, into library strategic planning. A notable example on improvements made at the Birmingham City University Library (Andrews & Eade, 2013) identifies the following benefits of journey mapping:

- *Increased understanding* of student expectations about how library systems worked
- *Changes in work practices* such as the enhancement of induction sessions and improved signage
- *Continuous improvement* approach based on the need to iterate
- *Future planning* and ability to use journey maps for envisioning ideal future states
- *Fresh perspective* involving user voice and lived library experience

Del Olmo and Morelli (2022) provided a further example from the context of EU-funded education projects where multidisciplinary project teams applied journey maps as a planning and reflection tool enabling them to communicate across disciplines and include a diverse set of stakeholders in the projects. In their example of managing funded research projects, they apply journey maps as boundary objects, a term we have covered in the persona profiling chapter. In this sense, the physical and tangible representations of the project journeys were used to cross communication boundaries between participants from different backgrounds who developed a shared understanding of the project expectations. They talk about the journey maps as a *plan* that helped the teams with common representation of the process, an *eye-opener* that facilitated frictions, a *map* for actions, a *shared language* for stakeholder involvement, an *anchor* that kept them focused and a *trigger* to inspire idea generation. What an excellent summary of the power of journey mapping!

Journey maps function as a collaboration tool showing the perspective of the user, the student or the staff member who is in the heart of the educational experience that is being designed. A word of caution is needed here as on many occasions we get tempted to map the process from our own perspective, rather than the user journey. It is possible to combine both, the experience and the process, in a more developed service visualisation called *service blueprint*. Blueprinting methodology or technique has been extensively applied in the public sector and is explained thoroughly in the Design in Government Blog (Ivey-Williams, 2016b) where Adam Lawrence makes a valuable point that: 'a user journey map is a representation of an experience, whereas a service blueprint shows the process necessary to create that experience'. In addition to the user journey, a blueprint shows the layers of the service delivery detailing service systems, actors and processes required to enable the successful functioning of the service system itself.

Blueprinting has been applied at the University of Derby (Baranova et al., 2010; Radnor et al., 2013) designing the complex transition from a student enquiry about university studies through to their enrolment.[1] This project mapped the student experience with each stage of the journey being detailed through the blueprint technique. The points where the service failed in the enrolment process were identified and captured through focus groups and surveys. Other Higher Education (HE) blueprinting case studies can be found in Ostrom et al. (2011) where we get insights into detailed blueprints of students' access to financial aid and of online and hybrid courses redesign.

In the next section I will share different applications of journey mapping, while outlining a range of purposes and benefits that can be readily adopted to any educational context. The examples below will focus on emotional journey maps that can be expanded into detailed blueprints to achieve service improvement or redesign.

Designing education with journey maps

In my practice, I always start with the emotional aspect of the journey mapping before moving to analyse the more functional and operational side of the service I am reviewing. The reason behind this is my focus on empathy in the visualisation process, as beautifully described by Segelström in his article on *communication with one's memory* (2009, p. 8). Journey maps, as a method to exercise and keep empathy in the design process, reveal emotional associations with what the learner remembers about their experience without limiting themselves only to study-related events. It provides a holistic narrative of what life events influenced their learning journey and the role of emotions in the learning process. In this way, journey mapping also serves a powerful reflection purpose enabling the learners to reflect on their own approach to learning and highlight potential areas of improvement that will be implemented by themselves, not only the design team. The self-reflective aspect of journey mapping is rarely considered in a service design context; however, it is paramount in the education context.

As we will see from the examples, journey maps will also fulfil other purposes, such as communication with those who have designed the learning experience and who are striving to make improvements.

The EDUJAM journeys

The context for the two examples of journey mapping practices in this section is a bi-annual design challenge event focused on transforming education founded by the Service Design in Education community. In 2022, EDUJAM[2] took place in the Victoria and Albert Museum in Dundee attended by more than forty educators, designers and students who came together for three days of co-creating the future of our education. The EDUJAM concept is based on a global public sector annual design challenge (Global Gov Jam)[3] focusing on public services innovation. Over the course of three days, participants, who come from a variety of backgrounds, work together in a collaborative, experiential and immersive way following design principles and putting the needs of learners and education stakeholders into the centre of the design process.

Life learning journeys

Upon arrival at EDUJAM, participants were invited to map out their life learning journey using the template below.

Participants were invited to take a seat at a roundtable and note down their individual learning memories and reflections in association with their feelings and emotions. The simple instructions provided to them were:

- Grab an EDUJAM sticker and place it on the timeline – YOU'VE ARRIVED!
- Take a seat, explore your EDUJAM kit and pick a colour pen and a black fine pen.
- Remember when ... start on the left side of the timeline and draw a circle for informal learning or a square for formal learning in either the top half of the paper (feeling happy, positive, excited) or in the bottom half of the paper (feeling scared, anxious or sad) and write down your memory using your black pen.
- Your memory will have a feeling, smell, people – write down whatever you remember.
- Now move on the timeline to your right, recording more learning memories of your life.
- Keep going until you arrive at the EDUJAM sticker point!
- Fantastic! Your learning journey is here! Now share with others and display on the wall!

Allowing the space and time to communicate with one's memory created a very welcoming and peaceful environment with time to settle into the new space and get ready for the learning weekend. When participants were ready to share, they

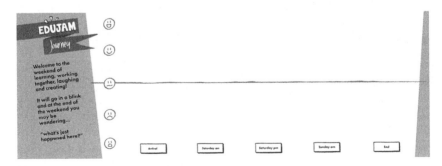

Figure 16.1 My EDUJAM journey

organically identified either another participant or one of the EDUJAM organisers and shared their life journey with them. The non-judgmental nature of this
activity married with the freedom to use the template as a drawing, doodling or
writing canvas led to very open communication and sharing of very personal and
intimate accounts of learning experiences within a group of strangers.

The life journey maps enacted the function of boundary objects facilitating
the sharing of personal information among strangers from different backgrounds, cultures and generations. The open sharing and vulnerability among
the participants led to the organisers' better awareness of the participants'
relationship with learning and established a shared understanding of the
EDUJAM community's sentiment for education and their motivation for
positive transformation. It also contributed to enhanced psychological safety of
the participants who were able to embrace group activities with greater ease.

Analysis of our first twenty-one journey maps revealed that the main themes
related to positive emotions of informal learning experienced in safe family
environments. The activities participants mentioned as fun and enjoyable in earlier stages of life were mainly riding a bike, swimming, drawing and dancing. In
later life stages participants identified positive emotions with activities of their
own choice associated with freedom and independence. The negative and frustrating parts of the learning journeys were mainly related to strict learning
environments where we felt not good enough, where performance was a focus
for learning, and where we felt ashamed, ignored or bored. One participant
mentioned "reciting books of old testaments" as a reminder of rote learning
without any ability to be creative. The suppression of creativity and need to
conform to systems and rules dominated the negative area of the journeys.

Such rich information achieved in such a short period of time within the first
two hours of a learning event! How might we as educators apply this technique to better understand our students, learners and learning event participants?

A service design appreciation of sequencing the nature of events emphasises
the importance of understanding what happens before we interact with a service, during the service itself as well as afterwards. When our students join our
university programmes, they come with a lot of previous learning that impacts
on the way they relate to their university learning experience. With the pressure
to deliver the busy university schedules, we seldom take time to pause and
reflect with learners on 'the before', which most likely leads to misunderstandings of expectations and can contribute to poor student experience.
Taking the time to arrive, pause and reflect and develop a shared language of
what we mean by learning can be a powerful approach to delivering a seamless
University student journey – as we discuss in our closing chapter.

I hope this example has inspired you to experiment with learning stories and
histories. The next example is also inspired by the EDUJAM weekend and we
will now have a look at how we applied real time journey mapping with the
participants to document their continuous learning and reflect on their
EDUJAM learning experience.

The EDUJAM experience learning journey

This example of utilising journey mapping for reflective purposes is a continuous experience mapping that resembles diarising. In HE it has become common practice to ask students to reflect on their learning, and reflective essays have been integrated as an assessment method that gives students an opportunity to capture their own growth. This practice, however, typically happens after the learning is completed and students often struggle to account for the significant learning moments that slipped their memory. The continuous reflection we applied in EDUJAM was incorporated as a daily routine with integrated moments of reflection supported by the template below to facilitate visualisation of the learning experience, enabling participants to record the learning events as well as emotions associated with them.

Participants received a series of instructions with the template and during the three days of busy activities there were scheduled moments for all to regroup and record their learning journey.

The instructions were as follows:

> So, let's document those memories and learning 'aha!' moments on your EDUJAM Journey timeline!

- Arrival – start on the left side of the timeline and draw a circle or a square to document your learning moment. What did it first feel like to sign up for EDUJAM? Where did you find out about it? What did you expect? Start in either the top half of the paper (feeling happy, positive, excited) or in the bottom half of the paper (feeling scared, anxious or sad) and write down your memory using your black pen.
- As we go through our EDUJAM learning journey, we will take some time to reflect each day to document our learning on our timeline.
- Keep your timeline with you and keep learning!
- On Sunday we will have a display of our learning and celebrate the making of yet another learning step of your life!

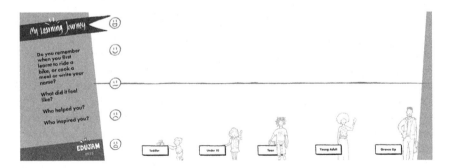

Figure 16.2 My learning journey

At the end of EDUJAM we recorded a collection of video accounts of participants sharing their learning journeys. Yet again, the holistic view of the participant's perception of the learning included their journey to the venue, their emotions associated with arriving at the venue, meeting the other participants, etc. The accounts varied from initial feelings of anxiety, owing to a post COVID-19 apprehension of participating in large events, to reflections of enhanced self-awareness and deep personal learning reflections openly shared with others: "There are also some challenges that I need to overcome, which are communication and co-operation with people from different professional backgrounds, although it is quite harmonious in a short period of time, it needs time to be honed in the long term deep co-operation".

In my personal practice as educator, I have implemented this method with my students within a module where the students receive a very similar template and we incorporate moments of reflection during the module to facilitate the approach to their final reflective essay. I have also applied this method to conference feedback. This is not as a continuous reflection but takes place during the last day of the conference, using visualisation of the learning experience as a means of personal reflection as well as a communication tool with conference organisers for future improvements.

Both EDUJAM examples are very versatile and applicable to diverse contexts. In these examples we have seen very personal journey mapping where each journey is associated with a specific person who develops that journey as a boundary object to share their insights with others and keep a personal memo of their own learning. The next example will provide a different angle on journey mapping, focusing on redesigning an existing service, using participants' insights, synthesised through a persona, as we will see in Chapter 17.

University degree programme learning journey

The last example has been inspired by a research project *Investigation into service design approach to the annual programme review practices* (2018–22) in which I applied a variety of service design methods to incorporate student-led improvements to university degree programmes. Emotional student journeys that mapped an experience of 'doing' a university degree were tested with over 135 students in three British Universities (Newton, in Huang & Hands, 2022, pp. 159–172).

Emotional journey mapping has proven to be a valuable approach when trying to understand the student learning experience to identify opportunities for improvement. The journey maps are created by the students who are participating in the degree programme in various moments of time to capture, for example, each semester or the programme as a whole. This approach works well when students work in teams and develop a student persona first and then map out the persona's learning experience over a certain period of time.

This method differs slightly from service journey mapping when we aim to record user's touchpoints as moments of interaction with the service provider. In the context of the programme review example, students map out any moments they recall as significant in their persona's learning experience. The value of understanding of this rather open approach is to acknowledge our students as human beings who are experiencing our degree programmes in the wider context of their university life, away from home, learning to live alone, often in a new country.

Below you can see an example of an emotional journey on a postgraduate management programme covering the time from the beginning of the programme in October until February, about half-way through the programme. Each of the points the students recorded can be zoomed in and expanded to its own journey map. Zooming in and out is very powerful and useful in journey mapping, as it allows us to explore various parts of the journey in greater detail and yet remain connected to the whole map that provides the overarching context.

If we take an example of the journey map extract in Figure 16.3, each moment ought to be investigated with further enquiry to understand how these moments impact on the overall experience, what happened at these moments in relation to the learning and how these points could be used as inspirations for improvements. As a facilitator of this participatory activity with your students, the key is to remain non-judgmental and employ an open

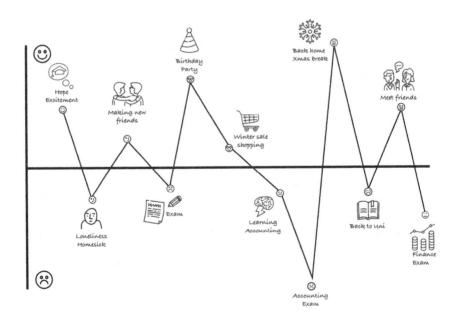

Figure 16.3 Student journey map

questioning approach to try and find out what happened, why, the impact and what could have been done better.

For example, the first two points are very important to consider for overall programme experience. Many of these students seem to start the programme excited and full of hope and then quickly slump, owing to homesickness. This may imply difficulties in engaging them in learning and also in extra-curricular activities. In this case, the challenge was to deliver career development sessions in this period of time that were very poorly attended and the low mood in the cohort helped to explain potential reasons for disengagement. Students suggested addressing this by incorporating a cohort activity to nurture the feeling of togetherness, helping to overcome the homesickness.

Another pattern that has featured in most of the cohort journey maps were the negative emotions associated with exams. This may be easily overlooked and regarded as a standard fear of exams. Enquiring deeper into what it is about the exams helped us understand students' apprehension about the exam format, the unknown venue and the timing of the exam. Students will be always concerned about exams but we can help manage the exam anxiety by being more explicit about the format, providing past examples of exam papers, ensuring that everybody knows where the exam venue is and adjusting the timing to avoid a very early start or late afternoon finish. These are small adjustments that can significantly improve the overall student experience on the programme.

The exam point can be expanded into its own journey and developed into a blueprint acknowledging stages of when students receive information about the exam, from whom, how it is communicated (via email, in the handbook), who is responsible for the exam preparation, who arranges the timing and venue and what do students do when they cannot attend the exam etc. The exam experience is a journey map in its own right and if, through detailed enquiry, you identify some major issues in this area, it is worthwhile zooming in and expanding the journey map to identify the root of the problem and visually depict where in the "exam journey" the issues occur.

Looking for recurring patterns in the journey maps of the cohort is essential and helps focus on priorities. It is also important to look at the positives and see how these can be enhanced. Most students' maps contained the joys of celebrating birthdays. This can be something that the whole cohort can embrace. On our programme, we incorporated digital GIF congratulations for everybody's birthdays and also for cultural festivals, such as Diwali.

Journey maps created by students referring to their degree programme have proven to be a powerful tool of reflection and communication between students and the programme team. There were certainly multiple boundaries that have been crossed, not only between students and staff but also between the students themselves as a heterogeneous cohort coming from a variety of cultures and academic and professional backgrounds. It created a sharing activity for a group of students who were able to recognise similarities in their experience and gain reassurance that what they may have perceived as their personal insecurity is actually shared by their wider peer group. Students have reported a greater sense of belonging, increased psychological safety and appreciation of being heard and listened to as a group. The journey maps provided a ground for programme improvements that were communicated back to the students through a series of visual posters in a "You said, we did" session at the end of the programme. Closing the loop in this very explicit way created a sense of commitment to the programme in the students beyond graduation as well as pride in the ability to input into the programme evolution.

Conclusion

Journey mapping is a well-developed method to synthesise user research and find out about the service delivery strengths as well as weaknesses from the point of the user. It can be a very powerful envisioning tool for prototyping the ideal future state of a service you wish to redesign or develop from new. The main purpose of journey mapping is typically as a visual communication between the user and the service provider, establishing the user's experience. In our education examples we have seen powerful applications enhancing the learners' reflection developing their sense of life learning history or a shorter learning event. We have seen how mapping a learning journey enhances empathy and provides opportunities for the learners' co-creation of education experience improvements. Journey maps as visual boundary objects do help crossing boundaries between our own memories and our own learning actions, between ourselves and our peers and between educators and their students who experience their learning in a complex university ecosystem though interactions with multiple providers.

Key learning points

1   Establish the purpose of why you are mapping a learning journey:

   • To help learners reflect on their own learning
   • To understand the learner's experience with an aim to improve it
   • To visualise complexity of service delivery and establish a shared understanding of the network of service providers
   • Or simply to create a sense of community and acknowledge diversity of approaches to learning

2   You may have more than one objective and one map may meet multiple aims.

3   Start with simple maps and don't feel too restricted by what to record and how. Your practice can evolve with time and experience. The key principle is to stay open minded without judgment and enquiring deeper into the ups and downs.

4 Do your own map of your life learning journey after reading this chapter or of your learning gained from the book. Have a go at using our simple templates and share them with your colleagues.

Notes

1 The project was led by one of our co-editors, Jean Mutton.
2 https://edujam.co.uk.
3 http://globaljams.org/jam/globalgovjam.

References

Andrews, J. & Eade, E. (2013) Listening to students: Customer journey mapping at Birmingham City University Library and learning resources. *New Review of Academic Librarianship*, 19(2), 161–177.

Baranova, P., Morrison, S. & Mutton, J. (2010) *Service Design in Higher and Further Education*. JISC CETIS, p. 6.

Cabinet Office. (2007) *Customer journey mapping: An introduction*. London: HM Government.

Crosier, A., & Handford, A. (2012) Customer journey mapping as an advocacy tool for disabled people: A case study. *Social Marketing Quarterly*, 18(1), 67–76.

del Olmo, M. V. & Morelli, N. (2022) Service journeys as boundary objects in participatory processes for multi-stakeholder engagement: The case of the easyrights journeys. DRS 2022. Design Research Society.

Følstad, A., Kvale, K. & Halvorsrud, R. (2014) *Customer journeys: Involving customers and internal resources in the design and management of services*. ServDes. 2014 Service Future; Proceedings of the fourth Service Design and Service Innovation Conference, Lancaster University, 9–11 April 2014 (No. 099, pp. 412–417). Linköping: Linköping University Electronic Press.

Huang, Y. & Hands, D. (Eds) (2022) *Design Thinking for New Business Contexts: A Critical Analysis through Theory and Practice*. London: Springer Nature.

Ivey-Williams, K. (2016a) Design in Government Blog: How to make a user journey map. Available at: https://designnotes.blog.gov.uk/2016/04/21/how-to-make-a-user-journey-map (Accessed: 1 August 2023).

Ivey-Williams, K. (2016b) Design in Government Blog: Why we use user journey maps in government. Available at: https://designnotes.blog.gov.uk/2016/03/30/why-we-use-user-journey-maps-in-government (Accessed: 1 August 2023).

Newton, R. (2022) Design thinking – Practice and Applications. In Y. Huang & D. Hands (Eds) *Design Thinking for New Business Contexts: A Critical Analysis through Theory and Practice*. London: Springer Nature.

Newton, R. (2023) Inclusive Programme Review Method: Co-Creating student learning experience with service design methods. Available at: https://wp.lancs.ac.uk/ipr/ipr-method (Accessed: 8 July 2023).

Ostrom, A. L., Bitner, M. J. & Burkhard, K. A. (2011) *Leveraging Service Blueprinting to Rethink Higher Education: When Students Become "Valued Customers", Everybody Wins*. Washington, DC: Center for American Progress.

Radnor, Z., Osborne, S. P., Kinder, T. & Mutton, J. (2013) Operationalizing co-production in public services delivery: the contribution of service blueprinting. *Public Management Review*, 16(3), 402–423.

Samson, S., Granath, K. & Alger, A. (2017) Journey mapping the user experience. *College & Research Libraries*, 78(4), 459.

Segelström, F. (2012) *Communicating through visualizations: Service designers on visualizing user research*. In Conference Proceedings ServDes. 2009; DeThinking Service; ReThinking Design, Oslo Norway24–26 November 2009 (No. 059, pp. 175–185). Linköping: Linköping University Electronic Press.

Segelström, F., Raijmakers, B. & Holmlid, S. (2009) *Thinking and doing ethnography in service design*. IASDR, Rigor and Relevance in Design. Seoul.

Smaply. (n.d.) Customer Journey Mapping. Available at: www.smaply.com (Accessed: 1 August 2023).

Stickdorn, M., Hormess, M. E., Lawrence, A. & Schneider, J. (2018) *This is service design doing: applying service design thinking in the real world*. Sebastopol, CA: O'Reilly.

Whittle, S. & Foster, M. (1991) Customer Profiling; Getting Into Your Customer's Shoes. *International Journal of Bank Marketing*, 9(1), 17–24.

Chapter 17

'Know thy student, for she is not thee'

User personas as a way to give agency to student voice

Radka Newton and Michael Doherty

Introduction

When we are designing our courses or programmes, we often think about our own knowledge, what we want to convey to the learners, what we feel is important. As conscientious educators we *do* consider the people we are designing for, especially if we have absorbed the dominant rhetoric of student-centredness. What, though, is this consideration based on and how do we keep these interests and insights front and centre when we are developing our educational practices? We might draw upon our own experience of being a student, which is likely to be highly unrepresentative. If we rely on reflections from our own teaching, then this knowledge will still be dotted with assumptions and be partial (both in the sense of incomplete and refracted through our existing perceptual lenses). If we use published scholarship of teaching and learning, how do we know that the findings will be of relevance to the cohorts that we teach? All these sources of knowledge are valid, but if we do not also take steps to really understand who our students are then perhaps the most important piece of the jigsaw remains missing.

Service design principles guide us towards a user-centredness that helps us consider who our learners are, what previous experience they may be coming with, what their expectations are and what is their context of learning. Taking time to consider the learners will help us determine many important aspects in our planning, not just related to content, but also for issues such as mode of delivery, scheduling, assessment preparation and physical or digital learning spaces.

Student-centred education

Placing students at the centre of learning is a well-accepted concept in Higher Education (HE). It emphasises the importance of learner autonomy, independence and student empowerment. A recent development of student-centredness is the concept of *engagement through partnership*, which encourages innovation 'through staff and students learning and working together to foster engaged student learning and engaging learning and teaching enhancement'

DOI: 10.4324/9781003383161-28

(Healey, Flint & Harrington, 2014). Work on promoting this concept offers examples of students contributing to the development of learning materials, co-creating parameters of assessment, driving discipline research, inputting into learning evaluation and participating in curriculum improvements.

An obvious question here is – why bother with user research and personas if you can just directly involve students in educational design decisions? We are enthusiastic about co-production, but there are potential shortcomings. Bovill (2017) points out that many case studies involve working with a small selection of students such as course representatives or volunteers. It is rarer for engagement to reach wider cohorts and provide a more inclusive mechanism for a diversity of voices. To put it bluntly, those students whose lives and perspectives we most need to understand are the least likely to be involved in co-production activities. The values underpinning co-production and user research and personas are the same, principally the core value of empathy. We argue that all these concepts and tools should be part of the repertoire of the modern educator in HE.

To relate and understand

Service design practices invite us to explore the sometimes messy reality of our students' whole lives and to recognise the existence of emotions, life events and the impact of wider systems on learners' readiness to learn. We recognise that learners come to us with prior education experiences and, for example, that the norms and rules they previously acquire are perhaps contradictory to the notions of active learning. Empathic understanding cannot close itself off from this holistic perspective. It involves more than having a supportive attitude. It requires particular types of research, knowledge generation and representation methods.

As scholars we pride ourselves on evidence-based research that informs many aspects of our practice as well as the creation of new knowledge. Conducting research into our own student population does not, however, come as a natural activity. We rely predominantly on data based on student surveys and other university and national statistics providing basic quantitative information. But as Kahu (2013) argues we neglect to gain insights into how students are feeling. Complementing the analytical data with these behavioural perspectives gives 'a much richer understanding of the student experience'. Likert scale surveys or student representative reports do provide some explicit information on what students think, but only when we go deeper and employ designerly techniques (Visser et al., 2005) such as observations or participatory workshops in collaboration with the students, are we able to gain insights on the personal sociocultural context, feelings, dreams and hopes of our students. The user research perspective in design offers a multi-layered approach to relating to and understanding our audience and helps us find answers to the most fundamental question: 'Who are we designing the learning for?' By understanding the expectations, motivations and concerns of students it is possible to transform the depth and meaning of the learning not only for our students but also for ourselves.

What are user personas?

According to Williams (2023), a user persona is 'a fictional rendition of character ... created to embody key characteristics of the anticipated users of a designed output'. Persona profiling or user personas are one of the empathetic techniques helping designers relate to and understand their audience to avoid the common mistake of assuming that everybody is like us and therefore that the best design is the one that meets our own needs. Personas are concerned with visualising and understanding users' goals and motivations and the relationship they have with the designed product or service. They can make 'the abstract concrete, engaging the visual and the tangible to show rather than tell' (Williams, 2023).

The software designer Alan Cooper developed the concept of personas as a design tool in the 1990s and explained that 'Personas are not real people, but they represent them throughout the design process. They are hypothetical archetypes of actual users, [often] defined by their goals' (Cooper, 2004). Pruitt and Grudin (2003) argue that their strength lies in their usability as a conduit for conveying a broad range of data not covered by other design methods. They are normally used as part of a wider design-led process (user experience mapping, ideation, prototyping) but they can be used as more of a standalone tool or exercise to help understand and focus on the needs of a cohort.

Meet Sofia

Figure 17.1 Student persona

Sofia is a postgraduate student from Asia who left home for the first time and feels very homesick. Her mum has not been well, and Sofia is worried about her. The distance is making it all very tough, but her mum keeps encouraging her to focus on her studies. She loves her degree and studies really hard, but she worries the lecturers don't think she is good enough. Because of the time difference, she can only call home in the early hours of the morning. If the classes are early the next day, she feels very sleepy and embarrassed. She doesn't mean to be disrespectful to the lecturer. She has to call home every day....

Sofia is a student persona created as a visual synthesis of a variety of data collected through multifaceted research. Sofia is not a purely imaginary person. Her profile is based on facts, observations and deeper investigation of student emotions and personal contexts. Her profile is a personification of real students at a real University. Sofia acts as a visual representation of student characteristics, fears, dreams and aspirations.

Do you feel you know her? Can you imagine that she is a student in your institution, on your programme? Developing a portfolio of personas that represent your students will provide you with a constant reference point ensuring the functionality, usability and relevance of your curriculum design reminding you that real people, humans with feelings, will be sitting in your classroom. To encourage empathy, personas have real names, some sort of visual identity and some amount of demographic information. But it is the psychological information, their concerns and motivations, that matters most; that gives us the focus to understand what the users want to gain.

Personas in education

While well developed in other applications of service design, it remains rare for personas to be used in the design of education. There have been some related practices outlined below.

While they did not use personas, Rogers et al. (2006) showcase the importance of learner needs segmentation and the 'shifts in the attitudes of individual faculty members toward different types of learners'. They demonstrated how, as part of this mindset shift, understanding diverse student segments influenced the governance structures in a university to make them more aligned with students' needs. These needs were seen a part of a continuum, a journey from recruitment to careers support.

An inspiring example of user research and personas comes from Lewis and Contrino (2016) describing the case of librarians who redesigned the library user experience. They carried out in-depth user research with an objective to challenge their own assumptions about how easy it is to use library resources, discover the struggles of the learners trying to access the library and understand challenges related to the wider education system linked to tasks initiated outside the library. Their personas were created 'using narrative to project depth, complexity and to view the user within a scenario rather than just looking at the scenario'. The personas were data-driven and included information on background, motivation and challenges, and their use resulted in changes to the library website and embedded information skills information within substantive modules.

A final example shows both the potential utility of personas on education design and some of the practical barriers to their adoption by academics. In this example by Lilley et al. (2012) we learn about a project that enquired into the needs of online learners and their preferences on receiving feedback. The project involved programme administrators, education technologists and tutors who created online student personas to synthesise and better understand their findings from surveys and interviews. This was motivated by a sense that there was a lot of data on students but that 'it did not provide an adequate sense of the people behind the numbers or the context in which they were studying'.

The case studies in the next section of the chapter will show how we incorporated personas into our curriculum design and what benefits this has had on our educational practice. We will also outline some potential pitfalls in the use of personas.

Our case studies

We developed our interest in applying service design mindsets and methods to HE, including using personas, quite independently of each other (Doherty & McKee, 2022; Huang & Hands, 2022; Newton, 2023). When we found each other's work we were interested in how differently we had used the same toolkit, and how personas drew on a coherent underlying ethos and method but were applicable in widely differing ways and contexts.

Design is a pragmatic and practical practice and there are enablers and barriers to service design adoption. We want to make it clear how our academic positions enabled us to practice service design. We were both in academic leadership positions that gave us the *authority* to decide (with others) what approach we took to curriculum design, what outcomes we were aiming for and how the outputs would be implemented. We also both framed our projects as scholarship enquiries with an aim to share our findings and influence a wider academic community. As such we had a unique opportunity to carve out some *time* as well as *access* to students and other collaborators inside and outside our institutions developing a robust body of data.

Both our projects' aims were to go beyond just incorporating traditionally received student feedback into our curriculum redesign *to engaging students in decision-making processes* and making them far more visible in the design process.

Legal curriculum case study

This case study outlines how service design methods were used as the framework for a major curriculum re-design of an undergraduate law degree, creating a new version of Year 1 of a law degree at an English law school. The team wanted to create a more coherent student experience across the programme, rather than just offering an agglomeration of individual modules that do not easily connect to – or build upon – each other. We also wanted to address issues of inclusion, with a specific focus on the ethnicity attainment gap and to promote attendance and engagement.

The law school was part of an established teaching-focussed (and research-active) post-1992 university, with a Year 1 law degree intake of around 180 students. The cohorts were from a diverse range of educational backgrounds, mostly from the North-West of England, with many commuting rather than living on campus. A high percentage were first generation to university and many students were from economically and educationally disadvantaged backgrounds. We used the Stanford d.school Design Thinking Process which structured the specific tools we used and provided a landscape and rationale for our development activities.

Reasons for using personas and how we did user research

We saw this curriculum re-design as a real opportunity to critically question existing practices and assumptions. Design thinking offered us a toolkit and mindset to explore what was more likely to work with our students and what would lead to greater engagement, attainment, intellectual development and future success.

We had ongoing research interests and projects within the team that were relevant e.g. on inclusive learning, addressing the BAME attainment gap and diversity barriers. We needed to consciously question and critique our assumptions, but we did have existing insight into our students with well over 100 years' experience in the school between us in teaching and student support. According to Stickdorn et al. (2018) this internal knowledge has a valid place in user research, and we supplemented this with desk research, i.e. the collection and review of existing research on issues such as the mental resilience of undergraduate law students.

The data sets that increasingly pervade HE help us understand some aspects of student experience but are often intended for different purposes (ranking, overview and audit). They also do not get under the skin of the lived experience of students. To find this rich information for our cohort we hired a third-year undergraduate to undertake *in-depth UX interviews* with a small number of year one students. We already had information from our students on things like the assessment regime, feedback, aspects of teaching etc., so we focussed our questions on things that we felt we did not fully understand. This included the relationship between our students' studies and the rest of their lives, e.g. what they told their friends and families about what they were studying, what their families felt about them being a law student. We explored the positive triggers that stimulate their learning, e.g. what they felt empowered to do now that they could not do at the start of the course. We also tried to identify 'pain points', i.e. the blockages in students' engagement with their programme. These were more likely to be practical (commuting costs and time, the need to work part-time) than academic (the content of the modules). Finally, we discussed the students' motivations and hopes for the future. Using multiple research methods (teacher perspectives, desk research, UX interviews) adds to the richness of the data set and allows a team to triangulate their findings (Stickdorn et al., 2018). The variegated information that we obtained went into the creation of three user personas – Terri, Nazir and Karen.

How we created and used the personas

We worked with students, through drafting, consulting and re-drafting, to co-create three user personas to represent a range of educational and social/family backgrounds, demographic characteristics, career goals and personal interests. We chose to have three personas as balancing the need to represent the diversity of experience, background and aspiration with the need for a limited number of characters that we could engage with. Each persona was summarised on one page which we kept visible and physically centred during our regular team discussions. Some personas are visually represented by a sketch, but we chose to use stock images as a way of making them seem more 'real'.

Large organisations will often undertake photoshoots to have multiple images of each persona, but a single stock image suited our project (and our budget). Each proposal was tested by considering how it would work for the personas. It may sound a little strange, but we became emotionally invested in *Terri Jackson, Nazir Hussain* and *Karen Ramsey*, we wanted to do our best by them in making our decisions and to give them a curriculum, pedagogies and academic support that would allow them to flourish.

Benefits

The benefits were at least four-fold. First, they helped us shift perspective from a teacher to a student view of issues. This teacher-focus is a particular risk when those designing the curriculum will be responsible for its delivery. Cooper (2004) identifies personas as principally a discussion tool, and we largely used them this way; "how would structuring the workshops this way work for Terri?" We felt that this shift helped us come up with innovative ways of thinking about how students learn in their first year.

Second, they provided diversity, not only in the basic characteristics of age, gender and race, but also in their wider life circumstances and different priorities outside of their studies. The personas, for example, had learning needs, caring responsibilities and difficulties in commuting to campus. They did not, though, operate as a simple checklist of learning challenges. As rounded individuals they also had strengths to draw upon – a good educational background, strong motivation, a supportive family – that introduced nuance and realism into thinking about these challenges.

Third, the personas acted as 'boundary objects', that is, as a shared basis for communication (Pruitt & Grudin, 2003; Newton & Doherty, 2023). All the members of the team would have an internal mental picture triggered by a phrase such as 'students with learning needs'. This picture would be a compound of the very different past experiences of the different team members. Unless this concept or category is taken out of people's minds and personified or in some other way made tangible (the 'boundary object') then there is a greater risk of talking at cross purposes and of misaligned assumptions. Indeed, the process of creating the personas helped us make our implicit assumptions about our cohorts more explicit and therefore open to question.

Fourth, personas can act as an external communication tool (Miaskiewicz & Kozar, 2011). That is, in giving clarity and weight to the reasons for particular educational decisions; "We went for option A because that will work better for Terri, Nazir and Karen than options B or C". This helped in discussing resourcing issues and other practical help that we needed from other parts of the institutions in implementing the curriculum.

All these things helped us in producing a curriculum design that was innovative in promoting active learning and independent study, in curriculum content that had greater relevance to our students' daily lives, in gaining institutional support for changes to timetabling that helped our commuting students and in structuring classes to optimise opportunities for connection and relation-building between students.

Management curriculum case study

This case study is situated within a context of providing academic leadership to a globally accredited postgraduate degree programme at a British business school. A programme director seldom has opportunities to meet the students apart from a few induction sessions and staff-student committee meetings. Yet they need to ensure that students meet learning outcomes and have an excellent learning experience and that staff teaching on the programme deliver stimulating and relevant modules. A student cohort is typically perceived as a homogeneous group of postgraduate management students and the key information provided about them is related to nationality, gender and age.

The challenge I was facing as a director was to support over fifteen teaching staff members who delivered individual modules on the programme and ensure the programme remained relevant for the growing student numbers. From the traditional student feedback through surveys (30 per cent completion rate) and student representatives, I gained a few insights into the challenges the students were facing related to the fast-paced nature of the programme and the intense assessment schedule. The programme also had an extensive career development component that was poorly attended.

The purpose of using persona profiling in this case was to become more familiar with the student cohort so that I could inform colleagues about student needs and implement a continuous programme review mechanism that would be more inclusive and complementary to the standard student feedback that we collect. I also wanted to challenge some assumptions that we had about our students. The main characteristic conveyed about this particular cohort was that they are ambitious, career and result-oriented. However, the feedback from the careers team, who seemed to be more attuned with the cohort, somehow contradicted this description and developing student personas seemed like an excellent opportunity to get a more representative and nuanced overview of who our students are.

Approach to personas development

Persona co-creation seemed like an appropriate method to create a cohort sense of togetherness and give me and the programme team an opportunity to meet students away from the study-related context. This is known a generative method – when you generate insights together with your users. The service design methods companion to Stickdorn et al. (2018) defines this as 'using the know-how of a group of invited participants to create a set of personas'. In this case my participants were my students, the direct beneficiaries, users and co-producers of the programme.

Students worked in self-selected groups of four receiving a very simple set of instruction – *'please, make me a typical student of this programme.'* Each team had an A3 card paper, selected a photograph for their visual student representation and picked other craft material to use. I was amazed how they launched into the activity, sharing, working together and laughing. Initially, I prompted the teams with questions like:

- What are their hobbies?
- What does their family say about their studies?
- What is their dream career?
- What are they worried about?

In time as my student cohort grew in numbers, I developed simple guidance for students to use more independently (Figure 17.2.) including factual as well as emotional prompts.

Outcomes

The visual representation provided insights into how the students saw themselves and what they considered important to share. It provided a near to

LEARNER'S PERSONA

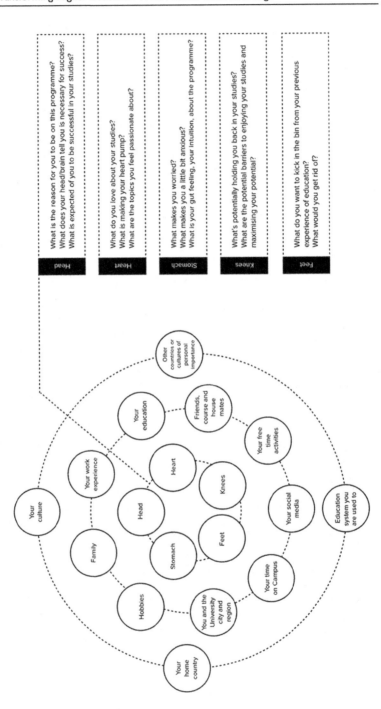

Head
What is the reason for you to be on this programme?
What does your head/brain tell you is necessary for success?
What is expected of you to be successful in your studies?

Heart
What do you love about your studies?
What is making your heart pump?
What are the topics you feel passionate about?

Stomach
What makes you worried?
What makes you a little bit anxious?
What is your gut feeling, your intuition, about the programme?

Knees
What's potentially holding you back in your studies?
What are the potential barriers to enjoying your studies and maximising your potential?

Feet
What do you want to kick in the bin from your previous experience of education?
What would you get rid of?

Figure 17.2 Persona profiling guide

cathartic experience of portraying their expectations, needs, fears and emotions as well as some facts about our student body. It also helped that there was a distance between what they created and what was highly personal to them. For example, they told a story of a student with pink hair called *Melanie Richards*, rather than their own story which they may have felt too emotional about. This is important in the context of including students of diverse cultures in this exercise, especially for those students where it is not culturally acceptable to openly disclose such personal information to an authority figure.

Students enjoyed presenting their visualisations of the personas and there seemed to be a real spirit of fun, community and a relaxed atmosphere, but also a serious commitment to informing our improvements. The no-judgment rule we adopted as staff members in these sessions was key to openness and trust. We learnt that our students are human beings, not only driven and ambitious future leaders with clear plans and confident extraverted characters. The personas demystified the homogenous assumption of a super-student and helped us recognise some aspects of students' lives that we had not taken into consideration when designing the programme.

From the variety of personas created, we were able to converge to a collection of reoccurring patterns such as: lack of self-confidence, significant self-doubt due to high family expectations, struggles with British academic cultures and the language barrier. Via the personas, students communicated how they wanted to spend their free time such as travelling to Europe, learning a new musical instrument or playing sports. Such insights have significantly altered how we think about designing the learning experience, how we structure career support, schedule assessment and communicate with our students.

Impact on our quality assurance process

The persona co-creation workshop has been integrated as an annual programme session for the whole cohort. The process of discovery never stops. Every year our students change, every year we strive to verify our assumptions and endeavour to discover our student body, immerse ourselves in their world, connect with them to reflect and be able to create a shared understanding of their programme expectations and experience and hopefully deploy these insights into our continuous programme improvements.

Melanie Richards, William Dong, Ivy Lee and many others have made it into the quality assurance reports. The annual programme review and our accreditation dossier proudly acknowledges our students as humans. Our external examiners often comment: "...you really know your students!"

Here are a few examples of improvements we have incorporated as a result of the heightened understanding of the student cohort:

- Career development sessions incorporated more self-awareness preparation with personality profiling diagnostics.
- Wednesday afternoons were left out of the timetable to allow time for social activities.
- The programme handbook was reduced from 70 to 20 pages with a recorded narrative of key information phrased in simple language: "What to do when you miss a class?" instead of "mitigating circumstances".
- The assessment schedule was revised to incorporate more preparation and mock practice.

Some drawbacks

There are some risks in using personas and potential missteps in their creation and application. Unless they are built on data and the right sorts of inputs, they may not be credible. Pruitt and Grudin (2003) point out that persona use does involve decision-making and that 'choices have consequences', i.e. if we foreground certain characteristics in our personas then we may obscure other characteristics present in our cohorts.

If the persona is presented merely as a CV or a resume, they will not have the sort of empathetic engagement we are looking for. It is possible to create good personas but then not to make effective use of them through decision-making processes (Pruitt & Grudin, 2003). Personas are highly context specific to a particular programme, cohort and time and the temptation to recycle them should be resisted.

Despite the significant impact that the persona profiling has had on our programme evolution, growth, quality and innovation, there is still a fairly small uptake of this activity across the institution. Pruitt and Grudin (2003) report institutional resistance to the idea of using fictional personas in self-consciously rationalistic settings like engineering, and the same has been found in HE applications (Lilley, Pyper & Attwood, 2012). Some of the scepticism in HE can flow from the belief (the assumption) of tutors that they already know and understand their student cohorts (Lilley, Pyper & Attwood, 2003). In addition:

- It can be hard to present the visual information in formal quality assurance documentation.
- Legitimising the value of such activity in the formal academic culture is still a challenge.
- It is perceived as time consuming.

Of course, there are some drawbacks to the persona co-creation method, but one day per year spent well with students has prevented a hundred sunken hours of trying harder and harder to deliver something that has no value to them.

Conclusion

As teachers we saw that we could not show respect for our students or real satisfaction in our efforts to facilitate their learning if we did not understand them *as people*. This reaching towards empathy and a desire to translate the high rhetoric of student-centredness into the regular practices of our teaching lives led us, independently, to the mindset and methods of service design. In the context of the drive in HE to engage students and staff effectively as partners in learning and teaching, we believe that taking a service design approach will take education design to a more fundamental concept of students as humans.

Persona co-creation as a method works well for creating a collaborative environment with an aim to involve students directly into a design or re-design of their learning experience. It contributes to trust building and empathy within the cohort as well as between students and staff. It gives voice to students who would not typically come forward with explicit feedback about their learning experience.

The two different approaches we undertook to develop personas demonstrate the flexibility and variety of the personas' application. Gathering and synthesising knowledge and understanding of our students through design research methods allowed us to make more informed decisions not only about what we teach but how we design environments in which our students can flourish as learners and as human beings.

Key learning points

1   Student personas are fictional, but they are not simply 'made up'. They are personifications based on rigorous research that is multifaceted, moving away from a reliance on traditional statistics and superficial demographic data.

2   There are many ways to apply student personas in education with the key objective of understanding who we are designing a module, programme or a support service for. The underlying value is empathy that offers a non-judgmental and relational platform for creating education that is human-centred not process-centred.

3   Putting students into the centre of education and working with them as partners is a well-developed concept in Higher Education, but there has been some shortfall in the understanding of practical ways to achieve this. User research and personas are effective and concrete tools that add to the repertoire of student-centred educators.

References

Bovill, C. (2020) Co-creation in learning and teaching: the case for a whole-class approach in higher education. *Higher Education*, 79(6), 1023–1037.

Bovill, C. (2017) A framework to explore roles within student-staff partnerships in higher education: Which students are partners, when, and in what ways?. *International Journal for Students as Partners*, 1(1), 1–5.

Cook-Sather, A., Bovill, C. & Felten, P. (2014) *Engaging students as partners in teaching & learning: A guide for faculty*. San Francisco, CA: Jossey-Bass.

Cooper, A. (2004) *The Inmates are Running the Asylum: Why Hi-Tech Products Drive Us Crazy and How to Restore the Sanity* (2nd ed.). Carmel, IN: Sams Publishing.

Doherty, M. & McKee, T. (2022) Service design comes to Blackstone's tower: Applying design thinking to curriculum development in legal education. In E. Allbon & A. Perry-Kessaris (Eds), *Design in Legal Education*. Abingdon: Routledge, pp. 67–80.

Healey, M., Flint, A. & Harrington, K. (2014) *Engagement through partnership: Students as partners in learning and teaching in higher education*. York: Higher Education Academy.

Healey, M., Flint, A. & Harrington, K. (2016) Students as partners: Reflections on a conceptual model. *Teaching and Learning Inquiry*, 4(2), 1–13.

Huang, Y. & Hands, D. (2022) *Design thinking for new business contexts*. New York: Springer.

Kahu, E. R. (2013) Framing student engagement in higher education. *Studies in Higher Education*, 38(5), 758–773.

Kouprie, M. & Visser, F. S. (2009) A framework for empathy in design: stepping into and out of the user's life. *Journal of Engineering Design*, 20(5), 437–448.

Lewis, C. & Contrino, J. (2016) Making the invisible visible: Personas and mental models of distance education library users. *Journal of Library & Information Services in Distance Learning*, 10(1–2), 15–29.

Lilley, M., Pyper, A. & Attwood, S. (2012) Understanding the student experience through the use of personas. *Innovation in Teaching and Learning in Information and Computer Sciences*, 11(1), 4–13.

Marshall, R., Cook, S., Mitchell, V., Summerskill, S., Haines, V., Maguire, M. & Case, K. (2015) Design and evaluation: End users, user datasets and personas. *Applied Ergonomics*, 46, 311–317.

Miaskiewicz, T. & Kozar, K. (2011) Personas and user-centred design: How can personas benefit product design processes. *Design Studies*, 32, 417–430.

Newton, R. (2023) Inclusive Programme Review Method: Co-Creating student learning experience with service design methods. Available at: https://wp.lancs.ac.uk/ipr/ipr-method (Accessed: 8 July 2023).

Newton, R. & Doherty, M. (2023) Beyond the survey: Service design approaches to inclusive programme review. *International Journal of Management and Applied Research*, 10(2), 199–215.

Pruitt, J., & Grudin, J. (2003) *Personas: Practice and Theory*. Proceedings of the Conference on Designing for User Experiences. Available at: www.microsoft.com/en-us/research/wp-content/uploads/2017/01/personas-practice-and-theory.pdf (Accessed: 18 March 2023).

Rogers, G., Finley, D. S. & Patterson, M. (2006) Transformation in higher education: a learner–needs segmentation leads to improved learner satisfaction. *Teaching in Higher Education*, 11(4), 401–411.

Stickdorn, M., Hormess, M. E., Lawrence, A. & Schneider, J. (2018) *This is service design doing: applying service design thinking in the real world*. Sebastopol, CA: O'Reilly.

Visser, F., Stappers, P., Van der Lugt, R., & Sanders, E. (2005) Context mapping: Experiences from practice. *CoDesign*, 1(2), 119–149.

Williams, C. (2023) Using personas, vignettes and diagrams in legal education. In E. Allbon & A. Perry-Kessaris (Eds), *Design in Legal Education*. Abingdon: Routledge.

Chapter 18

Seamless Student Journey

Fact or Fiction?

Jean Mutton and Christine Stewart

Introduction

We heard from Adam St John Lawrence at the start of this book that 'Service Design solves the right problem', which brings with it the opportunity to be more effective and efficient in our service delivery and stopping us from wasting our resources by looking in the wrong place to find solutions. The student experience will be enhanced, and we can make better use of resources by placing less drain on the service provision. By enabling the end-user to find what they need quickly and neatly, staff can direct more of their time and focus on ensuring that all students are getting the support they need to attain their goals. But how do we engage staff in this new way of approaching transformational change? What are the challenges they face and how have they been overcome, or not?

In the UK, there are a number of ways in which students are involved in feeding back to institutions about their own experience (the National Student Survey, for example) but we wanted to get an understanding of whether staff felt that the students at their university were getting an excellent experience and if not, how so. We set up a Padlet which we initially made available to attendees during an online conference presentation at a Lean HE Conference entitled 'LEAN + DESIGN: The creative application of Lean to strategically engage, collaborate, and succeed together', which was streamed from the University of Melbourne, Australia, in October 2022. We asked our audience of 40 staff from HEIs around the world to decide via an online poll: 'The Seamless Student Journey: Is it Fact or Fiction?' and the response was: 25 per cent Fact and 75 per cent Fiction. We were not surprised that the majority thought that a seamless student journey was a fictional concept. But what does 'seamless' mean? Just joining up services does not result in an excellent service experience, so what is needed? We also asked; 'what are the blockers and what are the enablers?'. Our audience was mainly Professional Services staff, who are only too aware of the challenges and barriers surrounding the delivery of a seamless experience given the large number of silos they encounter in their organisations and in their day-to-day operations.

DOI: 10.4324/9781003383161-29

This 'live' feedback and several of the themes which have surfaced in this book have led us to identity a series of provocations which may help you, as change makers, to address challenges that you may encounter as you set off on your journey to shape a better future for your students, your staff and your institution.

How might we address the siloed nature of HE?

'Services created in silos are experienced in bits, because services comprise multiple touchpoints across multiple channels and are experienced in their totality'. [1]

In our work across the higher education (HE) sector, we have encountered lots of desire to enhance the student journey using a range of methodologies and approaches such as Lean (which, put very simply, concentrates on the elimination of waste), Systems Thinking (which takes a holistic approach as well as focussing on the constituent parts of an organisation) and more latterly Service Design with its emphasis on co-creation, empathy and research. All these methodologies aim to join activities and processes together to deliver value to our students while making it simple and easy to provide a service. But we know that one of the challenges in all large complex organisations, such as universities, is to break down silo mentalities to foster a more holistic way of thinking with a focus on the felt student experience in its totality. This requires a management and business culture that builds ownership in the delivery of shared priorities. However, staff will often have their own personal as well as their departmental priorities and targets, and the same goals may not even be shared across the institution. The complex nature of historic processes, practices, systems and culture needs to be unpicked and re-aligned to the vision: making sure that all aspects of the University are working together to deliver and support the student journey.

So how do we tackle silo-thinking and silo-working? To help us to improve the end-to-end journey we should start by exploring what it is that the end-user wants and needs, giving us purpose and value in what we are trying to do. By mapping the end-to-end journey to understand all the pieces that go together to make the journey happen, we can begin to improve it by removing the lumps and bumps along the way. To do this, staff from the various constituent parts of the organisation need to come together to hear and see what the felt student experience is for their part of the process, and it is often an eye-opener for them. The importance of working with all the stakeholders to reflect on their place in the process and how the different pieces of the organisational jigsaw fit together to make the full picture should not be underestimated. Then when rebuilding the process, we should collectively understand the demand the end-user is placing on a service so that we can ensure that the right resource is in the right place at the right time to deliver what is needed. In this way, a non-judgemental perspective can be achieved – not an agenda driven by the Centre or a particular Faculty or Department but clarity and focus on what is important: there is a neutrality which this approach affords.

Figure 18.1 Student standing on islands representing silos

We heard earlier in the book about how making maps or personas, with your students and from their point of view, can be valuable tools. This is not only to find pain and wait points in systems and processes but also to support critical reflection on their learning journey. It is important to state at this point that these are outputs that won't necessarily lead to outcomes unless they are acted upon, revisited and revised regularly. They are merely platforms for surfacing problems or affording insights, which can act as springboards for personal or organisational development. Maps and other outputs which are created and then filed away are largely a waste of everyone's time. They may have had some impact in the moment of creation, but their full potential will not be realised unless they are iterated further and shared widely.

We need to recognise that it can be hard for staff in the many different departments, schools and faculties in a university to come together to take a student-centred view of a service experience: whether that is going through enrolment, submitting an essay or navigating their timetable. As facilitators of change, we need to be the best diplomats to draw folk in to ensure that no-one feels threatened and everyone feels heard, driving change at all levels. Coming together to create journey maps is one way to begin to break down these entrenched silos by creating an understanding of the whole, and how areas should collectively deliver improvement to both the delivery of the service and the experience of using it. We also need to understand the need for a change in mindsets.

How might we build a culture of open mindsets?

'We cannot solve our problems with the same thinking we used when we created them'.[2]

Over the years, we have heard and seen for ourselves, how staff in HE often jump to conclusions about what needs to be done, sometimes through organisational pressure for the 'quick fix' or because they are not encouraged or given headspace to explore what the issue really is. Learning to find the right question rather than looking for an answer to an assumed problem is a leap which many managers find risky. Staff have told us: "We don't have the time to do this sort of research", and even "We don't want to ask the students to participate in this project as we may be opening the flood gates". But if those flood gates stay shut, how can we enact meaningful change?

Far more powerful than any individual design tool is the creation of an open mindset and culture of continuous improvement, giving staff capability and confidence to make mistakes, fail and fail better next time: taking ownership of what they do on a day-to-day basis. Learning the importance of understanding the end-to-end process from raw material through to the hands of the customer is an easy thing to do when making an aeroplane – you just get your steel toe capped boots on and walk from the warehouse to the distribution centre. This is not so easy in HE, which is more like a bowl of spaghetti, where you start to unravel one end of a procedure and you find you are tugging on another 40 interrelated systems and processes.

This takes us back to the key question: 'what's the problem to be solved?'. One of the most important but often overlooked aspects of any change project is the initial research. This is too often skipped over or given a nod to, but not doing thorough research into what is happening to the felt student experience (which only be understood by working directly with students) can break or undermine your service delivery. It is surprising what you learn sitting in a main thoroughfare at your institution with a box of chocolates or a coffee voucher and a sign that says 'If you could change one thing about your university what would it be? Come and talk to me'. However, just asking them is not enough: research should be triangulated. As well as extracting data from surveys or holding focus groups, we should be looking and listening with an open mind, abandoning our assumptions and being alert to researcher bias. We don't want to end up 'doing the wrong thing righter' as system thinker John Seddon so succinctly put it.

How might we utilise technology (with a nod to Big Data)?

'The technology you use impresses no one. The experience you create with it is everything'. [3]

Sean Gerety

We all know of staff in HE who think that technology is the answer to everything, however, this approach can be a double-edged sword. A big part of making large databases such as student records systems fit for purpose is having the right data and having the data right. In HE there can be numerous Excel spreadsheets that are held locally by staff for their own purposes and that may not tie up with those held in the 'official' central student record systems. This can be a major barrier to collective understanding, and we'd like to declare a spreadsheet amnesty. Poor data can be a root cause of deep problems and we need to stick our heads above the parapet and look at where the data sits, who owns it, how is it used and what is it used for?

Earlier in the book, we saw how data on gender was handled with great sensitivity, to further a culture of inclusivity. Using a human-centred approach allowed the use of new data on gender to not only evidence the value which that institution places on inclusion but also addressed the needs of their diverse student community by working with them to design the right responses to meet their needs, deepening a sense of belonging and a feeling of being 'seen'.

We have heard how we should consider the holistic service experience – digital and non-digital; the tangible and the non-tangible. Is everything the user can access up to date and consistent? Where is the weakest link in the chain? At present, too many technological solutions are built on shaky foundations and more staff are turning to service design as previous attempts at sustainable change have fallen by the wayside and many an IT project has bitten the dust for want of thorough research, prototyping and testing. In bringing Intelligent Automation to the University of Glasgow with virtual workers, key questions for the team leading the change project were 'how do we measure benefits?' and 'what will success look like?'. By building on a sound basis through a service design lens, the project has broken new ground in moving toward a better student experience and embedding value in their service delivery.

How might we improve communications?

'The single biggest problem in communication is the illusion that it has taken place'.
George Bernard Shaw, Nobel Prize-winning playwright

People are easily confused, especially in a world they don't know. Fudged or conflicting messages will land badly, so communications need to be clear and consistent across all channels. Excellent communications – or rather the impact of poor or no communications – are not just a student issue, they impact on staff too. Internal communications need to be open and honest to build trust and ensure that there is consistency across the organisation.

In their non-student life, people are now so used to turning to search engines such as Google to find out how to do something, that they do so even when they are looking for help during their student journey. But how do they find what they need at that point? Here the name of the service can be key – it should clearly state what it is, what it is for, how it works and for whom. It needs to be in a form of words, determined by students, which will mean something to them. Rather than jump into determining the process flow of a service we should ask 'why would anyone want this' and 'how and why did they get here?'

When we are designing a process where a student needs to move through several steps, such as going through Enrolment, one key area to get right is signage, be it virtual or physical. We have seen signage which says 'This way to the online enrolment IT lab' with signs pointing in two completely different directions. As it happened, that IT lab could be reached via two sets of stairs, so both were accurate but also very confusing. Signage should be placed and laid out in a way that it takes you to where you need to be without fuss. The end-user will have been making lots of decisions while they moved through the corridors, making a series of decisions to get them to the right place. Too often these can become pain points or wait points. The same applies to navigating the way through a service process. How many steps are there? What is the rhythm and tempo of what is leading that person to their goal? If any of these are poorly designed, staff will end up with demand on the service which is not of value to anyone where a user (or more likely hundreds of users) bounce back into the process to resolve issues, leading to unhappiness in the service experience and wasting both their time and that of the staff.

How might we engage others to ensure sustainable transformational change?

'By encouraging participation early on in the implementation process, team members will feel responsible for the outcome of the change. This way, change isn't just something that's happening to them. It's something that's happening because of them'. [4]

Jeff Grabill

In general, staff working in HE care greatly about supporting their students. They want them to be happy, to succeed and achieve their goals, but staff can be both blockers and enablers. People will go to work each day to do the best job they can and have told us "We want to deliver good service to our students despite….". It is these 'despites' that can trip us up.

Too often staff behaviour is driven by target-setting parameters rather than what is needed and wanted at a human level and there will be processes that staff work with which are outdated and inefficient. Sometimes, services are delivered in a way that is of little benefit to either the user or the organisation but 'they've always been done that way'. We say to people: 'Be prepared to challenge everything. You may find however you are not popular'. But staff have told us they are often too overwhelmed to embrace and support change as they are firefighting just to stay on top of their workload and many find it hard to embrace uncertainty and to trust the process to lead them to a better outcome.

When innovating change, to prevent things from reverting to legacy systems (we are creatures of habit after all), staff should be given a safe space and drawn in as co-creators of the changes to what they will see as 'their' service. Often it will be front line staff who feel the pain of the end-user and who have fundamental insight into where the real problems lie, sometimes from looking at where workarounds have been put in because a process or system is not fit for purpose. If we can gain their trust to give of their precious time to review systems and processes from a human-centred perspective, the benefits will be felt by not only the end-user but also the service delivery team.

Staff have asked us: 'Where do I start?', and 'Doesn't this take a long time?' Sometimes a lone voice in an organisation will be itching to find a better way but won't know where to begin. We say, start with small fires, get some success, be visual and share then watch as others become interested in what has been achieved. They will be peeping over the parapet to see what is happening and they may want a slice of the action next time. This ripple effect should gain its own momentum and in due course, with the right support, education and experience, a learning organisation will rise, like a phoenix from the flames, that truly puts their students at its heart and centre.

But most importantly, how do we engage students in the co-creation of their own experience? We have seen the applications of utilising personas as alternative means to finding and capturing the student voice. Using persona creation and storytelling in a non-judgmental, neutral space will allow students to open up and share their felt experience. Backed up by research this can be a powerful way to find the right questions to ask, problems to be addressed and to overcome assumptions.

We heard earlier in the book about how making maps, with your students, from their point of view, can not only be a valuable tool to find pain and wait points in systems and processes but can also be used as a learning tool to support students' critical reflection on their learning journey.

We conclude that there is very much a desire to create a Seamless Student Journey that is simple and easy to deliver and intuitive to navigate, but both the student and the staff experience need to be in balance and in line with organisational strategy.

Summary

Our discussions around the Seamless Student Journey have been wide and far-ranging. We have covered many topics, raising issues that need to be dealt with and successes that should be embraced and shared. This has led us to a new model: the '3Ps: People, Purpose and Process'.

1 People – Cultural issues around fear of sharing, local experts and the HE penchant for silo working creates an increased number of handovers, bottlenecks and an unwillingness to stop and look critically at what we do. There also seems to be a disconnect between student and staff experience perhaps exacerbated by a lack of humility and a belief that we are better/ smarter than the student – meaning that we take more of a process view on how we operate rather than a human-centred one. In order to tackle this mindset, there needs to be a shift to co-creating 'with' not 'for' our student communities.

2 Purpose – There is often no shared perspective on the whole process and how everyone contributes. This lack of clarity of the whole and the misalignment of priorities and vision makes it difficult to secure buy-in to what needs to be improved. This can lead to local optimisation and ownership issues where either no-one takes ownership or people are unwilling to let ownership go.

3 Process – Outdated processes, systems and documentation make it difficult to unpick how things work and the implementation of new ways of working can be challenging. This is further complicated by the variety and needs of different subject areas, courses and programmes and also of the diverse student body. We never said it would be easy.

Overall, we are left with the impression that a Seamless Student Journey is an achievable goal albeit still some way off, however, this is not stopping institutions and individuals from creating a momentum for change using the tools and techniques of service design.

So, where will you start?

Notes

1 Polaine, A. 'Your product is a service and why that matters'. Available at: www.polaine. com/2021/10/your-product-is-probably-a-service-and-why-that-matters (Accessed: 2 August 2023).
2 www.brainyquote.com/quotes/albert_einstein_121993 (Accessed 6 December 2023).
3 https://olhamaikut.medium.com/the-technology-you-use-impresses-no-one-b663b 73fed4b (Accessed: 6 December 2023).
4 https://voltagecontrol.com/blog/the-blueprint-for-sustaining-organizational-change (Accessed: 12 December 2023).

Index

Note: *Italic* page number refer to *figures* and **Bold** page number refer to **tables**.

ABC Avalanche tool 67
Academic Workload Planning 130
accessibility 204
Adm2020 134
administrative staff 39, 138
Agile software development 42
Anderson, Kim 18
Artificial Intelligence (AI) 175
Assumption Mapping Framework 89, *90*, 95
assumptions 54–55
authoritative statements 12
automation service 17; challenges 183; choice and selection *177*; creation 176; current situation 181–182; Robotic Process Automation (RPA) 183–184; story of 181; unintended consequences 180; University of Glasgow 178–181

bad design 51
balanced scorecard, 121
'behind the scenes' process 7
blueprinting methodology 232, 233
Bohr, Niels 94–96
Bombardieri, Mila 15
booking events spaces 128
Bovill, C. 244
boundary object 99, 232, 235, 237, 240, 250
brainstorming 40
British Higher Education 78
Brown, T. 126
Business Enhancement Team (BET) 120
business needs for data governance 163

buzzwords 26

campus leadership 172
canvas: deploying 80; development of 79–80; prototyping and testing 80; stages 81–82
capstone portfolio project 61
case study: creating design principles 63–64; Innovation Lab and harnessing technology 127; learning management system (LMS) 87; legal curriculum 247–248; management curriculum 250–251; Murrie, Katie 63, 71–72; PhD student experience 87; Professional Development Award in Service Design 212–215; service design 145–147; student projects 127–128; Virdi, Sonia 61–62, 65–71, *72*
championing design principles 4
Change HEROs (Higher Education Re-Organisation for Students and Staff) 52; online course, development of 52–53
change management 171
changing mental models 110
charismatic leadership style 43
coaches, service design 107–108, **109**
co-creation process 32, 56, 70
co-design session 68
cognitive bias 94
collaboration and iteration process 7
collaborative activities 76; on canvas 83 *see also* canvas; course-led 82; with external organisations 77; primary research 78;

30-minute online visual interviews 80, 82; volume and scale of 78
collaborative innovation 14
collaborative online workspace 64
communications 262–263
community, role of 29
conceptual thinking 13
conduct research 162
constructive alignment 225
contextual interviews 220
continuous improvement 15, 120–123
continuous reflection 236
contribution process 70
Contrino, J. 246
conventional thinking *126*
convergent thinking 61
Cooper, A. 249
cross-organisational service-map 136–138, *137*
crowd-sourced insights *25*
cultural re-orientation 133
Curse of Knowledge 54
customer journey mapping 231
Customer Service Excellence Accreditation 232

data collection process 78
data-driven evidence 61
data-driven research 164
data enablement 171
data governance, business needs for 163
data integration methods 164
data security 172
Delalande, Phil 67
del Olmo, M. V. 232
design 4–9, 11, 13–15; agencies 3; and business as usual (BAU) 110–111; communication tool 19; curriculum 17; definition of 37; experience and technical requirements 164–165; external consultancy 163; inclusive 18; journey 91–93; notion of 1; principles 1; principles creation of 63–64; research tools 108; thinking 17; *see also* design thinking; human-centred design (HCD); service design
design brief challenge checklist 89–91
Design Challenge Charter 91
design challenge readiness framework 89–91
'design coach' 107–108
Design Council 3, 52, 60, 73, 92

designerly, 3, 95, 96, 244
designing education, with journey mapping 233
'designing for service' 75
design-led organisational change 77
Design Sprint model 86
design system 59–60; stages of 60; University of Edinburgh 61
design thinking 3, 17, 37; ecosystem for 86; methods and tools in 15; mini-sprint 196; and service design practices 5; for student engagement *see* student engagement; teaching and learning 190; with Warwick Secret Challenge *see* Warwick Secret Challenge (WSC)
Dewey, J. 93, 226
Dhir, Anne 3
digging deeper 28
digitalisation 5
digital pattern library 64
digital transformation projects 119
dimension of culture 173
direct discrimination 204
'Discovery Grants' 109
discovery/research phase 128
dissertation projects 224
diversity 18
divergent 61
Diversity, Equity, and Inclusion (DEI) organization 159
Doherty, Michael 13, 19
Double Diamond 60–61, 92, 105, 124, 130; aspect of 127; Design framework 52; pre-discovery research 64–65; Service Design Academy (SDA) 65–70
Downe, Lou 2, 36, 65
drawing inspiration: defining phase 6–7; deliver phase 7; develop phase 7; discovery phase 6; key learnings 8–10; making things easier 9–10; service design 10
Drummond, Sarah 23
Dunne-Watts, Nichole 15
Dyer, Sarah 15
dynamic of engagement 75

ecosystem 86; map *165*
Edinburgh Global Experience Language (EdGEL) 64, 66

education 27, 61–63, 71; accessibility 204; aspects of 2; inclusive design 204; institutions 14, 52; personas in 246–247; pleasures of 27; service design 27, 61–63, 71; student-centred 243–244; student engagement with 189; universal design 203–204
Education Incubator 102, **103**, 111
educators 35–36
EDUJAM 4, 10, 71, 233–234, *234*
Egan, Jenny 16, 145
Eilertsen, Karin 16
emotion 5, 11, 19, 25, 27, 44, 66, 95, 230, 231, 233–237, 239, 244, 246, 253
emotional journey mapping 123, 125, 233, 237
empathy 1, 2, 4, 10, 19, 23, 31, 40, 41, 47, 66, 70, 71, 94, 95, 104, 114, 129, 198, 201, 233, 240, 244, 246, 255, 259
engagement through partnership, concept of 243
enrolment process 50
Equality Act 2010 18, 209
ethnography 230
EU-funded education projects 232
"exam journey" 239
executive sponsor 159
experience 1–5, 11, 13–15, 36–38, 42, 44, 48–55, 57, 58, 60, 62–72, 79, 80, 82, 86–88, 91–97, 102, 104, 105–109, 112–114, 122–130, 133, 139, 143, 148, 151, 155, 161, 163–165, 167, 172–173, 221, 225–226; design 170–171; institution work 49; learning 203–207, 209–210, 212–215, 219, 220, 223; learning educational 18; learning journey 222; PhD student 87; positive WSC 124; of service design *see* service design; student *see* student experience; and technical requirements 164; university 175–178
experience learning journey *236*, 236–237
experiential learning models 42
experimentation 7
expert service design 159
exploratory user research 145

'fail fast' approach 7, 9
feedback 57, 220
final portfolio project 61, 63, 64
formal curriculum 226

formative assessment methods 225
Futurelib 150

Gasson, S. 12
gender 160
gender data enablement project 173
gender data project 159–161; data privacy 169; external factors and influences 160–161; gender and 160; impetus for change 159; visioning and organizing 159–160
gender identity 160; questions **170**
gender-inclusive campus: best practice recommendations 168–171; conduct research 162; data enablement 171; data security 172; designing for *162, 165*; discover and map technical considerations 164; experience and technical requirements 164; gender data elements **169**; gender data project 159–161; impacted community members 172; implementation 166–167; key learnings 172–173; privacy and transparency 172; recommended approach 161–167; representative reporting 172; risks and rewards *166*; structural changes in 158; support respectful communications 171; Trevor Project 158; user testing 165–166
generative method 251
generative pre-trained models (GPTs) 176
Geuy, Bernadette 16
Giacom, J. 12
Gibbs, G. 221
Global Service Jam (GSJ) 123, 124
Good Services: How to Design Services That Work (Downe) 2
Gov.uk's design principles 64
Grabill, Jeff 263
graphic design process 62
Grudin, J. 245, 254

harnessing technology 127
HCD thinking disposition model 96
Hidden Disabilities Sunflower Scheme 205
hierarchy of needs 11
Higher Education (HE) 38–39; administration and management 51; blueprinting case studies 233; design system *see* design system; human-centred design in 24; institutions 161;

institution work experience 49; people working in 1; reflective practice *see* reflective practice; service design in *see* service design; siloed nature of 259–261; student-centredness in 12
Higher Education Business Community and Interaction (HE-BCI) 78, 83
Hollowgrass, Rachel 16
Holmes, Kat 206
homogenising data 189
Human Capital Management (HCM) system 158, 159
human-centred design (HCD) 1; authoritative statements of 12; building capacity 13–15; collaboration and iteration 7; definition 86; design brief challenge checklist 89–91; Design Challenge Charter 91; design challenge readiness framework 89–91; and design thinking models 92; drawing inspiration in *see* drawing inspiration; early learnings and shift 122–123; experimentation 7; 'fail fast' approach 9; illustration process 6, *8*; immense value in 8–9; impact of 12–13; importance 180; interactive systems 12; 'learning-by-doing' approach 93; mindsets and identities 92–93; preparation 87–89; in real-world design challenges 87; and service design 10, 12, 66; 'situatedness' of 13; to work and empowering teams 91–92
'human flourishing' perspective 224
human motivation 11
human needs 16, 163
humble learning 94, 99

ideation 20, 37, 39, 40, 41, 44, 54, 67, 105, 124, 127, 130, 151, 184, 189, 245
'the Ikea effect' 32
illustration process: human-centred design (HCD) 6, *8*; stakeholders for 6; styles 6
implementation, service design activity 41
inclusion 18, 56
inclusive design 203, 204; approach *205*; in learning 205–206
inclusive education design 187
incorporate sustainability 76
in-depth UX interviews 248

individual and organisational learning outcomes 93
individuals' professional development 112–113
informal curriculum 226
Information Services Group (ISG) 62
informed assumptions 54, 109
ingrained mindset 152–153
innovation 14–15, 17, 26, 27, 37, 39, 44, 45, 48, 50, 61, 68, 75, 91, 96, 97, 102, 189, 195, 254; co-creation of 17; collaborative 14, 75–84
The Innovation Lab 15, 102, **103**; coaches to support participants 107–108, **109**; 'critical hope' 104; design and implementation 113–114; educators and students 107; elements *109*; 'embedded researcher' 105; five defining characteristics 105–109; and harnessing technology 127; pilot itself 108–109; programme **103–104**; project 103; real world setting 106; reflecting on three tensions 110–114; service design and business as usual (BAU) 110–111; structured service design programme 105–106; value of participating in 106
Institute for Advanced Teaching and Learning (IATL) 190, 191, 197
Intelligent Automation: choice and possibilities 177; Robotic Process Automation (RPA) 178; technology 175; University experience 175–178
intensity gradient 148
interactive systems, human-centred design for 12
Interconnected Services 134
Interdisciplinarity project 192–193, 197
internal communications 263
internalised mindset 27–28
'internal language' 133
interventions, reflective practice 220–225
iterative design process 150–151

Jackson, Jacqui 188
Jobs-to-be-Done theory 97
Joint Information and Systems Committee 50
Jones, Sharon 15
journey mapping 230; benefits 232; customer 231; designing education with 233; different purposes of 230; dimensions 231; EDUJAM 233–234;

emotional 123, 125, 233, 237; life
learning 234–235; service design
approach to 230; student 222–223,
227, 238; university degree programme
learning journey 237–240; user *see* user
journey map

Kahu, E. R. 244
Katz, B. 126
Kelestyn, Bo 17
knowledge exchange (KE) activities
75–77, 80
Kolb, D. 221
Kuzmina, Ksenija 15, 18, 104

lack of awareness 18
Lawrence, Adam 13, 66, 232
leadership teams 39
Lean Competency System (LCS) 121
Lean Higher Education (LeanHE) 122
Lean methodology 134
Lean thinking 121
learner 1, 2, 5, 12, 18–19, 23, 52–53,
59, 61, 65, 71, 72, 86, 87, 95, 104,
106, 187, 205–208, 210, 212–216,
218, 219, 230–235, 240, 243, 244,
246, 247, 255
learning-by-doing approach 86, 92,
93, 95
learning educational experience 18
learning loop 42–43, *43*, 44
learning management system (LMS) 87
learnings: inclusive design in 205–206;
journey 222; motivated behaviour for
209; summary 82–84; and teaching 76;
universal design for 206–207
legacy systems 50, *55*
legal curriculum case study 247–248
Lego® 59
LEGO models 124
Lewis, C. 246
life learning journey mapping 234–235
lightbulb moments 27–28
Lim, Christopher Sze Chong 18
'lo-fi first' approach 151
Lotus Blossom method 67
'low-intensity space' 149

Mace, Ron 203
'making HCD thinking visible' 95–96

map 35, 41, 50, 66–68, 80, 128, 137,
150, 164, 165, 173, 196, 223,
230–232, 234, 237–241
mapping 18, 25, 28, 47, 64, 66, 83, 84,
87, 89, 125, 135, 164, 193, 196,
211, 213, 220, 222–223, 226, 228,
232–240
management curriculum case study
250–251
market research 40
Marshall, David 16, 145
Maslow's foundational theory 11
massive ecosystem 51
method 15, 19, 28, 31, 36, 42, 62, 67,
78, 87–89, 91–96, 124, 128, 133,
144, 147, 191, 220, 221, 230, 233,
236–238, 240, 247, 251, 254, 255
McVitty, Debbie 23
'medium-intensity' space 149
Meinel, C. 86
Middlesex University: continuous
improvement at 120–123
'mindset disruption' 92, 99
mindsets 5, 14, 53, 56; challenge 41–43;
change in 48; definition 86; eat
methods 86–99; growth/designer
125; ingrained 152–153; internalised
27–28; user-centred design 47
Moran, James 18
Moran, Paul 47
Morelli, N. 232
Morrison, S. 187
motivated behaviour for learning *209*
'multiple means of engagement' 210
Murikami, Takeshi 7
Murrie, Katie 14, 59, 63, 71–72, *72*
Mutton, Jean 14, 19, 50–51, 122

needs 16–17
neurodivergent student 212
Newton, Radka 18, 19, 122
Ney, S. 86
non-profit organisations 76
Norman, Don 11
Northcote, Molly 4

observing method 128
Ogle, Daphne 16
one-size-fits-all approach 70
online canvas 80, 81
online course, development of 52–53
open-minded spirit 12

open mindsets 261
organisational culture 152–153

participant engagement 113
participant-learners 93, 95
peer institutions 163
performance indicators 121
personas 245–246; co-creation method
253, 254; created and used 249;
development 251–254; in education
246–247; profiling 254; profiling
guide 252; student 245
physical/digital models 41
physical violence 167
pilots: designing and running 138–140;
itself 108–109; services 139, 139
pioneering educators 5
place-based innovation ecosystems 75
Polaine, Andy 28
portfolio project 59, 61, 63, 69
positive feedback 172
post-hoc realisation 25–26
power of stories 31
practicing service design 215
privacy 172
problem, problem framing 161, 196
problem and solution space, guiding
principles 79
'the problem,' notion of 26
Professional Development Award (PDA)
59–63, 72, 212–215
professional services, people working
in 133
project-based learning 14, 75–76, 80;
complex networks of 78; impact
of 81; key role of 83; untangle
networks 83
pronoun options 169, **169**
Protolib 145–147, 151; impact of
154–155
'The Protolib Bunker' 150
prototyping 129; intensive phase of 80;
iterations **149**; 'medium-intensity'
space 149; reading space 148;
reframimg 44; service design
activity 41, 42
Pruitt, J. 245, 254
public institutions 134

quality assurance process 253–254

radical creativity 125–126, 129

reality check 44
reflective persona tool 223–224
reflective practice 18, 218; concept of
221; designing interventions 220;
interventions 220–225; onboarding
220–222; service design and 219–220;
student journey mapping 222–223,
227; student persona tool 223–224;
summative assessment of 225
reflection 18, 19, 84, 87, 95, 97, 99,
100, 108, 112, 147, 218–228, 236,
237, 239, 240
regional and national policies 2
representative reporting 172
research, design research 40, 108,
223, 255
research fellowship 27
research practices 76–78
research, service design activity 40, 42
resource ownership 134
Riddell, Jessica 104
rigid campus systems 168
ripple effect 31–32
Robertson, Jennifer 17
Robinson, Annette 47
Robotic Process Automation (RPA) 17,
175–178, 180, 181, 183–184
Rose, Phillippa 15

Salinas, Lara 14
Schneider, Jakob 37
seamless student journey 258–265;
improve communications 262–263;
open mindsets 261; siloed nature of
Higher Education 259–261; utilise
technology 262
Seddon, John 56
self-consciousness 127
semi-structured interviews 78
Senior Management Teams 77–79
serendipity 25–26
service blueprint 232
service, definition of 36–37
service design 2, 3, 10; activities 39, 44;
airport toilet 35–36; approaches 12,
133; assumptions 54–55; and business
as usual (BAU) 110–111; case studies
145–147; community and other
people role 29–30; concepts of 25–26;
crowd-sourced insights 25; and design
thinking 37; digging deeper 28; in
education see education; educators

35–36; embedding ideas 29; empathy phase in 129; epiphany 27; first steps into 123–126; foundation of 54; hearts and minds 135–136; ideation 40; implementation 41; internalised mindset 27–28; intervention 223; iterative design process 150–151; learning loop 42–43, *43*; learning points 137–138, 143; lightbulb moments 27–28; managing ambiguity 126; methodology 16, 133–134; methods 62; mindset *see* mindset; needs and chimes 29; post-hoc realisation 25–26; power of stories 31; practical application of 60; in practice 39–41; practitioners 10, 71; principles 37, 62, 71; 'the problem,' notion of 26; Professional Development Award (PDA) 212–215; project 143–144; Protolib 145–147; prototyping 41; radical creativity 125–126; and reflective practice 219–220; remember 24–27; research 40; ripple effect 31–32; sharing resources 30; Spacefinder 145–146; sticky making 28–30; strangeness 43; in supporting student wellbeing 155; tools and methodologies 158; tools and techniques 14; training 27, 57; transformative effects of 14; user centredness 124–125; working in 36
Service Design Academy (SDA) 59, 61, 63, 65–70; ABC Avalanche tool 67; Professional Development Award at 63; Sunflowers technique 67; work-based assessments 63
Service Design: From Insight to Implementation (Polaine) 28
Service Design in Education (SDinED) network 3, 4
service design programme 105–106
service design training 4
service leadership 140; elements of 140; functional model for 140–142, *141*; prototype for 141
service, Lou's definition of 2
service-oriented organisations 14
service pilots 139, *139*
sexual orientation 160
sharing resources, on service design 30
Shaw, George Bernard 262
Shostack, G. Lynn 28

Simon, Herbert 1
social constructivism 226
social learning 107, 115
social technology 191
Spacefinder 145–146, 153; impact of 154
SPARCK 3
Spokes, Pamela 14, 49
Spool, Jared 65
staff benefits 121
stakeholders 55; overcame challenges by 152–153
standard go-to method 133
Stewart, Christine 19
Stickdorn, Marc 37
storytelling 70, 73, 92, 173, 196, 200, 264
structured service design programme 105–106, 115
student-centred design 187
student-centred education 12, 243–244
student challenge roadmap *194*
student engagement 189, 191; with reflective practice 218
student experience 2, 14, 17–19, 25, 27, 48–50, 52, 87, 93, 95, 102, 122, 12, 127, 178, 179, 182, 189, 191–194, 196, 197, 199, 200, 212, 230, 233, 235, 239, 244, 248, 258, 259, 261, 262
student information system (SIS) 158, 159, 164, 166
student journey mapping 48, 222–223, *238*
Sunflowers technique 67
support respectful communications 171
sustainable transformational change 263
systems thinking 173

task force facilitators designed models 142
teaching practices 76–78
ten-week service design programme 102
30-minute online visual interviews 80, 82
3Ps (People, Purpose and Process) model 265
Tjeldnes, Svein Are 16
tool 14–15, 17, 19, 23, 24, 27, 40, 49, 52, 56, 57, 60, 61, 67, 72, 73, 83, 87–92, 97, 99, 107–109, 111, 112, 120–122, 150, 158, 173, 175, 177, 183, 184, 187, 189–191, 196, 199–201, 212, 213, 219–224, 226, 231, 232, 237, 239, 240
toolkit 13, 56, 111, 199, 200, 247, 248
training: impact of 70–72; pleasures of 27

transformational leadership styles 126
transformational learning 106
'transformative learner' 225
transformative re-organisation project 134
transparency 172
Trevor Project 158

UK Design Council Double Diamond
    model 86, 89
universal design 203–204
Universal Design for Learning (UDL)
    18, 206–207; disability support
    information to 210, *211*; principles
    214; Professional Development Award
    in Service Design 212–215; service
    design mindset and 208–212
universities: administrators 52; case
    studies 87; co-creation strategy 199;
    common approach in 134; converge,
    missions of *76*; digital transformation
    193; under Equality Act 2010 209;
    knowledge exchange 83; missions 75
university degree programme learning
    journey 237–240
University of Edinburgh 61, 63, 64
University of Glasgow 176, 178;
    automation service 178–184
University of the Arts London 77
unverified assumptions 54
user: experiences 14; personas 243–255;
    testing 165–166; *see also* user journey
    mapuser-centred design: mindsets 47;
    process 25; projects 12; right problems
    with 147–148
user journey map: define phase 67;
    deliver phase 69–70; develop phase
    67–68; discovery phase 66
user testing 165–166
utilise technology 262

value 1, 2, 8–9, 8, 10, 17–18, 23–25, 29,
    31, 38, 41, 44, 53, 55, 56, 62, 67–70,
    75, 78, 82–84, 86–95, 97, 106–108,
    110, 112–114, 121–123, 142, 147,
    151–154, 159, 171, 175, 177, 180,
    183, 189, 195, 200, 207, 219, 223,
    224, 238, 244, 254, 255, 259,
    262, 263
'value for money' 120, 121
verbal/physical violence 167
Virdi, Sonia 14, 59, 61–62, 65–71, *72*
Virtual Learning Environment 181
virtual learning environment (VLE)
    25, 95
virtual workers 177, 180
visual 9, 14, 64, 70, 75, 79, 80, 82, 84,
    89, 96–99, 121, 128, 137, 142, 164,
    169, 203, 213, 214, 219, 226, 240,
    245, 246, 251, 254, 264
visualisation 18, 40, 44, 64, 84, 232,
    233, 236, 237, 253
visual subject matter 213–215

Warwick International Higher Education
    Academy (WIHEA) 190, 191
Warwick Secret Challenge (WSC) 17,
    190–191; design thinking with student
    engagement 191; distinctiveness 195;
    first institutional innovation challenge
    193–195; improved 199–200;
    Interdisciplinarity project 192, 193,
    197; methodology 193; next for 200;
    proof of concept 192–193; replicable
    methodology 195–197; scaling of
    197–198; touch of secrecy 192;
    worked 198–199
Warwick Skills Portfolio Award 195
Webster, Merriam 37
wellbeing 155
Williams, C. 245
wireframe screen prototypes 164
work-based assessments 63
WREN model 96–99, *98*

Printed in the United States
by Baker & Taylor Publisher Services